FEATURES

WINTER 2026 • NUMBER 46

Plough

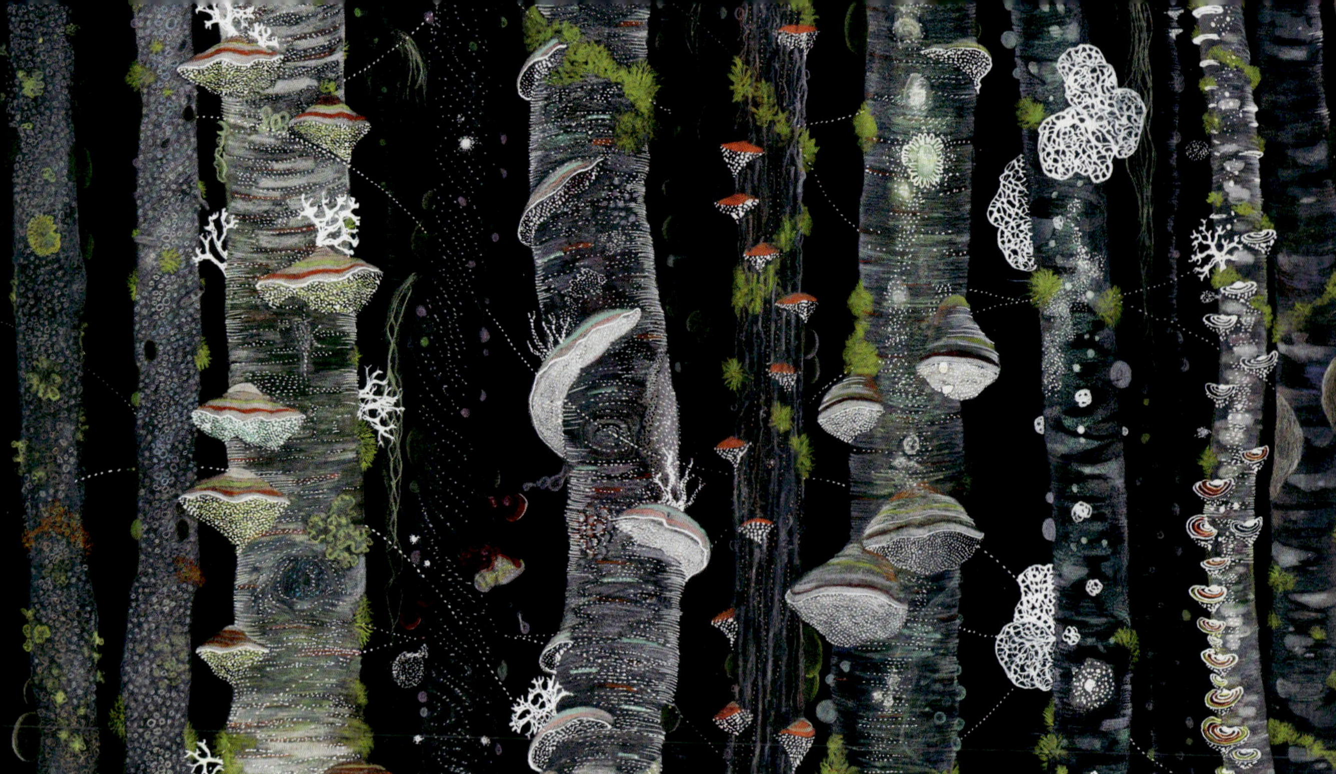

INSIGHTS

DEPARTMENTS

WEB EXCLUSIVES

Read these articles at *plough.com/web46*.

Artwork by Claire Burbridge. Used by permission.

Plough

ANOTHER LIFE IS POSSIBLE

Plough Quarterly No. 46: The Call of Beauty
Published by Plough Publishing House, ISBN 978-1-63608-190-8

EDITORIAL OFFICE
United Kingdom
Brightling Road
Robertsbridge
TN32 5DR
T: +44(0)1580.883.344

SUBSCRIBER SERVICES
Unit 6, The Enterprise Centre
Kelvin Lane, Crawley RH10 9PE
T: 0800.018.0799
plough@subscriptionhelpline.co.uk

North America
151 Bowne Drive
Walden, NY 12586 USA
T: 845.572.3455
info@plough.com

Australia
4188 Gwydir Highway
Elsmore, NSW
2360 Australia
T: +61(0)2.6723.2213

Plough Quarterly (ISSN 2372-2584) is published quarterly by Plough Publishing House, PO Box 398, Walden, NY 12586.
Individual subscription £24 / €28 / $36 per year.
Subscribers outside of the United States and Canada pay in British pounds or euros.

Front cover: Caspar David Friedrich, *Winter Landscape with Church*, oil on canvas, 1811. Public domain.
Inside front cover: Tōshi Yoshida, *Dance of Eternal Love*, woodblock print, 1994. Used by permission of Floating World Gallery.
Back cover: Lê Phổ, *Maternity*, ink and watercolour on silk, 1955. Image copyright ©AGUTTES, used by permission.

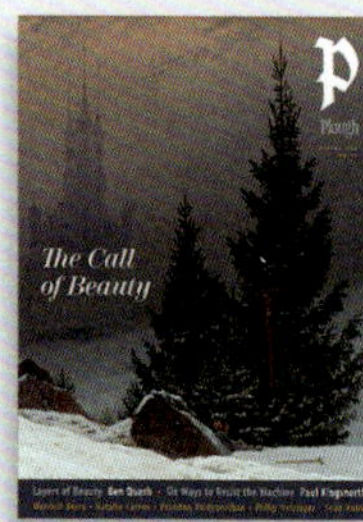

ABOUT THE COVER

Caspar David Friedrich's 1811 oil painting *Winter Landscape with Church* evokes many kinds of beauty – the natural beauty of pines against a winter sunset, the constructed beauty of the church in the distance and the ultimate beauty of Christ's sacrifice, as contemplated by the viewer in the foreground.

LETTERS

READERS RESPOND

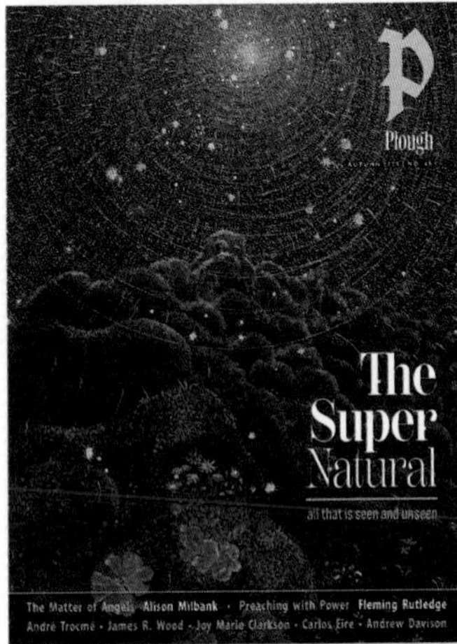

Readers respond to *Plough*'s Autumn 2025 issue, *The Supernatural*. Send letters to *letters@plough.com*.

I just got the first issue of my subscription, and I am poring over every article. You have put together a collection of words and stories that is giving me more hope than almost anything I've read in the last five years. Thank you for a deeply rich theological soil out of which is growing beauty and hope. So grateful to have found you. This magazine was meant to be in our office waiting room, but I am reading them first before setting them out!

Karah Thompson, North Carolina USA

On Joy Clarkson's 'Against Re-Enchantment': Spot on, Joy. We need to remember that the 'enchantment' of earlier times was often very oppressive and used to control through fear. Scripture shows the true interaction between the supernatural and the divine, offering freedom in Christ and opening our eyes to the beauty of his involvement and revelation in this world.

Aiko Ramdin, Nottinghamshire UK

On Sarah Crosby's 'Strange Gifts of the Spirit': I grew up (and still am) a Plain Mennonite, from within which culture 'the charismatics' are viewed with distrust. Though Mennonites vary from group to group, in my own group we hear preaching that suggests God will not speak to hearts apart from 'the church.' He will definitely never say to us anything that contradicts 1) the Bible, or 2) the church (which are sometimes assumed to possess equal footing).

But some years ago, I read a novel in which the main character dialogued with God. I remember nothing else about the book but the divine dialogue, because as I closed the book, I thought, 'I wish I could do that – talk to God and hear an answer.' Almost before I finished the thought, I had what I have come to call 'an immediate, Other response', which was, 'Why can't you?' So I've been talking to Him, and stilling myself to hear Him, ever since. You know what I will say next: He is mostly silent. But then … the responses. The humour, the quiet reproof, the sweet comfort and encouragement, the continual perfect answers, the surprises! Though of course I have no way of knowing, and lack the courage to ask, I like to think He is talking to many more Mennonites also, who are (unlike myself) wise enough to say little within our less charismatic culture about this astonishing inner dialogue.

Sheila Petre, Pennsylvania USA

On André Trocmé's 'A Time to Keep Silent, and a Time to Speak': Trocmé writes in a lively, even entertaining style. It's astonishing to read what he and his family experienced, including personal tragedy, as he lived through some of the most tumultuous times in recent history. While sometimes encountering doubt, he held tightly to his faith in God, a faith he would almost certainly credit for his survival and that of his family. His is a story of courage and faith filtered through history.

Glynn A Young, Jr, Missouri USA

On Fleming Rutledge's 'Preaching with Power': Yes, we want preachers to serve God's Word in their sermons, to put aside their egos and bring a message from God. But doesn't the incarnation and God's image in humans call for the preacher to show up as a fully human servant bearing the message to the congregation? I'm all for expository preaching, for making sure that God is the subject of sermons and for bringing a message from the Lord. But does that message not come through the whole person, whose heart, soul, mind and strength is in partnership with God to equip the saints? In short, let's keep the paradox of God's Word and the human expression of it intact, rather than trying to erase the human part. That's neither possible nor scriptural.

Gary Looper, Denver, Colorado USA

On James R Wood's 'The Politics of Pagan Christianity': As a historian familiar with 19th-century France and its rising social conflicts, I find this article both troublingly relevant and hopeful at the same time. Thank you for your work on this. May God give us some de Lubacs in our own day, and may the church awaken to its betrayals of the gospel.

Kathleen A Mulhern, Englewood, Colorado USA

On Mary Townsend's 'Your Friends Are Not in Your Phone': Dear God, this is the first piece that speaks to what I felt when I finally deleted my Twitter account. And then, when I found I had replaced the endless scrolling and group chats with short-form video, I uninstalled Instagram. Then Facebook. Then YouTube.

How comforting it's been to be bored and lonely again. I think the phone trains us to an allergy of discomfort – it provides an anaesthetic, sedating comfort against feeling too much or thinking too hard. Distraction, it turns out, is the ultimate addiction.

When you asked, 'Where have the people gone', that really struck me. There are pockets, for sure, but for the most part everybody is lost in a deeply private, curated, protected, comfortable world. How real is it? I'm sure it varies, but for me, it wasn't real. The friends through the screen were real, but not in the phone, and that's the only way I knew them. Great piece. Subscribed to *Plough* for more like this.

Anton Hengst, Long Beach, California USA

I believe the 'addiction' is not to the device, but to the apps and use of the device. The analogy that comes to mind is that a bottle can be filled with fresh, clean water or Jim Beam. The author seems to think that the bottle is the source of the addiction, so if there are no bottles around to hold the whiskey then one is safe from addiction. My view is that the phone is just a tool, a device that delivers content. It has amazing capacity (good, I believe) to be a useful tool for many things. I can text or email a friend, share photos, be reminded of appointments, see what the best route to my destination is, monitor my house alarm system, etc. I can also waste incredible amounts of time (like people do with TV) scrolling mindlessly through useless content on TikTok, Facebook, Snapchat or Instagram. Why the widespread addiction? Social media tech companies design their apps for maximum engagement – eyeballs on the screen generate ad revenue. These companies employ neuroscience to hack our brains using techniques that trigger dopamine responses – hence, the difficulty with putting the phone down.

As I've postulated, this isn't a device issue, it's an app and usage issue – a user issue, if you will. I personally haven't ever been a big fan of social media, and I terminated my Facebook account over ten years ago. My smartphone is an indispensable tool that I use for my own and others' benefit. And a *Plough* article like this is one of those beneficial connections for me.

John Geffel, Oregon City, Oregon USA

About Us

Plough is published by the Bruderhof, an international community of families and singles seeking to follow Jesus together. Members of the Bruderhof are committed to a way of radical discipleship in the spirit of the Sermon on the Mount. Inspired by the first church in Jerusalem (Acts 2 and 4), they renounce private property and share everything in common in a life of non-violence, justice and service to neighbours near and far. There are 29 Bruderhof settlements in both rural and urban locations in the United States, England, Germany, Australia, Paraguay, South Korea and Austria, with around 3,000 people in all. To learn more or arrange a visit, see the community's website at *bruderhof.com.*

Plough features original stories, ideas and culture to inspire faith and action. Starting from the conviction that the teachings and example of Jesus can transform and renew our world, we aim to apply them to all aspects of life, seeking common ground with all people of goodwill regardless of creed. The goal of *Plough* is to build a living network of readers, contributors and practitioners so that, as we read in Hebrews, we may 'spur one another on towards love and good deeds.'

Plough includes contributions that we believe are worthy of our readers' consideration, whether or not we fully agree with them. Views expressed by contributors are their own and do not necessarily reflect the editorial position of *Plough* or of the Bruderhof communities.

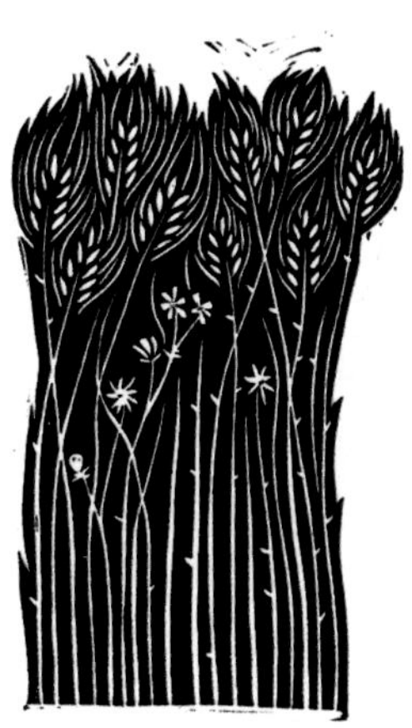

On Benjamin Crosby's 'Am I a Christian If I Don't Have Spiritual Experiences?': I find this article rather strange and certainly not very helpful. The author seems to have been taught to see a religious life as some sort of competition with grades attached. Christ categorically rejected this sort of thing and provocatively said, 'The last shall be first and the first shall be last.' Also, he singled out children. If the author believes each person is guided by God (something I do not believe myself), he could have comforted himself with the reflection that a deep spiritual experience was not for him, either because it would disorient him as such experiences do, or because he didn't need it. Direct experience of the divine is precisely what religious organisations the world over conspicuously lack, which is why those who have had such experiences find themselves disliked equally by the rationalists/sceptics *and* by the official churches. Montefiore, the late Bishop of Birmingham, said at a Bible study I attended, 'I am suspicious of anyone who claims to have had a spiritual experience.' Well, thanks very much! One reason why I shifted to the Quakers, who are a little less negative. Imagine the president of the Royal Society of Engineers saying, 'I am suspicious of anyone who claims to have made an electric motor.' And to boot, 'I am not sympathetic to anyone who even *wants* to make an electric motor.' The churches are the last ones to see the emptiness of current materialistic Western society or to think that the remedy might in some sense be a joyful 'religious' experience.

Robert Mules, Shaftesbury UK

On Hannah Rose Thomas and Rachel Miner's 'Mothers of Srebrenica': I was fortunate enough to receive a widow and her two children from Srebrenica in July 1995. I was working with Lutheran social services in Florida when we received an emergency call that a mother and children needed immediate protection. The widow and her two boys spent their first night in the United States in my guest room. She had been raped, and her youngest child was the offspring of that horror. The other child had witnessed the horror. The night they spent with us, she sat up all night with the light on, while the boys curled up on either side of her and slept.

After we found a place for them to stay, we helped them get settled. She got a job and the boys started school, and they all had enough to eat. None of them spoke any English when they arrived, but about a year later, I got a call from her, and she spoke enough English to say thank you and tell me how well they were doing. She rebuilt her little community after that genocide the best she could. I will never forget the honour of being able to help.

Owene Courtney, Blowing Rock, North Carolina USA

STATEMENT OF OWNERSHIP, MANAGEMENT, AND CIRCULATION
(Required by 39 U.S.C. 3685)

Title of publication: Plough Quarterly. Publication No: 0001-6584. 3. Date of filing: October 1, 2025. 4. Frequency of issue: Quarterly. 5. Number of issues published annually: 4. 6. Annual subscription price: $36.00. 7. Complete mailing address of known office of publication: Plough Quarterly, P.O. Box 398, Walden, NY 12586. 8. Same. 9. Publisher: Plough Publishing House, same address. Editor: Peter Mommsen, same address. Managing Editor: Sam Hine, same address. 10. Owner: Plough Publishing House, P.O. Box 398, Walden, NY 12586. 11. Known bondholders, mortgages, and other securities: None. 12. The purpose, function, and nonprofit status of this organization and the exempt status for federal income tax purposes have not changed during preceding 12 months. 13. Publication Title: Plough Quarterly. 14. Issue date for circulation data below: Fall 2024–Summer 2025. 15. Extent and nature of circulation: Average No. copies of each issue during preceding 12 months: A. Total number of copies (net press run): 18,891. B.1. Mailed outside-county paid subscriptions: 15,127. B.2. Mailed in-county paid subscriptions: 0. B.3. Paid distribution outside the mails including sales through dealers and carriers, street vendors, counter sales, and other non-USPS paid distribution: 1270. B.4. Other classes mailed through the USPS: 0. C. Total paid distribution: 16,397. D.1. Free distribution by mail: Outside-county: 1,225. D.2. In-county: 0. D.3. Other classes mailed through the USPS: 0. Free distribution outside the mail: 48. E. Total free distribution: 1,273. F. Total Distribution: 17,670. G. Copies not distributed: 1,221. H. Total: 18,891. I. Percent paid: 92.80%. Actual No. copies of single issue published nearest to filing date: A.: 20,600. B.1.: 15,119. B.2.: 0. B.3.: 2,642. B.4.: 0. C.: 17,761. D.1.: 1,242. D.2.: 0. D.3.: 0. D.4.: 49. E.: 1,291. F.: 19,052. G.: 1,548. H.: 20,600. I.: 93.22 %. Electronic copy circulation: Average No. copies of each issue during preceding 12 months: A. Total No. Electronic Copies: 131. B. Total paid print copies plus paid electronic copies: 16,528. C. Total print distribution plus paid electronic copies: 17,801. D. Percent paid: 92.85%. Actual No. copies of single issue published nearest to filing date: A.: 83. B.: 17,844. C.: 19,135. D.: 93.25%. 17. Publication of Statement of Ownership: Winter 2026. 18. I certify that the statements made by me above are correct and complete. Sam Hine, Editor, September 15, 2025.

FAMILY & FRIENDS

AROUND THE WORLD

Photograph courtesy of Food in Community. Used by permission.

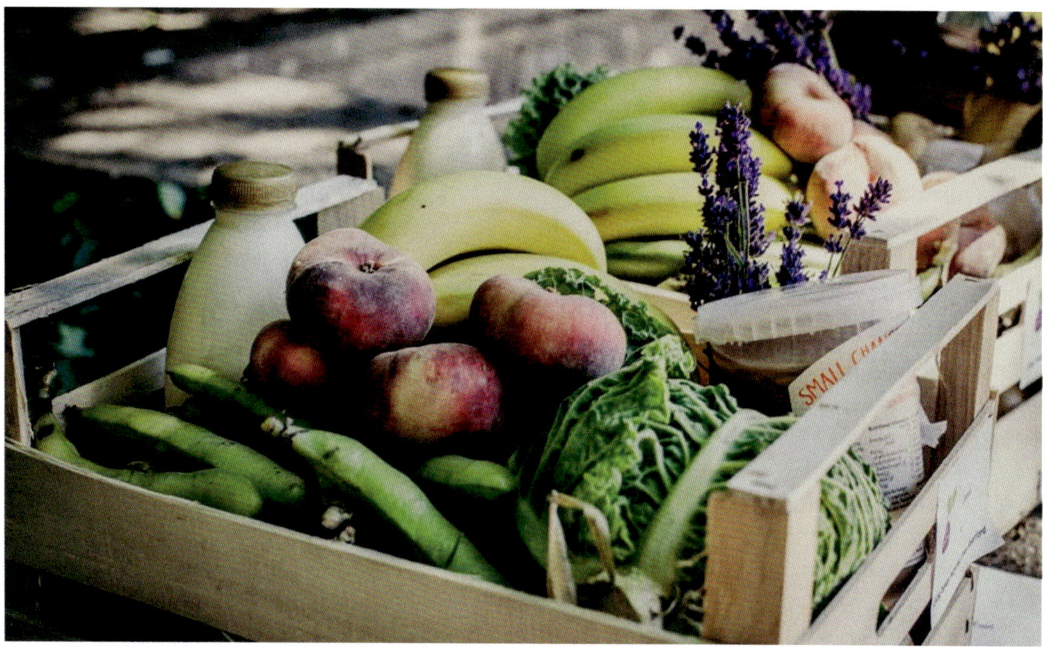

How We Feed Each Other

Two community projects weave together care for nature and sharing good food.

Sophie Caldecott

Eating is such an everyday act, it's easy to forget the startling intimacy of it until something disrupts your habits. Eating spaghetti, for example, is a very different experience in the company of a stranger or a crush, as you self-consciously wipe sauce from your chin. Sharing food centres our common humanity and is often the most effective way that we can express care for one another. It also requires a certain level of vulnerability; whenever we eat, we're trusting what we consume won't kill us, something that I'm reminded of every time I eat with my friend with Coeliac disease.

It's fitting that residents of my hometown of Ashburton, on the edge of Dartmoor National Park in Devon, came up with the idea of installing a community fridge in 2020, during the height of the Covid pandemic. Against a backdrop of general anxiety about how to feed ourselves and the loss of the many social and spiritual gatherings that cement human connection, a group of volunteers from the Ashburton Climate Emergency group proposed this endeavour to address food waste.

The fridge has been up and running since March 2021. Volunteers pick up the bulk of the food dispensed via the fridge from supermarkets with excess food that is close to its sell-by date. Locals are also able to share surplus produce they've grown, or sealed food that they've bought, as long as it hasn't been tampered with. (Due to health and safety rules, someone can't, for example, bake something at home and put it in the fridge without a food hygiene licence.)

There's a certain degree of trust that needs to be established in initiatives like these, where no money is changing hands. I've noticed the need in myself to overcome an irrational worry about whether or not the food is 'safe' to eat, simply because I haven't paid for it. This instinctive recoiling from free food was so unconscious in me at first that I was only able to confront it when my daughter, with all the innocent honesty of youth, asked, 'Is it clean?'

We must trust the good intentions and experience of the people involved in the running of the fridge. We must also use our own senses to check that the food hasn't gone off and is still good to eat, more than

Sophie Caldecott is a writer and poet and has worked as creative director of Verily *magazine.*

Food in Community (see next page) operates, among other things, a fresh food box programme to provide for families in need.

we are used to doing when presented with food in a supermarket.

Sometimes – as when a large delivery of leeks is dropped off – the news ripples through the town, the fridge acting as a conversation starter between people who wouldn't usually talk to each other. Cya Parker, one of the key organisers, tells me that she has heard of new friendships being formed as people bond over what they've found in the fridge and exchange recipes with each other. She's heard from fridge-users that they have also tried new fruit and vegetables because they were available.

The fridge is located in the centre of town and is open access, 24/7, free for all to use without requiring proof of financial need. It has become a much-loved feature and is used by people from every demographic, which means that there isn't the same stigma attached to it as there is to other community food projects, such as food banks.

The environmental charity Hubbub estimates that there are over 700 community fridges around the United Kingdom now, going some way to address the 6.4 million tonnes of edible food that the United Kingdom throws away every year. Ashburton's community fridge saved 38 tonnes of food from landfill in 2024.

ABOUT **20** MINUTES' drive away in the nearby town of Totnes, another initiative is flourishing. Food in Community was set up in 2013 as a way of providing for people in the area who were struggling financially and faced, as director David Markson described it, 'the indignity and inadequacy of provision … [having to queue] to receive a plastic carrier bag of poor-quality food.' Their idea was simple: team up with local organic farmers to collect surplus food from the fields. This process, known as gleaning,

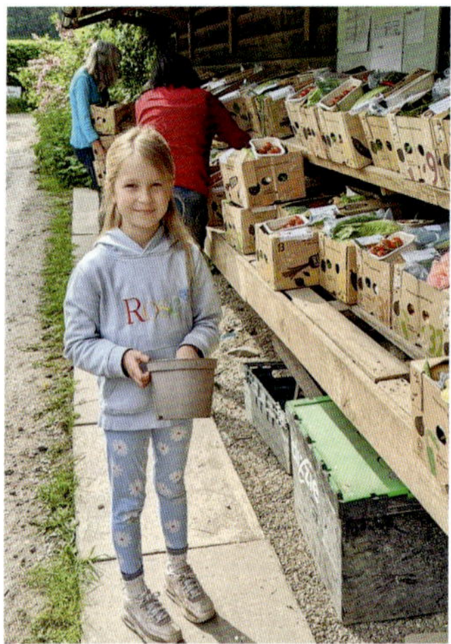

Photograph courtesy of Food in Community. Used by permission.

ensures that surplus crops are put to good use and that high-quality organic produce can be delivered to households in need who are signed up to the free service.

As around 40% of recipients are registered disabled, the direct delivery to the homes of people in need is vital. These people struggle to get to food pantries, community fridges and other projects designed to feed the community.

Food in Community repurposes over 150 tonnes of crop surplus each year. They have plans, David tells me, to quadruple that amount with a new community food processing project that is underway thanks to a £1.5 million farming grant that they recently secured to fund the initiative. 'Project Beetroot' will be a not-for-profit surplus food processing centre working with local organic farms to reduce food waste and the South West's carbon footprint while increasing food security and providing training and jobs.

Both the community fridge and Food in Community weave together care for the environment with a belief that high-quality food should be available to everyone.

This is the secret to their success. The charitable model that suggests a passive recipient is turned on its head when the recipient of free food becomes someone who is also actively engaged in the process of reducing food waste and helping to tackle climate change.

Feeding each other remains a radically vulnerable act, highlighting our interdependence and our often embarrassing, awkward bodies and needs. As so many of us discovered when we weren't able to gather to share meals in 2020, the spiritual and relational nourishment of these shared meals mirrors the more tangible physical nourishment. It's no wonder that a meal is at the centre of Christianity; the very first relationships of our lives are forged by feeding and being fed. Where there is hunger, there is life, and wherever we can come together to respond to this hunger, there is still hope for humanity.

Monica Ribar Cornell, 1942–2025

Bidding farewell to a pillar of the Catholic Worker movement.

Coretta Thomson

Plough lost a close friend and kindred spirit this summer. Monica Cornell, the wife of peace activist Tom Cornell, spent most of her life with the Catholic Worker, the lay movement founded in the 1930s by Peter Maurin and Dorothy Day. The movement is known for its houses of hospitality and for practising the works of mercy.

For the last 30 years, Monica has been the heart of the Catholic Worker's Peter Maurin Farm in Marlboro, New York. Her hospitality, from her home-cooked meals to her practical care of guests and residents, made the farm a place of welcome. Most of all, she is remembered for her expansive love – the attention given to each new face, her personal interest in every story.

Photograph courtesy of the Cornell family.

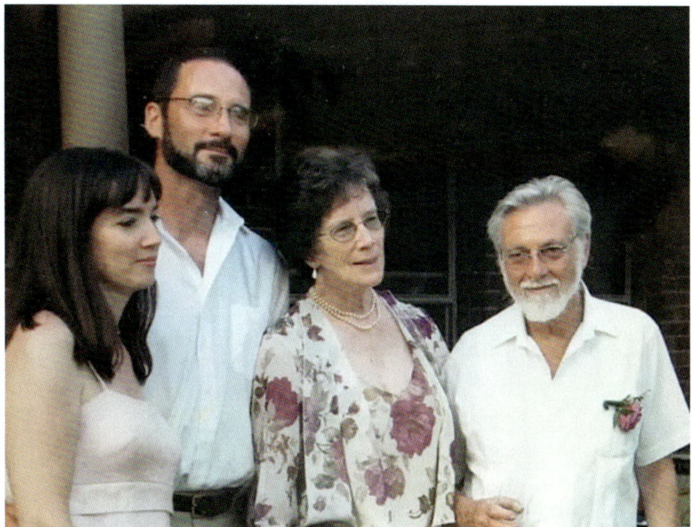

Monica's Catholic Worker journey started before she was born: her parents met in Cleveland while setting up one of the first houses of hospitality. The constant stream of volunteers that flowed through her childhood home expanded and shaped her worldview, as did the *Catholic Worker* newspaper.

Monica was raised before Vatican II. Although she embraced – even grew to embody – the Council's reforms, she felt her church sometimes compromised on the reverence and personal practices of piety she found central to a life of active service. Her early search reflected her commitment: a postulancy with Maryknoll, a formation course with Ladies of the Grail and two semesters at a Catholic college, before she joined the New York Catholic Worker at age 21. She arrived in Manhattan the day of the 1963 Birmingham church bombing, a fact forever etched into her memory.

It wasn't long before a fellow worker, Tom Cornell, took interest in her, and the two began dating. Dorothy Day, who felt personally responsible for this daughter of old friends, once accosted Tom after an evening visit, demanding, 'Young man, are your intentions honourable?' Not every couple can boast such a matchmaker! Tom and Monica married in July 1964, and settled in a nearby apartment furnished by donations.

When their children, Tom Jr and Dierdre, were small, the family lived in various rented apartments around New York City. Tom worked for the Fellowship of Reconciliation and joined the grassroots activist peace movement, publicly burning his draft cards – a symbolic act that landed him in federal prison for six months. Like her mother before her, Monica hosted a steady stream of Catholic Workers in their house, her vocation of the home anchoring Tom's actions on the street.

When the Cornells moved upstate in 1972, this arrangement continued. Tom travelled widely, supporting young conscientious objectors through Pax Christi (which he cofounded) and demonstrating against both the Vietnam War and the proliferation of nuclear weapons. Monica kept the home fires burning. Their house was always open to guests – visitors from all walks of life who helped shape their children's worldviews.

When Tom Jr and Dierdre left home, the Cornells decided to start a new Catholic Worker location. In Guadalupe House – a former convent in Waterbury, Connecticut – they cared for people dealing with addiction and homelessness, abandoned seniors, young soup kitchen volunteers and a foster child. Long-term residents recall the couple's love and gentle mentorship.

After ten years in Waterbury, Tom and Monica, joined by Tom Jr, took on the New York Catholic Worker's upstate Peter Maurin Farm, in part because the Cornells were getting older, but also because Monica was drawn towards Peter Maurin's vision. Maurin, who died in 1949, had described urban houses (Day's preference, and the more common model today) as intended 'for the immediate relief of those in need.' But ultimately, he said, the long-term solution would be found in 'farming communes where each one works according to his ability and gets according to his need.'

Besides sustaining a welcoming home, Monica joined local religious networks, attended farmers markets, and spent as much time as possible with her five grandchildren. Her spiritual life centred around devotional reading and the lives and feast days of the saints. Tom served as a deacon in their local parish until shortly before his death in 2022. He read daily from scripture, prayed the Psalms and maintained a lively interest in doctrinal interpretations and current events.

For decades, Monica and Tom have been friends with members of the Bruderhof, the community that publishes *Plough*. With a lifetime's worth of friends, they always seemed to have time to meet one more.

Coretta Thomson is an editor for Plough *and oversees its Spanish-language publications.*

Monica and Tom Cornell with their two children, Tom Jr and Dierdre.

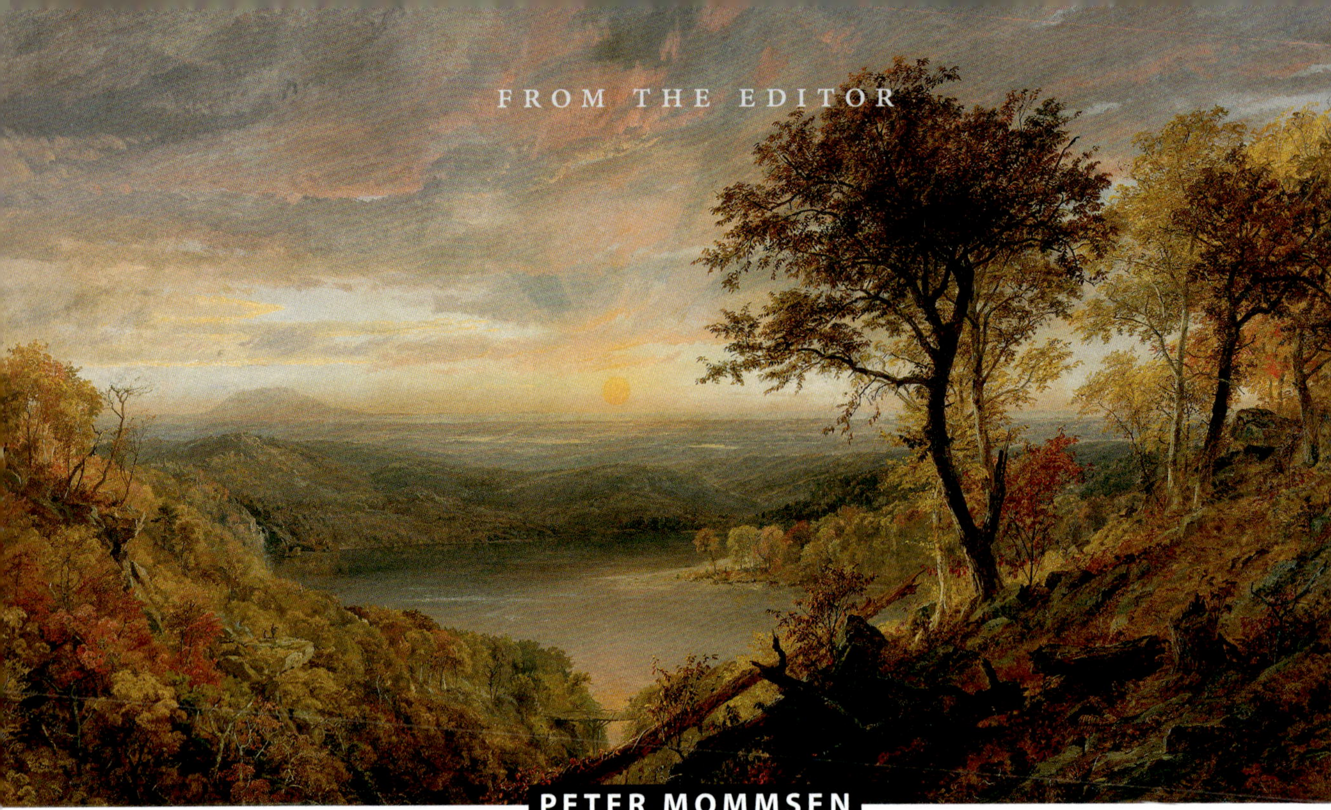

PETER MOMMSEN

The Call of Beauty

If beauty is the promise of joy, is it a promise we can trust?

There was a time when meadow, grove, and stream,
The earth, and every common sight,
To me did seem
Apparelled in celestial light.

—william wordsworth

On early mornings in autumn, when I take my dog into the sugar maple wood behind our house, I can easily see the world through young Wordsworth's eyes. A crimson glow has started spreading over the Hudson Highlands when Ajax rousts the eight-pointer who likes to bed down in the hollow. This happens most mornings, and the unworried buck sails away over the undergrowth, white flag flying. Ajax leaps in pursuit, until a misgiving – *Don't chase deer* – checks him mid-stride, and he glances back guiltily. We head to the lake, whose surface is steaming and flecked with yellow leaves. As usual, the great blue heron is frog-hunting in the rushes. Sensing us, he breaks off and flaps without hurry to the far bank. We wait side by side, watching the largemouth bass rising.

Then the sun swings up. Linguists say the word for dawn is among the oldest in the Indo-European languages; she's a goddess, whose reconstructed original name, *Ausōs*, gives us *Easter.* Ancient humans must have felt what we can feel now: dawn is so beautiful, she must be holy. The animals are so beautiful too, so akin to us and so unlike, that their beauty must *mean* something. What?

Jasper Francis Cropsey, *Greenwood Lake*, oil on canvas, 1870.

Christianity has a ready answer: beauty is an emblem of the divine. From the New Testament on, Christians have seen in the beauty of creation a sign of the beauty of the Creator – an Artist who, in turn, gazes on his work with delight: 'And, behold, it was very good' (Gen. 1:31). For patristic writers, the Psalms furnished warrant for this theology of beauty: 'The heavens declare the glory of God; and the firmament sheweth his handywork' (Ps. 19:1). By this way of thinking, the world's beauty, which calls for our love, is ordered so as to draw us to love its Maker; beauty becomes an invitation to faith. That's why, according to the theologian Hans Urs von Balthasar, 'Christianity is *the* aesthetic religion *par excellence*.'

Church fathers such as Cyril of Alexandria especially turned to the Book of Wisdom, an anonymous scripture that originated in the Jewish community in Alexandria, likely around the time of Christ. Nature-worshipping pagans are fools, Wisdom teaches, because 'they were unable from the good things that are seen to know the one who exists, nor did they recognise the artisan while paying heed to his works.' The wise, by contrast, love the natural world because it teaches them to know the 'author of beauty' by way of analogy: 'For from the greatness and beauty of created things comes a corresponding perception of their Creator' (Wis. 13:6).

The Book of Wisdom urges us to see the world as freighted with meaning. *This* dawn, *this* forest, *this* deer, *this* dog, *this* heron: each is a poem about God. As the 12th-century Byzantine monk Peter of Damascus elaborates:

> By contemplating the beauty and use of each thing, [a man] is filled with love for the Creator. He surveys all visible things: the sky, the sun, moon, stars and clouds, rain, snow and hail ... the four-legged animals, the wild beasts and animals and reptiles, all the birds, the springs and rivers, the many varieties of plants and herbs, both wild and cultivated. He sees in all things the order, the equilibrium, the proportion, the beauty, the rhythm, the union, the harmony, the usefulness, the variety, the motion, the colours, the shapes, the reversion of things to their source, permanence in the midst of corruption. Contemplating thus all created realities, he is filled with wonder.

As Wordsworth put it in the title of his poem, our experiences of beauty come to us as 'intimations of immortality.'

But even the beautiful natural landscape is not all peace and light. Where Peter of Damascus looked at the world and saw 'order', 'proportion' and 'harmony', the modern mind wonders how to reckon with the underlying violence: Darwinian competition for survival, Tennyson's 'nature red in tooth and claw.' The maple woods may *seem* lovely, but any given tree may be in competition against the rest for access to nutrients and sunlight. The noble-looking deer likely harbours hideous parasites and, come winter, faces a one in three chance of death by disease, starvation or coyote. When the largemouth bass breed next spring, 99.8% of their hatchlings will perish before adulthood, many cannibalised by their own siblings.

With these disconcerting facts as backdrop, evolutionary psychology dampens our attempts to find transcendent meaning in even our lovelier experiences. The pleasure of viewing a pristine landscape, for example, results from genes inherited from our hunter-and-gatherer ancestors, according to a much-cited hypothesis by the biologist Gordon Orians. He posits that prehistoric humans evolved to prefer verdant grasslands dotted with trees and offering water sources because such habitats promised ample food and made predators easy to spot. Thus, a landscape will please us to the extent that it resembles the fertile areas in the East African savannahs where our species originated. Beauty, by this theory, doesn't exist except as a genetically coded subjective response.

As for beauty's potential as a source of moral

or spiritual meaning, doubt has been cast well beyond the bounds of evolutionary psychology. As the theologian David Bentley Hart writes, there is 'an undeniable ethical offence in beauty.' Partly, that's because the devotees of beauty – connoisseurs, patrons of art and music, practitioners of *l'art de vivre* – have generally belonged to rapacious elites. But, Hart continues, the problem may lie with beauty itself:

> There is an unsettling prodigality about the beautiful, something wanton about the way it lavishes itself upon even the most atrocious of settings, its anodyne sweetness often seeming to make the most intolerable of circumstances bearable: a village ravaged by pestilence may lie in the shadow of a magnificent mountain's ridge; the marmorean repose of a child lately dead of meningitis might present a strikingly piquant tableau; Cambodian killing fields were often lushly flowered; Nazi commandants occasionally fell asleep to the strains of Bach, performed by ensembles of Jewish inmates; and no doubt the death camps were routinely suffused by the delicate hues of a twilit sky.

Fascist works of art offer a radical illustration of beauty's moral ambiguities. Take the films of the acclaimed cinematographer Leni Riefenstahl, who created propaganda for the Third Reich. Her *Olympia*, a visually magnificent documentary of the 1936 Olympic Games in Berlin, celebrates the beauty of athletic bodies in motion. Its technical innovations continue to influence the imagery of sports and fashion – as does its peculiar quality, diagnosed by Susan Sontag, of being 'both prurient and idealising.' This is a beauty that reduces human beings to gorgeous, vaguely pornographic specimens, interchangeable and soulless. Such beauty defines itself by what it leaves out, and who: a year after the film's release, the regime with which Riefenstahl was collaborating began its campaign of 'mercy killing' of people with disabilities. In the 1960s, a former Nazi sympathiser would thank the cinematographer for making films showing 'the most beautiful human beings, and not the cripples.'

While this is an extreme example, it illuminates why distrust of beauty is warranted, even in more innocuous settings. Any beauty that excludes humankind's imperfection and vulnerability is prone to becoming subhuman. And even the wholesome beauty of nature is only a partial truth in a world where children starve in war zones or are trafficked to abusers.

Yet stubbornly, beauty remains. It's there in the snowy egret I saw this morning, a white gleam circling over the lake where the heron usually stands. It's there in the exquisitely poignant modulations of a Bach chaconne. It's there in acts of moral greatness that have the power to shock us with a glimpse of splendour. I'm thinking, for example, of the moment on 21 September of this year when the US activist Erika Kirk spoke at the memorial service for her murdered husband, Charlie Kirk, before an audience of millions. She said this about his killer:

> I forgive him. I forgive him because it was what Christ did, and it's what Charlie would do. The answer to hate is not hate. The answer we know from the gospel is love and always love. Love for our enemies and love for those who persecute us.

Only an extraordinary feat of faith could have given her the strength to do that – a feat much like that of Felecia Sanders who, in the 2017 sentencing hearing for the perpetrator of the mass shooting at Mother Emanuel church in Charleston, South Carolina, said 'I forgive you' to the murderer of her son, Tywanza Sanders. Such actions, which transcend their time and context, bear witness to divine beauty. To quote Hart again: 'Nothing else impresses itself upon our attention with at once so wonderful a power and so evocative an immediacy. Beauty is there, abroad in the order of things, given again and again in a way that defies description and denial with equal impertinence.'

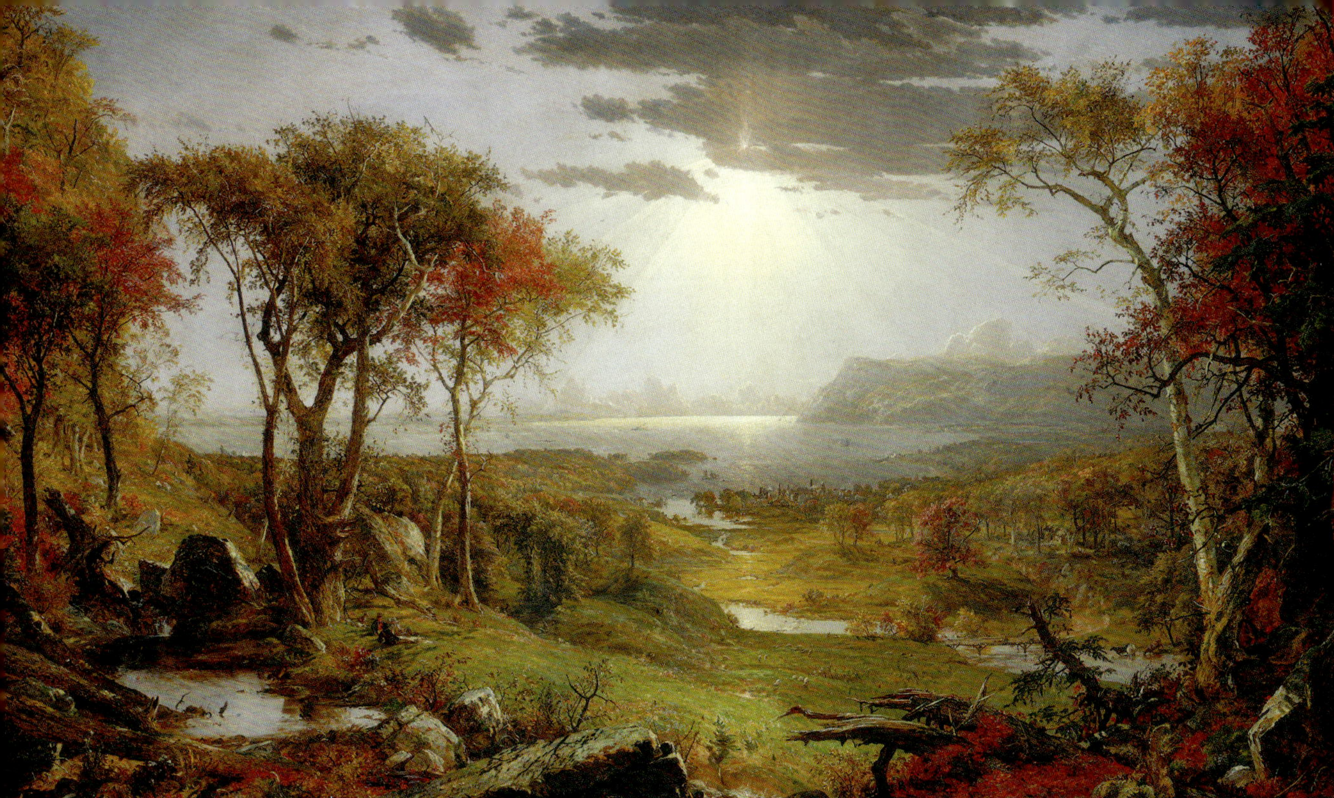

We can't help perceiving it, and it will not leave us alone.

For Christians, the solution to the problem of beauty is a Person, the one on whom Felecia Sanders and Erika Kirk relied. 'Late have I loved you, O Beauty so ancient and so new!' Augustine exclaims of Christ in his *Confessions*. As the Logos who was with the Creator in the beginning, he is the Book of Wisdom's 'author of beauty', the origin of all that is lovely in the world. And as the incarnate Son of Man, his beauty was that of a particular Jewish baby, born in obscurity and laid in a manger, who would go on to willingly suffer an ugly death to redeem creation from its sins and horrors.

Few have written as eloquently of this beauty as Mother Maria Skobtsova. Born a Russian aristocrat in 1891, she settled in Paris, took monastic vows and spent the last 13 years of her life serving the city's poor, dying in 1945 in the gas chambers of Ravensbrück. In one of her writings, she imagines Christ slipping out of a splendid church to walk the streets and 'mingle with the crowd: the poor, the lepers, the desperate, the embittered, the holy fools.' Wandering in the midst of degraded humanity, he seeks out 'the poor and the maimed, prostitutes and sinners', and sees even in their spiritual and physical deformity the spark of his own beauty:

> Does He not see in our ugliness, in our impoverished lives, in our festering sores, in our crippled souls – does He not see there His own divine image and a reflection of his eternal glory and eternal beauty? And so He will return to the churches and bring with Him all those whom He has summoned to the wedding feast.

For Skobtsova, Christ's is a beauty that summons us with infinite love. Understood this way, Stendhal's famous definition of beauty as *la promesse du bonheur*, the promise of joy, points to a fundamental truth about reality: because beauty is Christ, all manifestations of beauty exist to bear witness, whether dimly or gloriously, to his promise that love will have the last word.

Jasper Francis Cropsey, *Autumn on the Hudson River*, oil on canvas, 1860.

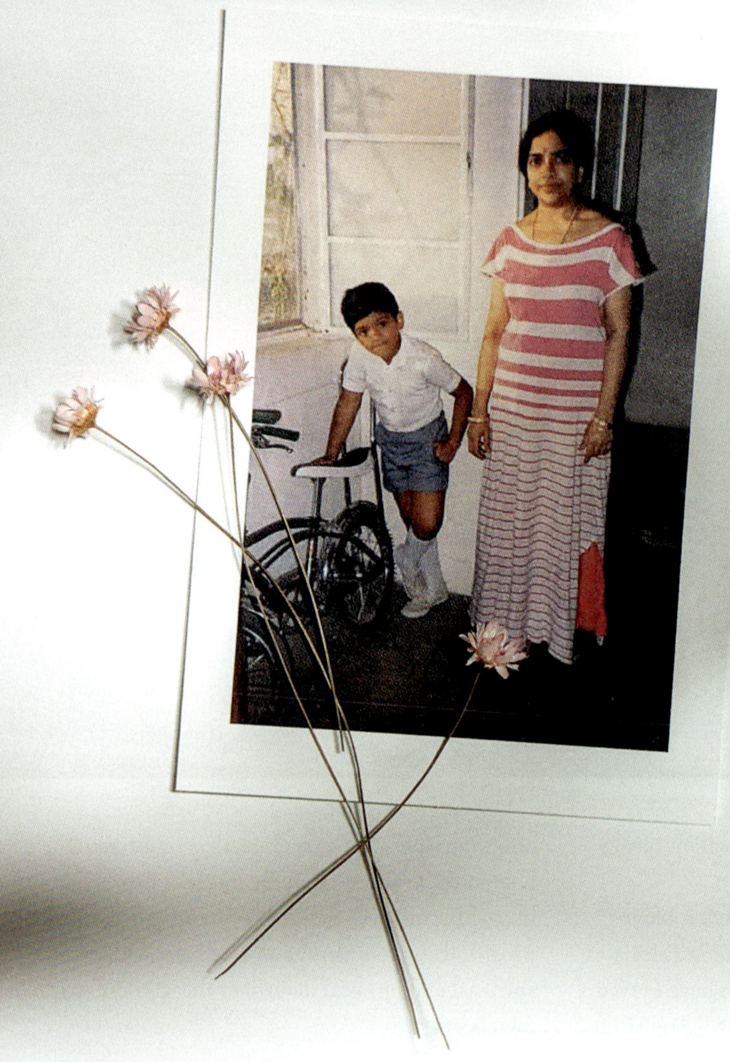

When Radiance Breaks Through

My mother's mental illness changed the way I see human beauty.

BRANDON VAIDYANATHAN

AROUND EIGHT IN THE EVENING, I wrap up my toddler's bedtime story and tell him it's time to call *Tata* and *Pati* – his grandfather and grandmother, as they're called in Tamil.

The routine is the same every night. My father answers my WhatsApp call and shouts across the room to my mother: 'Come, talk to the children!' It's already dawn in Bangalore, India, where my parents live. My mother's standing a foot away from the television, watching a live devotional broadcast from a Hindu temple. She needs glasses but never wears them, so she hunches towards the

---

Brandon Vaidyanathan is a professor of sociology at The Catholic University of America, and director of the Institutional Flourishing Lab. He lives in Maryland USA.

screen, eyes squinted. When my father calls again, she acquiesces and hobbles over to the phone as my father holds it out.

'Show me your toy – what toy you have today?' she asks my four-year-old in English. He hoists his latest Lego creation. Today it's a spaceship with a red wing on one side and a blue one on the other. 'Mmm, very nice, very nice', she says as he describes what it is. For three, maybe four seconds, her eyes catch light, as if a window somewhere inside her has opened. Then the shadows return. She turns away and tells my father in Tamil, 'OK, take it away, take it away', and goes back to the TV. We'll try again tomorrow.

If you had asked me when I was my son's age what beauty was, I would have pointed to my mother. In a photo from when I was four, I'm standing next to her, holding my green bicycle. I can still feel her running beside me in the desert heat of Oman, where I grew up: one hand on the tall sissy bar, steadying the bike and laughing as I finally figure out how to balance myself without training wheels. It's one of my only memories of her being plainly, effortlessly happy. In another photo from those years, I'm standing on the couch and kissing her cheek while she beams at the camera. But I have no memory of that moment, or of ever having kissed her. Those kinds of moments would soon disappear as my mother became severely mentally ill. And as her schizophrenia progressed, untreated, what changed was not only her, but also the way I processed beauty.

THERE ARE TWO TYPES of beauty. One is what I would call *scripted beauty*. This is the beauty for which we have cultural scripts – the kind we recognise and reward. We see it in physical attractiveness, beautiful objects, in picture-perfect homes with doting couples and smiling family photos. Scripted beauty doesn't have to be superficial; it can be laden with meaning and yearning, and its absence in one's life can feel oppressive. The second is what I call *revealed beauty* – the kind that usually remains obscured, yet sometimes discloses itself unbidden in moments of radiance and recognition where something surprising breaks through.

It matters to be able to tell these two kinds of beauty apart. Scripted beauty has its place – it helps us stick to shared norms and orders our lives. But if we stop there, we confuse beauty with conformity. We end up wounding those who can't follow the scripts, and become oblivious to their beauty. The full worth of a person is never evident on the surface; it remains obscured from our eyes. And in chasing after scripted beauty, we lose sight of this deeper kind. We don't know how to look for it – we may not even realise it is there.

If you had asked me when I was my son's age what beauty was, I would have pointed to my mother.

My mother, over a few short years, went from working as a physician to spending her days alone at home, gripped by a fierce worry, scanning the room with the intensity of someone who senses an enemy nearby, spending hours speaking to invisible presences. I never learned what triggered her illness. Her night shifts working alone at the hospital probably didn't help; she resigned when I was six. Perhaps it was the long days subsequently spent alone at home, without extended family and friends, without the scaffolding of language and custom. Life in Oman as a guest worker can make

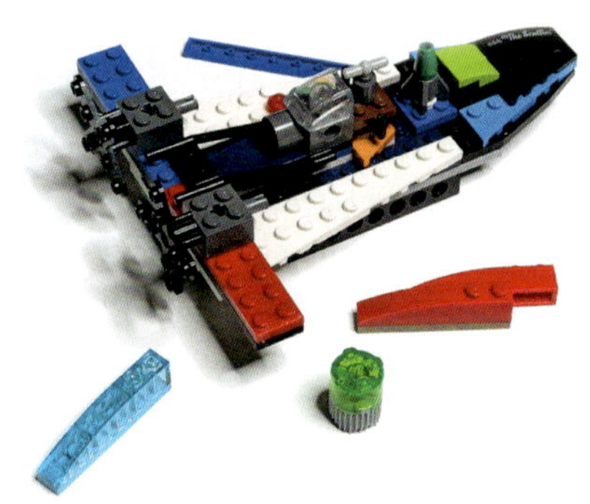

Lego spaceship created by John Goodwin.

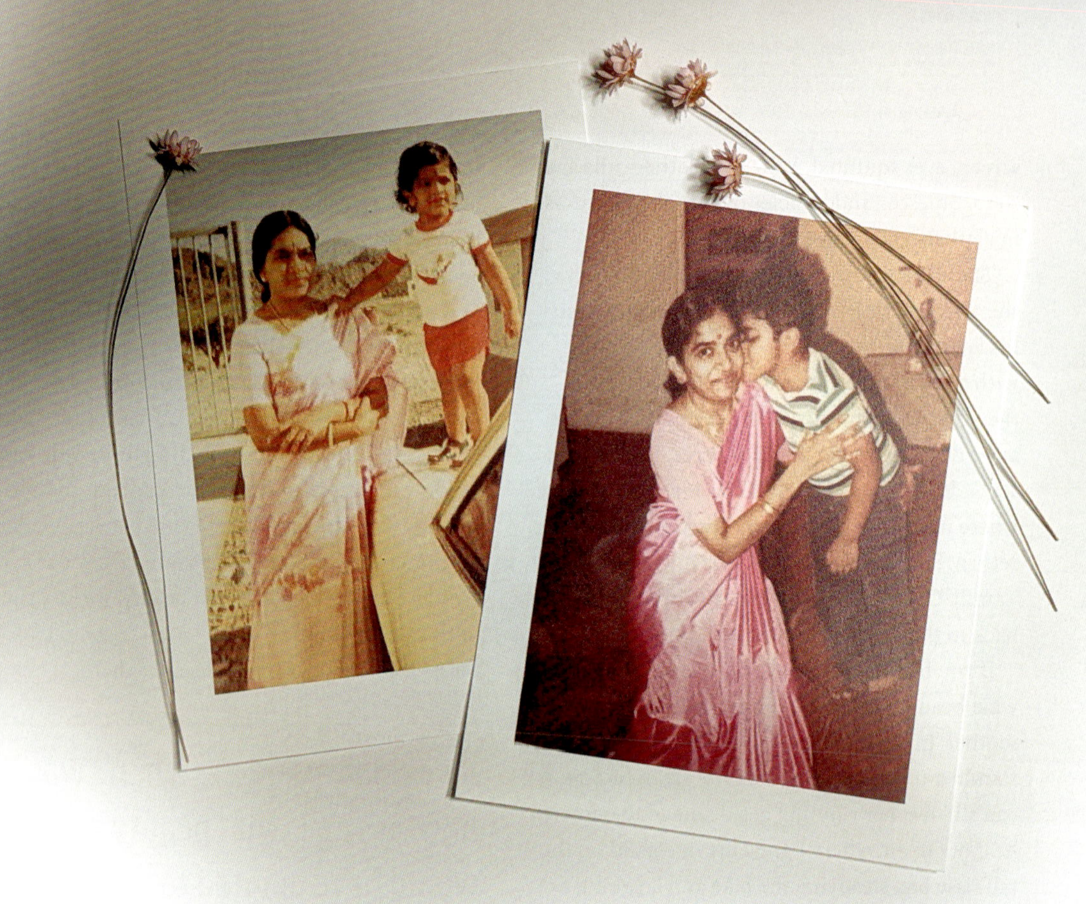

anyone anxious – you're always a foreigner, never at home, your visa one capricious administrative decision away from being cancelled, forcing your return to a home country where stable work is even more precarious. Genetics, neurochemistry and other unknown stresses were likely at work, but I didn't know any of this, and couldn't have seen it from the outside.

It probably didn't help that we were Brahmins, the highest rung in the Indian caste system. In our world, the mind was everything. Leading a respectable life meant becoming a physician, an engineer, a scientist. Here was another form of scripted beauty: you were supposed to excel in mathematics, to prove the power of reason. My mother's proudest accomplishment was the gold medal she won for topping her class in medical school. That was the kind her community knew how to admire. It featured prominently in the classified advertisement her family placed in the newspaper to elicit marriage proposals. But what happens to your worth, to your beauty, when you lose your mind?

One afternoon, I came home from school to find her shouting at an invisible visitor. A magician had appeared in our flat, she said, and he was responsible for making my father lose his job. She spoke to him in Tamil and English, eyes wide, lips tense. When my father suggested seeing a psychiatrist, she flared with blazing eyes: 'You think I am mad? I am a doctor! Gold medalist!'

I was unaware that anosognosia – the inability to recognise one's own illness – is a common feature of schizophrenia. To me it just seemed like stubborn denial, which only deepened my frustration. My own speech hardened into contempt and curses. I had decided that the woman in front of me was a problem to be managed, and resented her – and my father for not hospitalising her.

The Bollywood films my mother regularly watched presented mothers as tender and self-sacrificing, feeding their sons with radiant affection.

I fantasised what it would be like to grow up in a home where friends were invited in, where you could feel you belonged. My friends' mothers greeted us with warmth, and drew us into their orderly living rooms. 'Come, come, sit', a friend's mother sang out as she set out a real meal on a dining table, where the family – unlike ours – ate together. It was the beauty of a hospitality that was recognisable and expected, and one that was absent in my home. My mother scowled and grumbled when she fed me; she ate in the kitchen by herself, standing hunched over the counter, muttering to herself. None of this fit the script. And so, none of it was beautiful, and it repelled me, producing shame and disgust.

That disgust wasn't only my response to my mother; it became a way of reading myself. If beauty was the condition for belonging, then its absence meant exclusion and rejection. I learned to recoil not just from her but from what I feared I might become, and eventually from anything in me that didn't match the script. The standards I used to judge her became the ones I applied to myself.

This further fuelled my resentment towards my mother. Had she only fit the scripts of hospitality and affection, I convinced myself, I could have been more popular in class. Nothing wrong with a tidy room or a welcoming host – in many homes those are the first languages of beauty. But I used those standards to punish the person whom they no longer fit. Presentability became the conditional price of love.

One way this form of beauty infects society is through what psychologist Renee Engeln calls 'beauty sickness.' Our appearance-obsessed culture trains us to measure ourselves and others by very particular forms of beauty – at the cost of health, freedom and even love. Engeln's research focuses on the effects of beauty standards on women, but I saw the same mechanism at work in my own life. Such standards, Engeln shows, are often reinforced not just by media but by family members when judging their spouses and children. In my own home, I measured my mother by the scripts she could no longer perform. When beauty is reduced to what is legible only through our scripts, we spend our energy scrutinising what is on the surface and lose the capacity to perceive a person's worth.

My father and my younger brother, by contrast, never seemed to wrestle with this blindness. Somehow, they were able to recognise in my mother a beauty that I could not see. I don't know why it came more easily for them – whether temperament, habit or grace. For me, it took a conversion.

Our appearance-obsessed culture trains us to measure ourselves and others by very particular forms of beauty – at the cost of health, freedom and even love.

Shortly before I turned 19, through an unexpected confluence of events, I became a Christian. It is too complicated a story to tell here. But it opened me to a new kind of beauty that is not scripted. What I call revealed beauty is this radiance – the way reality shines forth as what it truly is.

I encountered this kind of beauty through people and experiences that unsettled my old criteria for scripted beauty: a mentor in church who saw in me more value than I could see in myself;

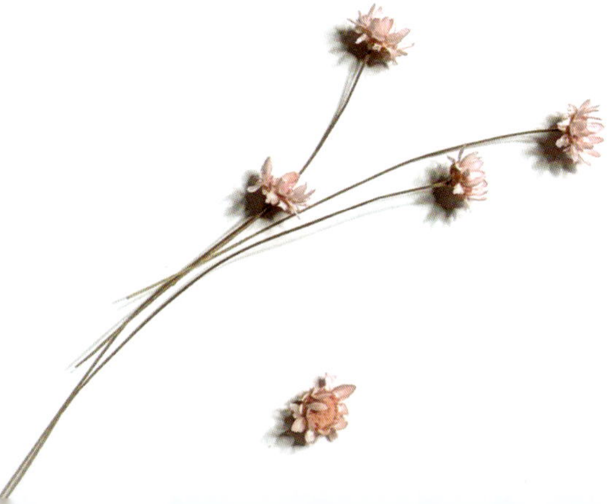

learning about Mother Teresa, who could look at the poorest of the poor and see Jesus; volunteering at L'Arche communities and befriending people with developmental disabilities in whom I met an undeniable joy and dignity. Becoming Christian

Seeing beauty in my mother again is an obligation of attention. It means refusing to make legibility the price of love.

entailed the recognition that my worth did not lie in performance, polish or conventionally scripted beauty. Rather, it was given – by Someone who loved me and beheld me as beautiful. And if that was true of me, then it was true of my mother. To accept that God delighted in me was to accept that she was just as precious in his eyes, regardless of her capacities. As a result, I began, slowly, to see my mother differently, and learned to find in her another kind of beauty.

Thomas Aquinas identifies radiance or *claritas* as a key criterion of beauty: the splendour of an object that makes its inner essence intelligible. A psychiatrist recently told me that this concept aptly describes where she finds beauty in her work, in moments when she recognises the flickers of personhood that illness can't erase – the brief glances and gestures when her client's true personality shines through. It's not the clarity of order or perfection, but that of beholding the person beneath the symptom. And it's truly something to delight in.

My mother was only diagnosed about ten years after the onset of her illness, when my father managed to trick her into a hospital visit. But the medications intended to help her mind ended up wreaking havoc on her stomach. After years of failed attempts, her psychiatrist concluded that my mother's life would be happier without medication.

Today she cannot hold a conversation for more than half a minute. Even in person, she turns away just as quickly as on the phone. But there are regular moments, such as when my toddler thrusts his latest Lego creation towards the camera, that her face becomes briefly transparent with joy. In those few seconds, her attention – which her illness often engulfs – is given wholly to another person. I suspect in those moments she encounters beauty as well.

Seeing beauty in my mother again is an obligation of attention. It means refusing to make legibility the price of love. It means holding together the facts of her illness and the honour due to her person. That means calling her every day with my children, and even travelling across the oceans on a long and uncomfortable flight once a year, in the hope of an encounter – so that they may see in her not just the strangeness but also the spark.

Scripted beauty is easy to process; it trains us, enchants us and helps us order our lives. We need it. But we neglect another form of beauty that is more demanding. It may not flatter our expectations and indeed may even offend them. It demands more of our eyes. It arrives unbidden, and asks for patience and humility. It arrives in weakness rather than strength. And perceiving it might require some kind of conversion – whether of faith or of attention.

To value such revealed beauty is to train ourselves to attend to what is easily missed, to wait for the radiance to surface. It is to recognise that presence is more important than presentation.

I used to think beauty had abandoned my mother. But I was wrong. What had disappeared was the scripted beauty I had been trained to look for. Learning to look again has taught me to wait for the revealed beauty that breaks through in her eyes. That beauty has not healed her illness. But it has helped me remember what it means to be her son.

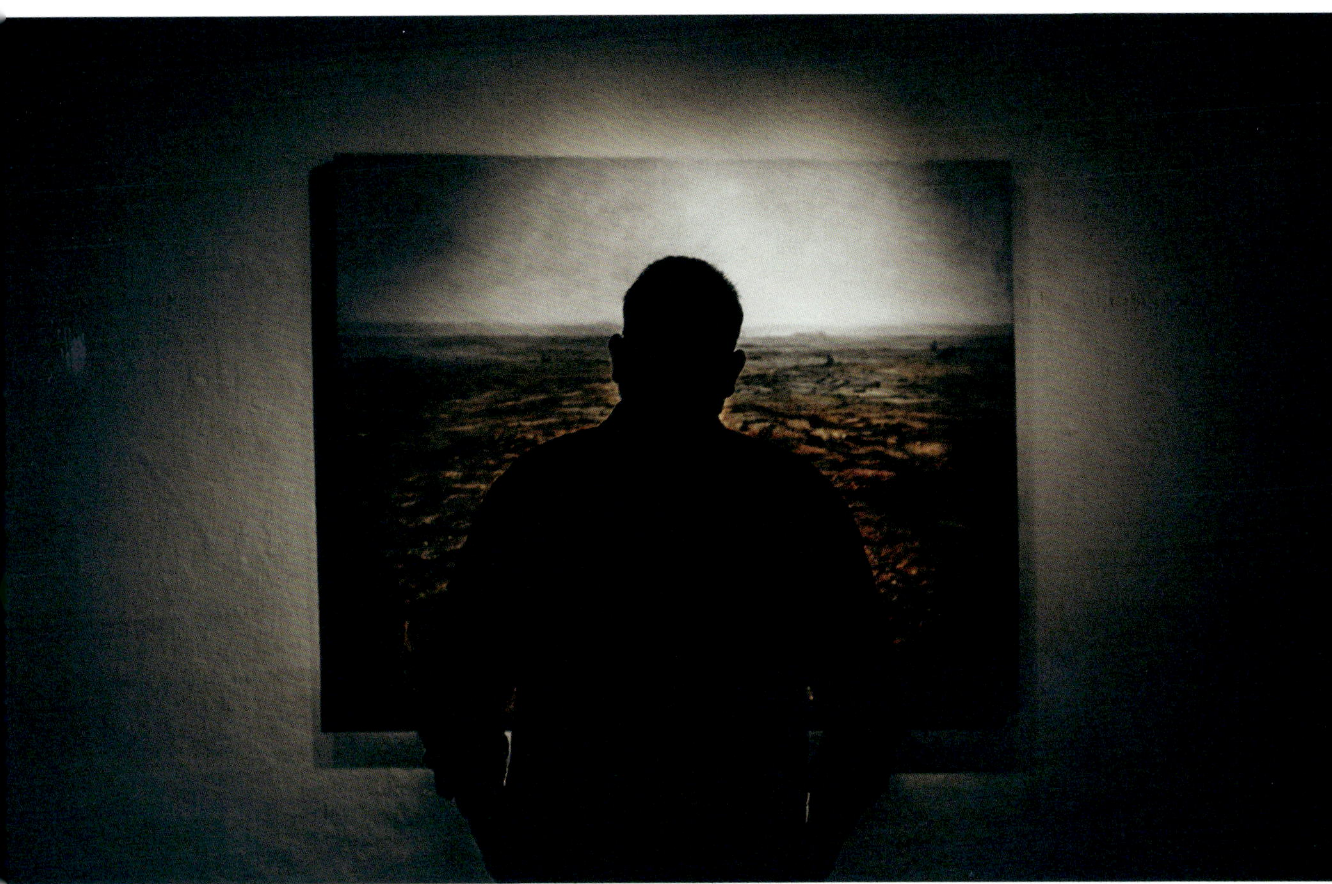

When Sight Becomes Adoration

Can a painting save you?

SEAN RUBIN

Photograph by Josep Pines on Unsplash. Used by permission.

My parents raised me in the faith, but my mother raised me in museums. When I was still travelling by stroller, she would take me on the Command Express bus from our neighbourhood in Canarsie, Brooklyn, into Manhattan to the Metropolitan Museum of Art. Later, when she recalled these trips, she told me that going between any two points within the Met had taken forever, because I would ask her to stop in front of nearly every painting so she could tell me about it. I can never remember a time when I didn't love art. Even though I am nearly 40 years old, I am still not sure if I love art for my own reasons, or if I love art because my mother loved it, and so it is a way of loving her.

My mother was born into a Roman Catholic family in 1951 and christened Denise Barbara Lanthier. She sang and chanted Latin in the choir

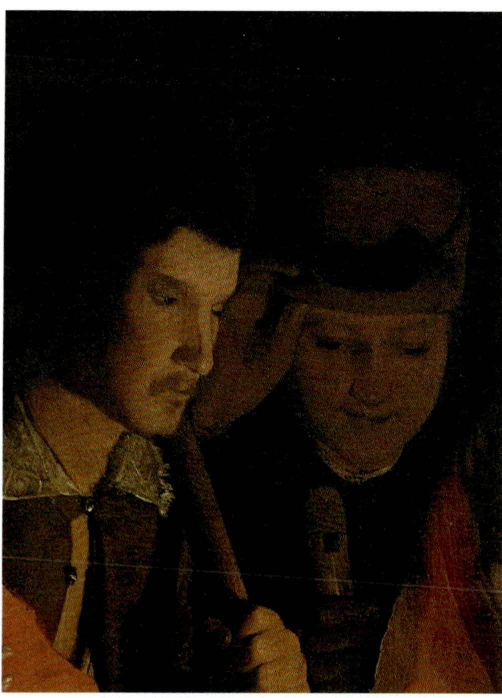

in a massive Romanesque Revival church on Flatlands Avenue in Brooklyn. At one point, the parish was so fruitful that it outgrew the sanctuary; her neighbourhood was told they would be leaving that grand building and would thereafter celebrate mass in a cinema. Around the same time, the Second Vatican Council dispatched her beloved Latin chants. And so my mother went from chanting the liturgy in a beautiful ancient tongue, in one of the most beautiful buildings in that part of the city, to sitting in a glum cinema and hearing the priest drone on in what Brooklynites insist is English. She began to ask questions.

As a young woman, my mother's escapes were art museums and Judaism. She would wander the galleries of the Brooklyn Museum, enjoying the art and imagining attending parties in its massive halls. Then she would take a short walk from the museum to 770 Eastern Parkway, the global headquarters of Chabad, and wait in line to receive a dollar from the Rebbe because she was looking for the blessings of Abraham. She had loved the Bible stories her mother would read before bed, especially the stories from Hebrew scripture. Her home life could be difficult, and I think she loved those narratives because they featured tales of miraculous escape – God was always choosing people, pulling them out of where they were and sending them to live more abundantly. At the same time, the things she valued, especially education, made her an outlier at home. She felt better understood by the Jewish families in her neighbourhood. Jewish friends even told her she had a Jewish soul. She fantasised about being adopted by a Jewish couple – or maybe she had been somehow switched at birth.

She tried to convert to Judaism, but she was never successful. For one thing, she always had to do the most involved version of everything. She only wanted to join Chabad, the Hasidic movement known for its vocal belief in a coming messiah. The rabbis she talked to were less inhospitable than politely confused. What Chabad will do, (almost) no questions asked, is give you a Jewish education. My mother received an excellent one, but from there she had nowhere to go. She stumbled through a spiritual odyssey, with a lot of almosts – she almost joined an ashram, until the guru announced his intention to arrange marriages among all the members; she almost was kidnapped by members of the Unification Church (the 'Moonies'), until she threatened to bang down a door; and she almost married a nice Jewish boy, until he turned out not so nice and she broke off the engagement. She did receive a dollar from the Lubavitcher Rebbe, Menachem Mendel Schneerson, one evening on Eastern Parkway. I'm not sure how many people

---

Sean Rubin is the author and illustrator of several books for children, including Bolivar, This Very Tree *and* The Iguanodon's Horn; *and an illustrator for Brian Jacques'* Redwall *series. He lives with his family on a farm in central Virginia.*

Georges La Tour, *Adoration of the Shepherds*, oil on canvas, 1644 (detail).

leave the Christian church to await the Messiah with Chabad. It cannot be a large number. But my mother wanted a messiah. Her relationship with Jesus was never one of rejection, but of disappointment. The Jews had been promised a king. So far as she could tell, Jesus wasn't it.

By her late 20s, she was spiritually adrift and living in California, far from her Brooklyn family. She had accepted that she'd never become a Hasidic Jew, though she still held faith. The 1970s were nearly over, and across America, people were becoming born-again, whatever that meant. One evening, during a routine call back to New York, her sister was almost hysterical about something called the sinner's prayer, saying that if she didn't accept Jesus into her heart, my mother was going to hell. At the time, my mother took this to be the latest volley in a long history of sibling power struggles. But for the first time in a long while, a particular window had been pried open – even if only a little.

My mother had a wonderful and sometimes confusing gift, which is that even if she had little interest or understanding for something you were passionate about, and even if she disagreed, it didn't prevent her from encouraging you. She also loved Christmas shopping. That year, while shopping for her sister, she found a book called *The Christmas Story in Masterpieces*, introduced by David Rossoff. This was a coffee table book filled with reproductions of European paintings from the Renaissance onward. In my mother's eyes, it was the perfect gift. If her sister was betting everything on this Jesus business, she could at least pick up some culture along the way.

As my mother looked through the book, she found paintings from the nativity cycle, accompanied by quotes from the Gospel of Matthew. She paused over a painting of the Slaughter of the Innocents, juxtaposed with Jeremiah 31: 'A voice was heard in Ramah, lamentation, and bitter weeping; Rachel weeping for her children refused to be comforted for her children, because they were not.' Then she turned a page and saw Georges La Tour's *Adoration of the Shepherds.*

The painting is straightforward enough. The infant Christ, apparently illuminated by candlelight, is shown in a wicker manger, a lamb still trying to pull some hay from beneath the sleeping baby. Christ is surrounded by five figures, mostly shown from the waist up – the Virgin Mary, three shepherds and Saint Joseph, who holds the candle. The light shines on all the figures, although tellingly, the middle shepherd is mostly in the dark. The adoration of the shepherds was never the most popular motif. If you painted an adoration of the magi, you could do all the gold and crowns and camels – exciting stuff, interesting to look at and you could charge your patron extra. When you painted an adoration of shepherds, you were mostly painting shepherds – dirty, smelly shepherds. But that was the point. As Philip K Dick said, 'The symbols of the divine show up in our world initially at the trash stratum.' In the book my mother was holding, a caption on the opposite page offered a reasonable interpretation of the painting: '*A smirking peasant boy in the background touches his cap, as if to a passing bigwig, unable, perhaps, to understand the implications of what he sees.*'

My mother told me this story often enough that I can still hear it in her voice. 'I realised I was the peasant with the smirk! I never disrespected Jesus. Why would I? He had been a good moral teacher, and then he was killed. I finished reading the rest of the book, and when I closed the cover I yelled out, almost involuntarily, "Oh my God – Jesus is the Messiah!"'

Some people come to Jesus easily. Some get thrown from horses on the Damascus Road, whereafter they are dragged into the kingdom kicking and screaming. And then there's Denise Lanthier, who had to start over at Abraham and work her way through all of redemptive history, as illustrated by old European masterpieces.

The epiphany completely upended my mother's

life. She eventually did say the sinner's prayer, and she also moved back to New York and began graduate school in art history – inspired, as you might imagine, by her experience with La Tour. When she met my father, a nicer Jewish boy named David Rubin, she changed her focus to early and elementary education. My dad had accepted Jesus a few years earlier, when someone in a pool hall told him to read Isaiah 53. They were married as Christians, although they said their vows under a chuppah, and the pastor prayed in the name of Yeshua at their wedding. She became Denise Lanthier Rubin in 1983 and a mother in 1986, the same year she earned her master's degree. I thus grew up in a house where we celebrated Jewish and Christian holidays, and where I was taught from the cradle to love Jesus, the Messiah of Israel.

MY MOTHER PASSED AWAY unexpectedly in the summer of 2025. In the days and weeks after, I found myself thinking a lot about La Tour's *Adoration of the Shepherds*, and why it was through this image, among so many, that God had revealed himself to her that Christmas. It may have helped that the painting was unfamiliar. The book she gave her sister was filled with the grandest Botticellis and El Grecos, but she would have known those already. It may have also helped that the painting is just *very good*. Extraordinary, even. La Tour is hardly a household name, but that's our failure, not his. His favourite trick was lighting a scene by candlelight, and then hiding the candle behind a figure's arm or hand, so that the warm glow seems to radiate not from a flame but from the Christ Child, or a leaf of paper, or even from the faces of gamblers. He was clearly influenced by Caravaggio, although at times La Tour's pictures can feel like a quiet critique of Caravaggio's melodrama. Caravaggio lights everything like it's the Conversion of Saul, in a manner often compared to theatrical spotlights. La Tour's lighting is diegetic, coming from a light source within the painting.

At this point, in the freshman art history paper, you'd spin a theological yarn out of these two different lighting styles. You'd probably mention that the source of Caravaggio's light is so high and removed from the figures, it must surely suggest God himself, whereas La Tour is focusing on the simple humanity of his subjects. You may even claim Caravaggio's light is transcendent, but La Tour's light is immanent. Along with the theologian and musician Jeremy Begbie, I would suggest that setting these categories against each other is boring, first-year theology stuff. Instead, try looking at these artists in terms of two categories proposed by Begbie to explain the vision of divine transcendence revealed in the New Testament: God's otherness and God's uncontainability. Carvaggio's light captures the first category in a fairly obvious way. The light touches the figures, but from somewhere remote, quite literally beyond the frame. The light is other, even if it illuminates everything. But what of La Tour?

In La Tour's *Adoration*, the light is both other and uncontainable. Other, because upon closer inspection, the light in his painting isn't exactly of our world. At first, it's easy to attribute the warm glow to the candle in Joseph's hand. But his attempts to shield the light don't seem to be working, and the light falls mostly on Jesus – so much so, the light actually appears to be coming from the baby. Thus the artist invites a question: Does the light come from the infant, or the flame? Or perhaps both? It's easy to attribute the miraculous to material causes, even when you have more proof of a miracle than of the mundane. The viewer can't really see the candle – the wax and the flame are mostly implied, while the infant is completely visible. I think that's part of the idea behind the painting. If you want a materialist explanation, by all means assume the candle is lighting the scene. Most candles don't shine that brightly, but then again, neither do most infants. Maybe the baby really is just a baby. Or maybe you're missing the implications.

This all makes the *Adoration* a particularly brilliant meditation on the Incarnation, via John's Gospel. *In Christ was light, and that light was the life of men.* If the light is divinity, by covering the flame with his hand, Joseph evokes the Incarnation beautifully. Try as he might to control it, the uncontainable light of God still shines through human flesh. (Which reminds me – you know when you were little and you put your hand over the bulb of a flashlight, and your flesh glowed a deep orange, especially around the edges? La Tour was a master at painting that effect.) Looking back, my mother's quarrel with God was always about the truth of who Jesus was. For most of her life, she had believed he was just a baby. And then, suddenly – the true light shone in darkness, and the darkness did not overcome it. Of course Jesus would meet my mother at Christmas.

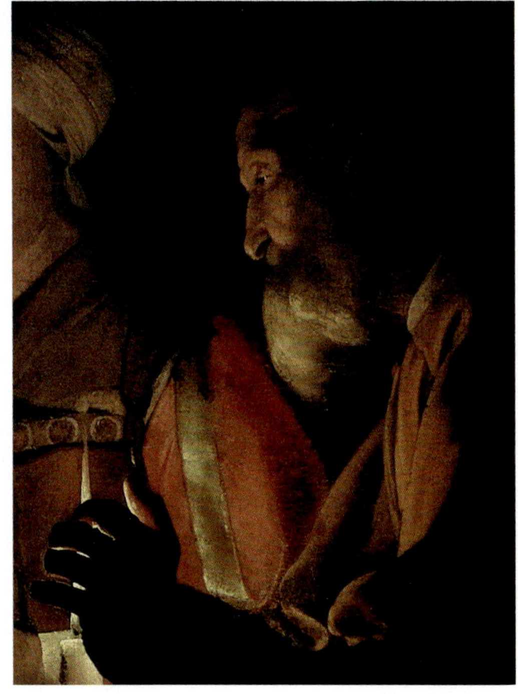

I FOUND THE PAINTING years later, in the Louvre, while I was studying abroad in Europe. I had made a pilgrimage to the quiet gallery mostly ignored by the throngs of tourists who come to take bad pictures of the *Mona Lisa* through bulletproof glass. For me, La Tour's *Adoration* was far more important than the *Mona Lisa*. We never hung a reproduction of the painting in my childhood home, but I suspect the painting had a continuing influence on my mother, perhaps beyond what she shared with me. Or maybe she was drawn to it because of currents already moving within her. When I returned to the painting recently, I began to notice certain resonances not only with her journey back to the faith, but with the vocation to which she devoted the rest of her life – education.

The most profound resonance involves what the philosophical theologian Judith Wolfe refers to as 'perceptual training': exposing oneself and one's children to God, his word and his church, in order to form one's senses to see things rightly. The *Adoration* was a pointed invitation, almost a challenge, to see rightly – if only you could. My mother was a lifelong educator, primarily known for teaching art and Latin, especially to elementary students. She was working on a Latin lesson plan the night she died, a detail that makes total sense to those who knew her. She cofounded a classical Christian school because she loved classical education, although not the kind tied to contemporary political movements. Instead, she loved the trivium because it taught children to identify and understand what was good, beautiful and true. She never cared for the jargon of higher thinking skills or 'teaching children how to think', which was very much in vogue during the early part of her career. For her, education was never a disembodied intellectual exercise. It was always about perceptual training, helping children to love the lovely. I think back to her teaching a church history class to 13 and 14 year olds, the students debating pre-Nicene

Georges La Tour, *Adoration of the Shepherds*, oil on canvas, 1644 (detail).

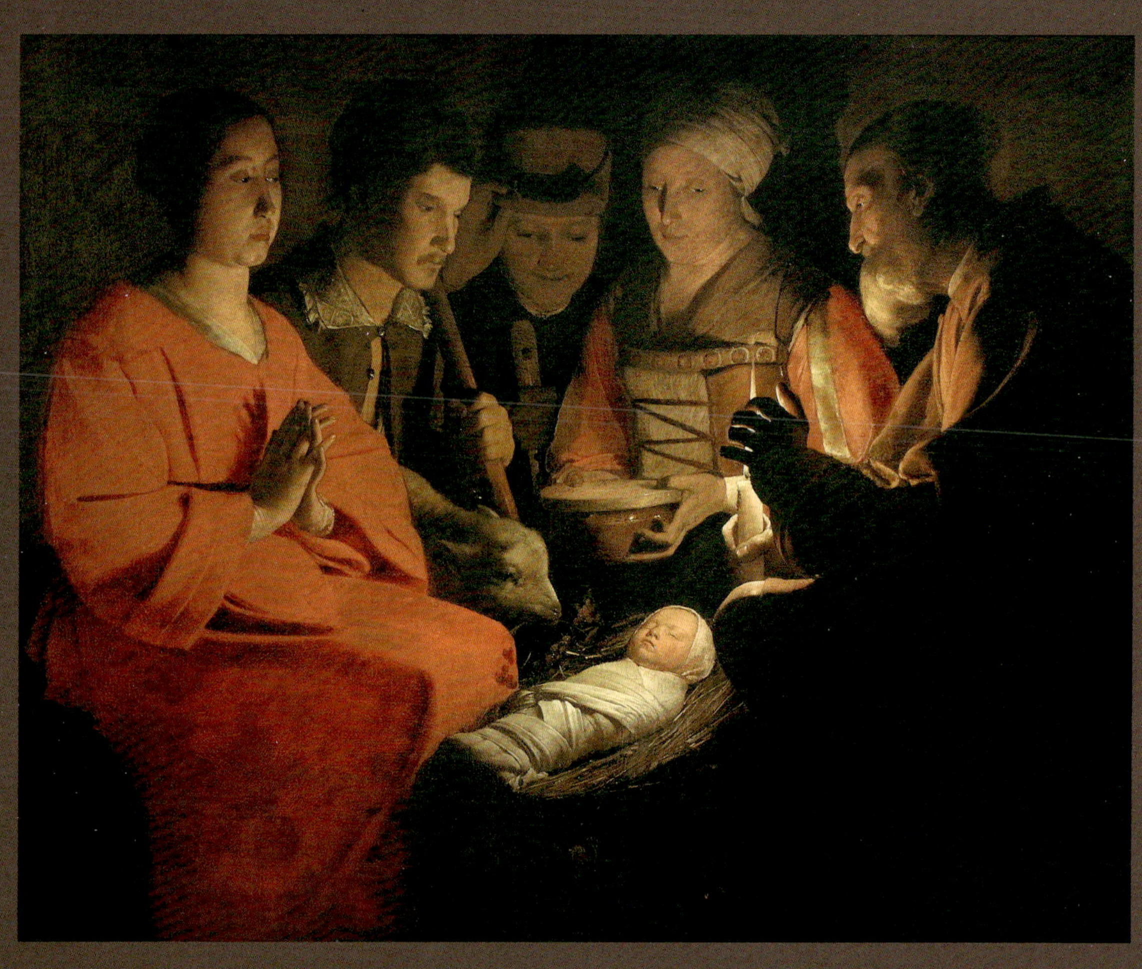

heresies while drinking tea or hot chocolate and listening to Gregorian chants on a CD player. The senses were always engaged. As Judith Wolfe points out in *The Theological Imagination*, this kind of education cultivates something akin to what we call 'taste' – a taste for God, and perhaps a sense of where best to find him.

If education is about learning to see rightly, there is no better way to learn how to see than by looking at art. But what art should you look at? My mother's own taste was immaculate. I've thought back on what she would show me in those museums, even going back to when I was in a stroller. Her favourite artists were those of the early Renaissance, although she would often point out that the line between the late Middle Ages and the Renaissance was really just a piece of Northern Italian chauvinism and myth-making – thank you Vasari. She gravitated towards Fra Angelico, Fra Filippo Lippi and of course Botticelli. She loved artists who could pull off particularly sympathetic depictions of women and children, and she loved Flemish tapestries and the insular manuscript tradition. She was often partial to the version of the thing prior to its full development – always early, never late. She preferred the Romanesque to the Gothic, Baroque music over Classical, the Lindisfarne Gospels to the Book of Kells. She collected Shaker furniture and Amish quilts, yet paradoxically she adored Byzantine art – especially the icons, the saints in their jewel-coloured robes on warm, gilt backgrounds. She loved altarpieces of all kinds. Most of all, and perhaps predictably, she loved images of the Annunciation, the Nativity and anything involving angels. Around her birthday, 29 December, she would insist on going into Manhattan, either to visit the Cloisters museum or to see 'the tree' – which for her was not the Christmas tree in Rockefeller Center, but the tree in the medieval court at the Met on Fifth Avenue, decorated in stately Neapolitan angels.

The Met was my mother's favourite classroom, and I was chief amongst her disciples. I can picture her in the Met's Greek and Roman galleries, her students following her like a flock of ducklings, or maybe on a day trip when I was a teenager. We'd peer through the halogen gloom and perform a sort of differential diagnosis on the image of a saint – an older man, holding the baby Jesus in one arm while holding a hammer and nails in his opposite hand – Joseph, the patron saint of Sicily, her favourite. The best art was art that illustrated scripture. She would tell her students that many Christians in the Middle Ages simply couldn't read, and so the paintings, the stained glass windows, sometimes even the church building itself were their Bible. Thus, to learn to see Christian art rightly was to comprehend Scripture – to encounter the Word made flesh, and finally understand its implications. Which is not to say she believed images were imbued with supernatural powers – at least, not in the mystical sense of the supernatural. For the most part, she would gently roll her eyes and shake her head if you suggested that contact with icons could heal illness. In the later years of her life, she seemed less dismissive of these possibilities, but they were never very important to her because they missed the point. To say a work of art was capable of healing in this way was to reduce the image to a mere object. The real power of the image was its content and its meaning, and how the artist conveyed that meaning to the viewer.

Looking back, I can see that my mother had been doing theology from the start. Paintings, windows and tapestries were her texts, but her subject was always her Creator. She knew, from her own life, that you could find Christ in a work of art, or rather that Christ would find you. And while a painting could certainly mediate a transcendent experience, it could also proclaim God's power unto salvation. That is why she loved art, and why she taught others to love it and to see it rightly – not just to look but to participate in the miracle, lest we smirk and doff our hats, not understanding what we see.

Georges La Tour, *Adoration of the Shepherds*, oil on canvas, 1644.

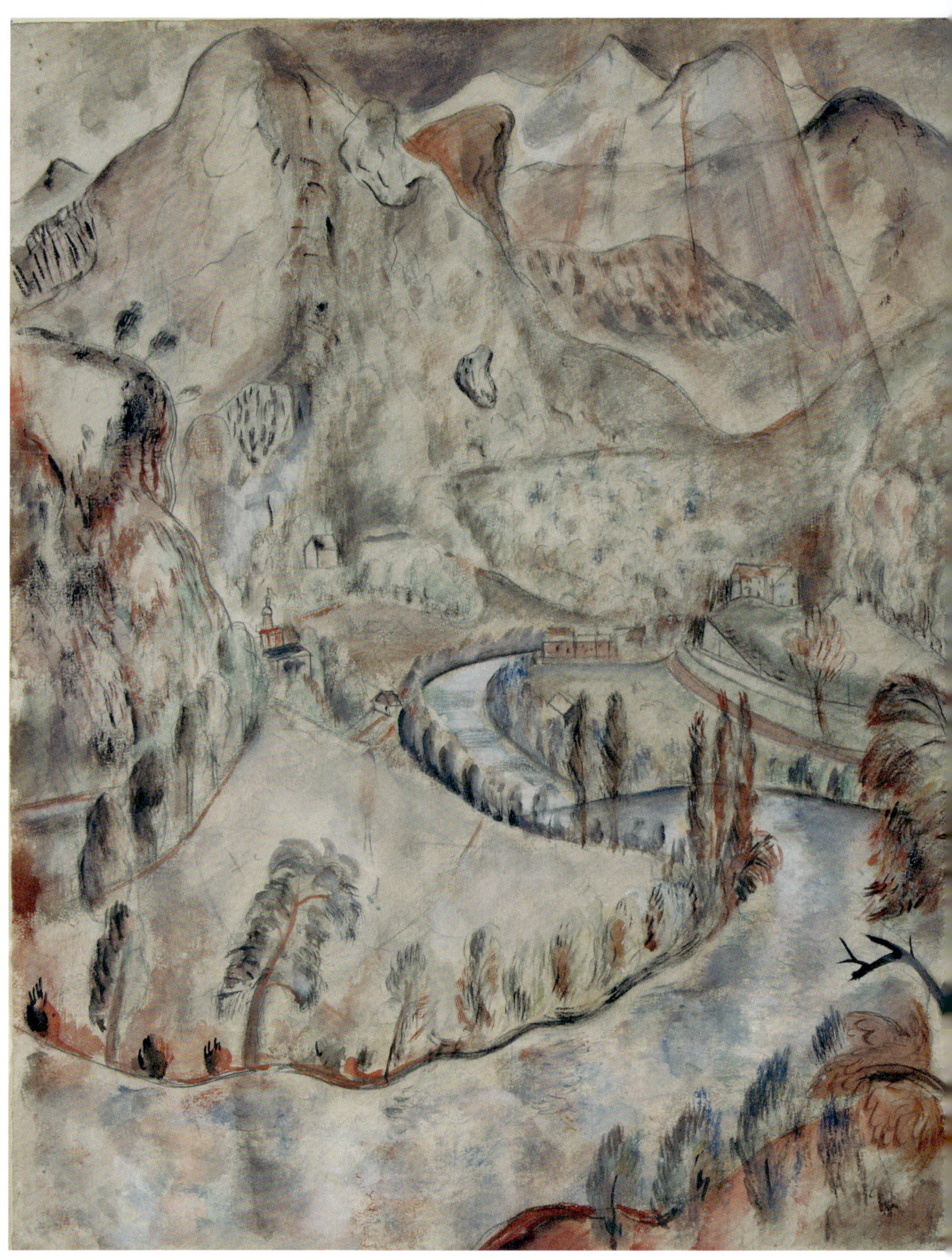

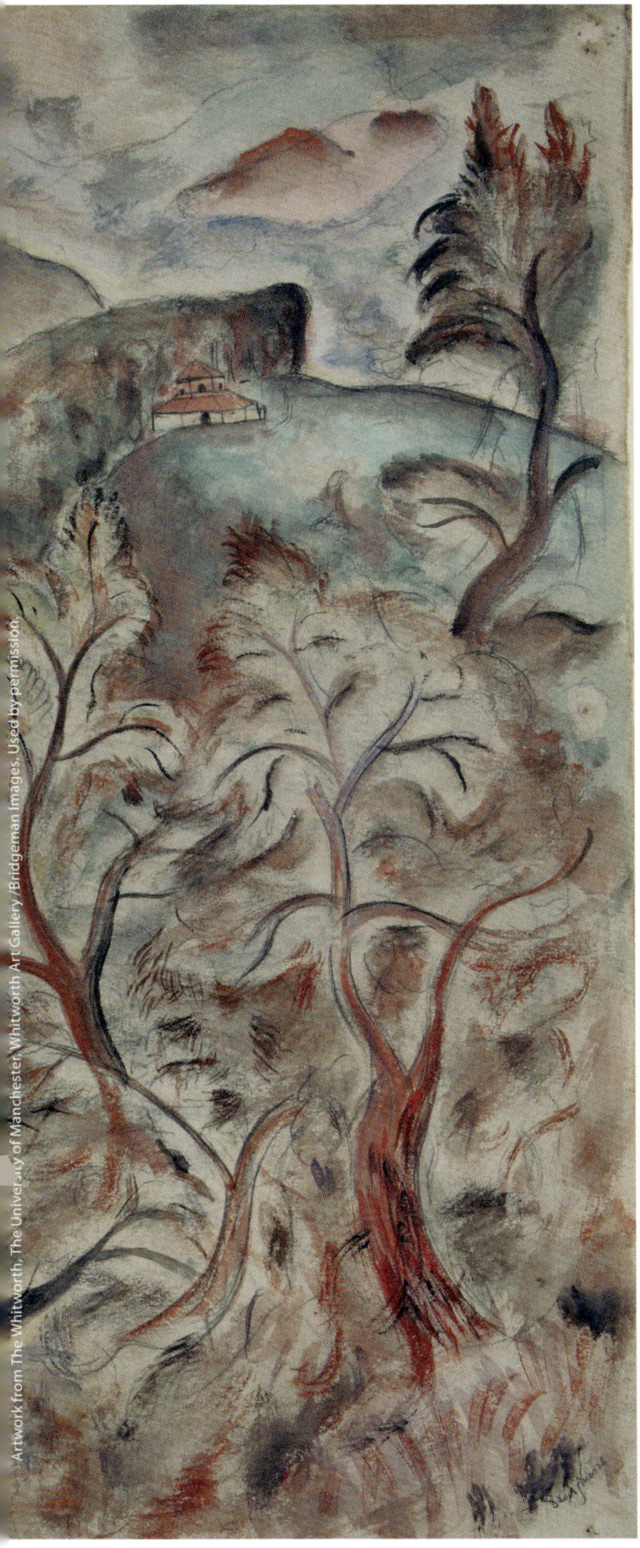

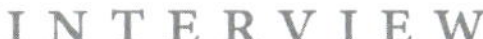

Layers of Beauty

How does beauty shape the Christian imagination?

BEN QUASH

Plough: How do the Christian scriptures speak about beauty?

Ben Quash: In the Greek of the New Testament, the language of beauty and the language of goodness are often pretty much interchangeable. For example, in Mark 14:6, Jesus says the woman who anoints his feet has done something beautiful. In English it is translated as a 'beautiful thing', but the word in Greek is *kalos*, which means 'good'; literally, Jesus commends her for a 'good work.' That's interesting! The equation of moral or spiritual goodness with beauty is characteristic of the few references in the New Testament to beauty. This closeness between goodness and beauty anticipates later medieval discussions of beauty as a transcendental property of being, something rooted in existence and ultimately in God.

Professor Ben Quash holds the chair of Christianity and the Arts at King's College London, and is the director of the Visual Commentary on Scripture, a project he runs in collaboration with the National Gallery in London.

David Jones, *Montes et Omnes Colles*, watercolour and pencil, 1928.

By contrast, in the Old Testament there is a profusion of words for beauty, and part of learning how to manage them is to realise that some are applied primarily to creatures, and some are applied only to God. There are characters who are notable in Old Testament terms for their physical beauty, including the young David, Abigail and Absalom, although it did the latter no good because his 'beautiful' long hair is what caught in a tree and caused his death. So, there's already an awareness in the Old Testament that the beauty of appearances can also be a perilous thing.

Then there's an idea of integrity as beauty. Job is described as having this quality of integrity. It's the same word that's used to describe acceptable sacrifices in the temple. They must be without blemish. In other words, and this is really interesting to me, beauty in that context doesn't mean something idealised and removed from the ordinary. In the Old Testament terms, this kind of beauty is precisely being what you're meant to be. So, a lamb without blemish is just a really lamby lamb; not some kind of exceptional lamb, different from all the other lambs, but a lamb with all the right bits in all the right places. And that's, I think, a nice reminder to our own 21st-century culture to question its obsession with standing out, and its search for a beauty that somehow sets you apart from others.

Finally, in Psalm 29, we are invited to worship the Lord in the beauty of holiness. The word there is a different word from that used to describe the beauty of human appearances. It's the language of splendour. And then there's the unique language of glory – *kabod* in Hebrew – which is only used of God.

How does Plato understand beauty, and how does that shape the Christian tradition's account of beauty?

That's an evolving debate – especially, actually, when it touches on the arts. But, generally speaking, for Plato, the realest things are the noncorporeal ideal Forms; the material things we encounter in this world are merely shadows of the real. When he's discussing beauty, he recognises it as part of the created world, and sees our encounters with it as less than ideal. They're mediating (in different respects and to different degrees) the ideal beauty of the One. Through beauty we can begin a journey towards the One, but it is only through abandoning the material world that we ascend.

There's a great deal of this that Christianity will take up and use. The Platonic idea promotes an ascent from attention to the created order around us towards the source of that beauty, and in Christian terms, that source is the Creator, the giver of all life, the one who graces all things with their beauty. The crucial difference between Plato and Christianity is that in Plato the radical transcendence of the ideal Form plays too easily into a dualism: the created world is bad and needs to be escaped, and the spiritual world is good. There might be a mediation going on in our experiences of beauty, and you can make a journey towards the ideal Forms through it. But there's a sense that the world of material things is denigrated.

The Christian gospel of the Incarnation, on the contrary, has this powerful affirmation of the material order as God's chosen language for disclosing his beauty to the world. And that the glorification and the exultation of this created world and of human bodies as part of that created world are absolutely at the centre of the gospel. There's no sense in which you must leave them behind once you climb the ladder of beauty. They're taken up. The ladder is taken up too. And I think that that's a very important difference.

How about Aristotle?

There are interesting differences with Aristotle, the other great heavy-hitter in terms of ancient Greek philosophy. For him, a lot of what beauty is about is the coming to fruition, or realisation of potential. And that gives him a much more positive approach to the arts. Plato is, perhaps unfairly, often

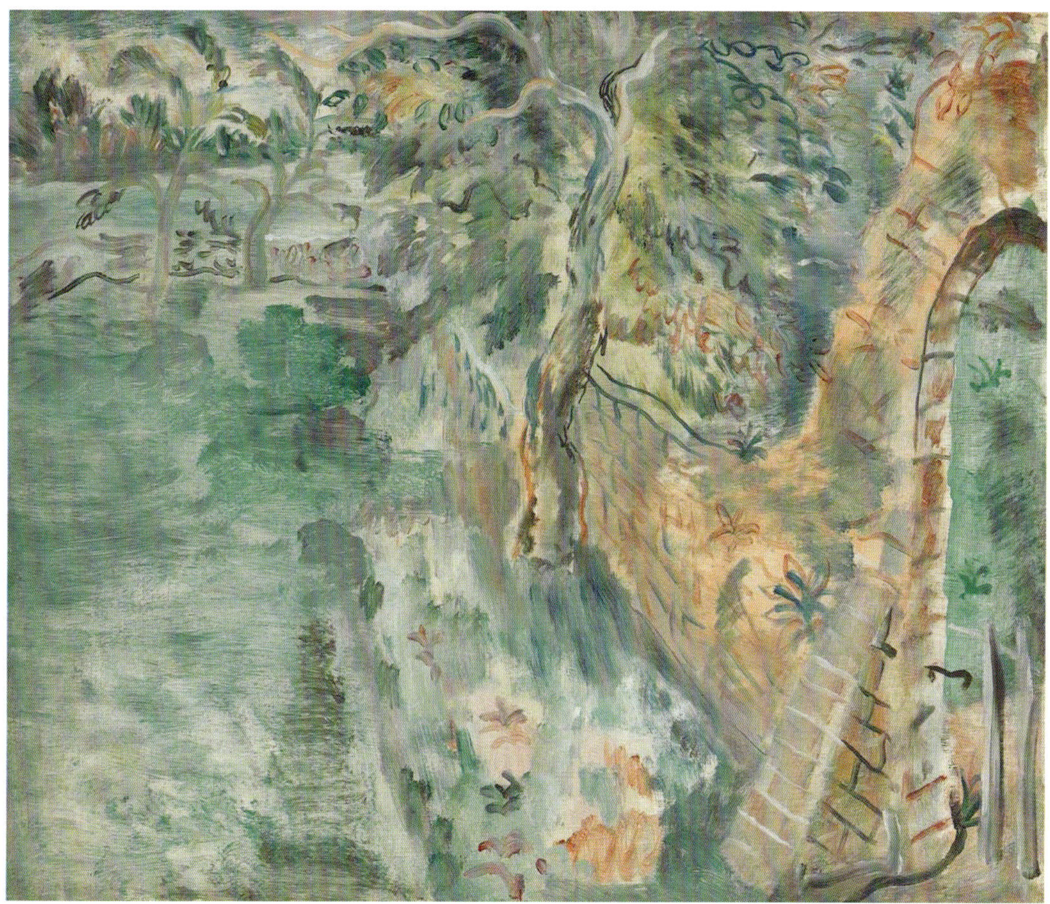

regarded as an uncompromising enemy of the arts because of the last book of *The Republic,* in which he says that there's no place for artists in the ideal city because they deceive us, and that imitations are always deceptions because they're lesser than the true object they're mimicking.

Aristotle is much more clearly positive about the arts, and I think it's partly because he sees one of the functions of artists as being to bring the potential of things to realisation – unlocking a block of stone's potential to be a sculpture, for example. He also sees a moral value in artistic representation. To take a literary example, when watching Greek tragedy, we're presented with, yes, imitations of situations that might be real in human life, but through them we are able to reflect on questions about right action in the world, and they therefore perform an educative function, a pedagogical function which serves the good. And that is part of the actualisation of our own potentiality as human creatures towards the good. You can see I've already slipped from a discussion of beauty into a discussion of the arts, because even then, they're constantly weaving in and out of each other.

Who is your favourite theologian of beauty?

Thomas Traherne. It almost brings me to tears when I read Traherne. He was a 17th-century poet and the most exquisite writer of prose. An Anglican mystic really, writing remotely in the West of England. Not a great deal is known about

David Jones, *Walled Garden*, oil on board, ca 1930.

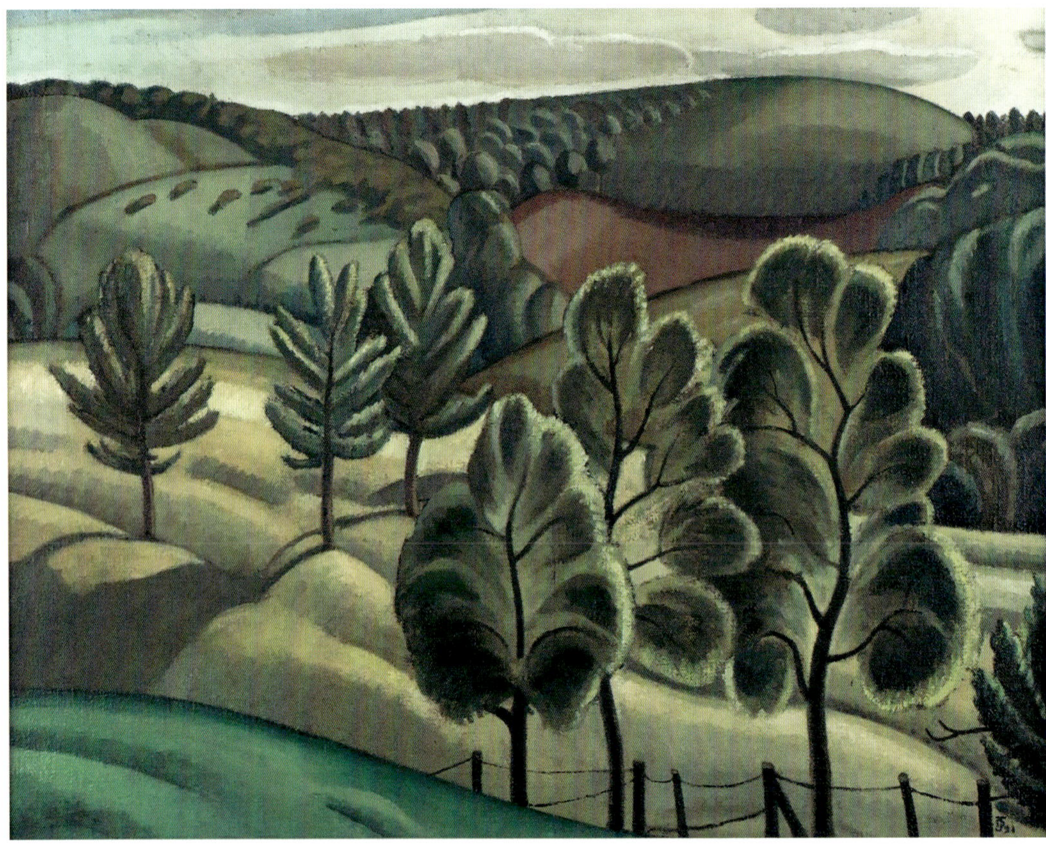

him. Many of his works are lost, but some have been found quite recently. He writes in the spirit of the metaphysical poets like John Donne and George Herbert. And beauty runs as a constant thread through his writings. He's intoxicated by it! It colours the way he sees everything around him in the world. This is in a way that is sort of platonic, but also so affirming of the material world. He talks about the Creation as the 'frontispiece of eternity': it's that front page of a book which is charged with the promise of what lies within. So, when we look at the world, we're seeing only the frontispiece, but it's not obscuring; it's promising. It's promising what's to come. And everywhere he looks, he sees eternity announcing itself. He can meditate ecstatically on the tiniest thing, on a humble fly, and see the respect and glory of its iridescence as already a foretaste of glory. It's amazing.

I think Traherne's influence runs through the Romantics to some degree. I feel there's a Trahernean spirit in Coleridge, whom I love as well, and people like Gerard Manley Hopkins, I suspect. And then it runs into the 20th century. It's a tradition I call mystical empiricism. The empiricism bit is looking at the world and its objects, its creatures, with intense attention. Not idealising them but really looking at them as they are. And it's mystical because precisely in that close attention to the very particularities of things, you find yourself suddenly feeling yourself to be in touch with ultimacy, with grace, with divine self-communication. These creatures are conduits of God's presence and purpose, precisely in their unique particularities. Observation of them becomes a sort of mystical form of encounter with the divine. That's what Hopkins is doing when he looks at the windhover

David Jones, *Landscape in Kent*, oil on canvas, 1921.

flying or the kingfisher 'catching fire.'

David Jones, the poet and painter, is one to whom I would point as one of the great appreciators of beauty in that tradition in the 20th century. And so much of that is caught up with the natural world, and with attention to it. It's not one of these intellectual ideas of beauty that you might find in a more anti-materialistic platonic tradition, but the contemplation of particular things in the world, the roses outside your window, the changing leaves outside of mine, that gesture beyond themselves to the real.

Traherne is writing at the time of the birth of modern science. This is where the very first steps towards organised natural science are taking place as a sort of distinct discipline with its own methods. But he's at that brief moment, that cusp, where there's no distinction between natural scientific method and praise. It's like doxological science. It's science that gives glory. And within the next 50 to 100 years after Traherne was writing that won't seem to be a possibility anymore. It's a door that gets closed. But for Traherne, an encyclopedia can be punctuated with exclamations of praise at every point. You're kind of mapping the world, learning about the world and constantly referring it to God in praise. I long for a doxological science. A science that can be the recognition of beauty.

From teaching and working with you, I am inclined to think that your account of beauty is deeply formed by the English landscape. Would you say that's true?

I draw deeply on the layeredness of long-inhabited place. That sense of, as Gerard Manley Hopkins puts it, a landscape 'plotted and pieced', 'fold, fallow and plough'; the layering of long habitation, collective habitation and the relationships that therefore evolve between human and non-human creatures. The soil, the fauna and the flora play very much into my own instincts about what I find beautiful and from which I draw theological conclusions about the bounty of God and what constitutes a wise life.

The English landscape has been very poorly treated in recent decades. Modern farming techniques are very damaging to it, and the biodiversity

---

Traherne talks about the creation as the 'frontispiece of eternity': the front page of a book which is charged with the promise of what lies within. It's not obscuring; it's promising. Everywhere he looks, he sees eternity announcing itself.

---

of England is far less than it was 100 years ago. There are real issues that we face, and one can all too easily be overly romantic about it. Nevertheless, in the literary traditions as well as the theological traditions that love the English landscape, I find a complex mutuality of human and non-human, built up over centuries, culminating in a compelling account of what beauty is.

One of the theologians from whom I learned a great deal was Dan Hardy, originally an American theologian who then spent most of his academic career in the United Kingdom. He used to contrast the English garden with the campus at the University of Virginia. The latter's original architecture was very classical and still is, at its core. And he said that was an architecture that spoke of the exclusion of wild nature under the impress of reason. So human reason, as it were, puts wild nature outside, keeps it at a safe distance. You would originally look down the lawn of the University of Virginia campus and nature would be in the distance, while everything would be under rational human control inside the perimeter. And eventually, even that view towards the outside was blocked off by more buildings.

And he said, this is a kind of metaphor for a way of relating to nature as wild, dangerous, other, irrational. And beauty was all those nice pediments and columns with their correct spacing.

By contrast, the English garden is much more reciprocal and messy. Its beauty lies in the fact that there are endless negotiations going on between the plants as they find the right space to get some light and water – but also, the human inhabitants who work with the plants to make them to be their best. These spillages and entanglements suggest a very different relationship with the natural world. And it's in such relationships that beauty sits. It's not just a measurable thing that you look at and say, this is a ratio of three to five, this is a beautiful ratio. It's much more of an intuitive, instinctive sense of how things are hanging together well or not. Those sorts of judgements appeal to me more. They are more organic and properly expressive of a love of the world as it is, rather than making it something it isn't. So that's a long way of affirming what you've detected in me: I like this kind of organic, messy, interactive, reciprocal beauty. I see that as English beauty.

David Jones has a lovely little essay reflecting on the English garden in the second volume of his writings (*The Dying Gaul*, which was published after his death). He thinks there's something distinctively English about that sort of garden, and he sees precursors of it as well in certain kinds of English painting and tapestry from medieval times, but he thinks there's a continuous tradition that's still alive.

Talk of beauty can sometimes seem very abstract or ivory tower, but you make it seem very integral. How does our idea of beauty affect our day-to-day lives?

This takes us back into the language of relationship. A belief in beauty may be awoken in us by what we experience around us, and sustained by ongoing ways of relating to what's around us. By the same token, faith can be something that often feels very vulnerable to evidence. Hopkins talks about the encroachment of certain kinds of toxic, destructive, wilderness-destroying forces. And Jones similarly laments the uniform nozzles of factory-made bottles. He seeks for the Logos in these things – and in the pylons strutting across the landscape – and cannot find Him.

Hopkins and Jones are aware of this vulnerability. They're aware that one could say it's just wishful thinking to believe that beauty is some kind of ultimate thing that the world tells us about. But I think that often – as with faith – to live in it and to live *into* it is to find confirmations of it. And that changes the way you live. The belief that beauty seeks to speak to us should make us more gently attentive, more patiently attentive and more optimistically attentive – more hopefully attentive, actually. For hope is more than optimism. It's a *disposition*, not a feeling; a disposition that sometimes we need to hold ourselves to. Something we need to actively pursue. That sort of determination will take the form of better relationships, not just with the things we look at (whether artworks or natural objects, the things we might categorise as *aesthetic* objects), but it will affect the way we relate to each other, and the kinds of communities we make. Because there's beauty in all relationships. Relationship, in a sense, is beauty. Good relationship is beauty. And that will include the relationship between two notes, or three notes, in a composition. The relationship between two colours in a painting, the proportions of an architectural space. But it extends to other forms of relationship, other kinds of good proportion. In the hierarchies of our social organisations, in the forms of mutual and reciprocal care and the distribution of responsibilities that any human family or society needs, where we seek to play our part in relation to others. When those things work, they are beautiful.

This interview was conducted by Joy Marie Clarkson on 2 October 2025, and has been edited for length and clarity.

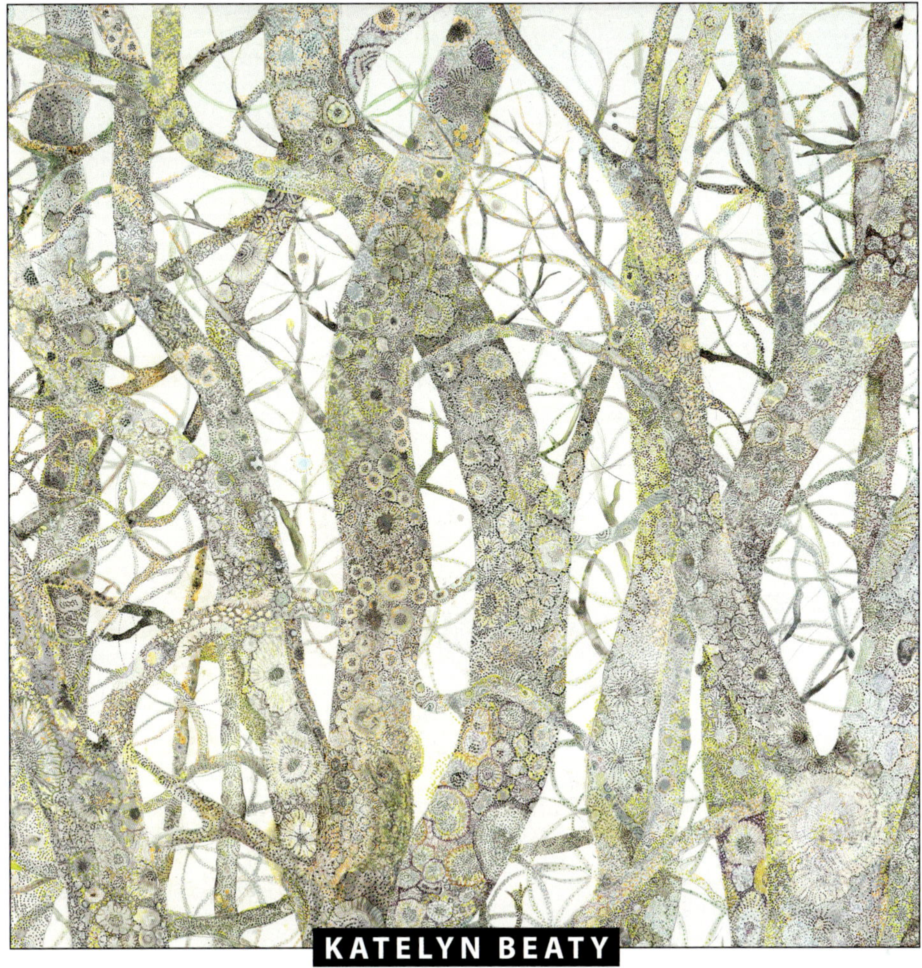

KATELYN BEATY

Respect Your Elder

Getting to know a tree may change your relationship to the natural world.

THIS SUMMER, for the first time, I began paying attention to trees. It's odd that I hadn't previously noticed the wide variety of species that covers 30% of the globe. I've been birdwatching my whole adult life, and a good place to see a bird is somewhere in a tree. Why had I neglected to appreciate and catalogue all the types of trees in the same way I have with birds for 20 years?

Noticing trees started in much the same way as noticing birds: by looking up. There was the tree below the underpass on my nightly walk

Claire Burbridge, *Unified Field 2*, watercolour, pen and ink, and salt crystals on Yupo paper, 2022 (detail).

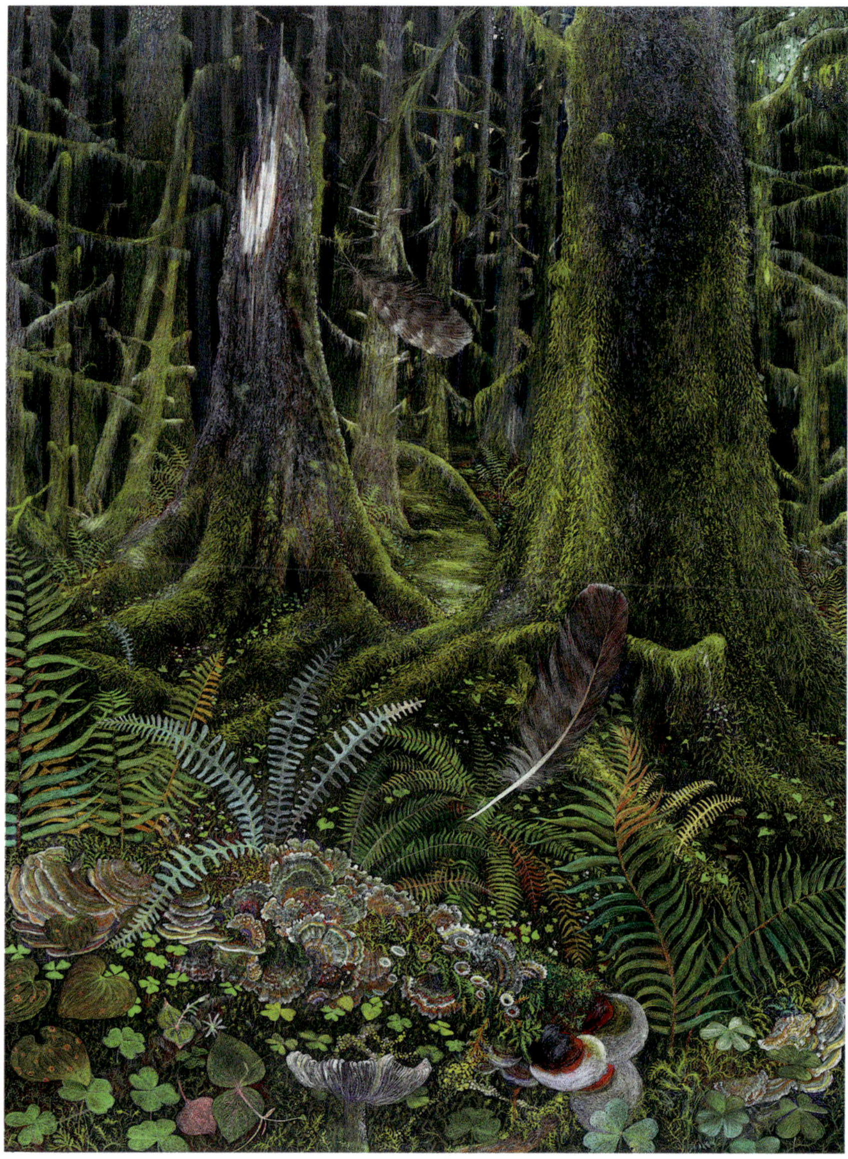

this summer, its plate-sized leaves fluttering in the humid air. With help from my phone camera and the *Trees of Ohio* field guide, I learned it was a northern catalpa, also known as the 'cigar tree' owing to its long, tubular pods. A neighbour's front yard featured a tuliptree, which has elegant, heart-shaped leaves and is among the tallest trees in North America. The buckeye was relatively easy to identify, given its smooth brown chestnuts and the preponderance of buckeye paraphernalia in Ohio, where Buckeye season usually refers to football or a decadent peanut butter confection.

The giant that stands in my front yard made itself known by shedding its bark in clumps one weekend in July. A large piece of that sycamore now adorns my living room mantle. When sycamores shed their bark, they are getting rid of their brittle exterior layer so that the fresh and pliable

Claire Burbridge, *Forest Knoll*, coloured pencil, 2023.

layer underneath can emerge like a smooth canvas against the sky.

It's easy for us to ignore trees. Beyond their ubiquity in our parks and backyards, we devalue them because they are so unlike humans. Trees lack a brain and central nervous system. They can't get up and move (which is what makes birdwatching, by contrast, so fun – like a hunt without the actual hunting). We grow in spurts, while trees grow slowly, sometimes over centuries. They don't have faces. And their breathing is our converse, taking in carbon dioxide through pores on their leaves and bark before releasing oxygen into the atmosphere.

This last fact, though, helps us to see trees as more than ornamental cover in a world meant mostly for humans. We and other creatures depend on trees in order to breathe clean air. A majority of the world's animal species live in forests. Deforestation means we are losing the equivalent of 27 football fields of forest per minute; as the forests go, so do these species, which causes disruption at every level of the earth's ecosystem.

Trees have provided innumerable human resources since premodern times, from timber to food such as fruits and nuts, from medicinal compounds to dyes and fibres and paper. Trees provide natural air conditioning in cities, blocking the heat from being reabsorbed by pavements and buildings. 'Green space' is also known to ease mental distress and even decrease crime. Plus, trees graciously let us lean up against them to read a book and find rest.

The Overstory, the sprawling 2018 novel by Richard Powers, tells the stories of several people whose lives and fates are bound up with those of trees. A forestry researcher named Patricia Westerford, a character inspired by the real-life scientist Suzanne Simard, stumbles upon a wild discovery: maples that are being attacked by invasive insects are able to send out airborne signals to other maples. In response, the surrounding trees pump out insecticide and thus stave off the insects. To Westerford, this demonstrates that 'The biochemical behaviour of individual trees may make sense only when we see them as members of a community.'

She labels her paper 'Trees Talk to One Another.' They don't speak in the way people do, of course. But what other than a language do we call a system of signals transmitted and received? Could trees possess intelligence that we are only beginning to understand?

Westerford is initially ridiculed; to say that trees 'speak' is to misunderstand natural processes, critics say, to assign human traits to non-human things. Shunned out of her field, she escapes into the forest until years later, when other researchers replicate her finding that trees trade signals and come to each other's aid, sending chemicals through the air.

Perhaps it's our modern impulse, the myth that we exist as individuals, that blinds us to the interdependence of other creatures – and to our interdependence with the rest of creation.

It is no wonder that people in the modern era are turning and returning to the natural world for spiritual sustenance. Technology has made our lives easier on many fronts. But it has also trained us to see life as a thing to be manipulated rather than a gift to be received. The internet lures us deeper into a non-material, and thus anti-human, space. Our screentime has fuelled mental health decline, loneliness and outrage cycles that line the pockets of tech CEOs. The astonishing acceleration of AI we see today is only the most

---

Katelyn Beaty is the editorial director of Brazos Press and the author of two books. Formerly print managing editor at Christianity Today *magazine, she has written for several mainstream and faith-based media outlets and currently writes a Substack called* The Beaty Beat. *She lives in Ohio.*

recent step in a long series of steps that is heading us further away from the material world, which is to say the home God has given us and calls good.

Our modern longing to reconnect with creation has taken the form of activism, starting with the environmentalist movements of the 1960s and coalescing in various climate change initiatives today. But our hunger for nature can also look more quotidian: watering a houseplant, planting a sapling or growing vegetables in our backyard. Caring for even a corner of the plant world, we fulfil the ancient command given to humans in the Garden where it all started: to tend, nurture and protect non-human life as God's representatives on this fragile earth.

The poet and essayist Wendell Berry has been a voice in the wilderness warning about our loss of connection to the living world. In his 1969 essay 'A Native Hill', Berry writes of his relationship to the plot of land in Kentucky where he has rooted himself for many decades:

> And so I go to the woods. As I go in under the trees, dependably, almost at once, and by nothing I do, things fall into place ... I feel my life takes its place among the lives – the trees, the annual plants, the animals and birds, the living of all these and the dead – that go and have gone to make the life of the earth. I am less important than I thought, the human race is less important than I thought. I rejoice in that. My mind loses its urgings, senses its nature, and is free.

Berry reminds us that people are only part of the creation – an important part, but also not bestowed with the 'main character energy' we usually operate with. Owing to their sheer, immovable size, trees dwarf us in ways that a goldfinch or a ficus plant do not.

Last spring I visited Sequoia National Park in California, home to some of the oldest trees on the planet. Many of the sequoias predate the life of Jesus. I was visiting before peak tourist season, and one afternoon it felt like I had the forest to myself. I stood amazed before the trees, but also intimidated; an average sequoia measures six metres in diameter and towers 300 feet in the air. No wonder the naturalist John Muir called them 'King Sequoia' and 'the greatest of living things.' Standing next to a massive tree can humble us down to size.

In Genesis, humans are created as the crown of creation after a long line of created beings. Like the plants and animals God created before them, humans are 'soil-breathed, soil-dependent creatures animated by divine breath', says theologian Norman Wirzba. The Hebrew word for human, *adam*, comes from the word for soil, *adamah*. Misreadings of the creation mandate have been used to support wanton destruction of forests the world over. But a doctrine of unfettered human expansion has ended up being bad for people too. 'We have lived by the assumption that what was good for us would be good for the world...We have been wrong', writes Berry.

> We must learn to cooperate in its processes, and yield to its limits. But even more important, we must learn to acknowledge that the creation is full of mystery; we will never entirely understand it. We must abandon arrogance and stand in awe.

In other words, our earthly good is bound up with the good of all creation.

J R R Tolkien created a universe where trees, or tree-like beings called Ents, play a crucial role in the battle against evil. In several passages of the *Lord of the Rings* trilogy, he goes into great detail (some would say too much detail!) about the forests and trees of Middle-earth. At one point, Frodo comes across a mallorn, a type of tree akin to a beech that grows in Lothlorien. As he reaches out to feel its bark, Tolkien writes, 'Frodo felt a delight in the wood and the touch of it, neither as forester nor as carpenter; it was the delight of the living tree itself.' The treeness of the tree, rather than its utility, awakened joy, both for the hobbit and his creator. Elsewhere, the destruction of the forests of Middle-earth is attributed to Saruman and his unquenchable hunger for power.

It is no surprise then that Tolkien loved trees. In a letter from 1955, he writes, 'I am … much in love with plants and above all trees, and always have been; and I find human maltreatment of them as hard to bear as some find ill-treatment of animals.' He wrote portions of his epic sitting under the branches of a particular black pine in the Oxford Botanic Garden. In the last known photo of him, he is leaning against the old pine. He named it Laocoon. It was felled in 2014.

I AM INTRIGUED BY THE IDEA of naming trees in the way Tolkien did his beloved pine. I don't mean knowing the names of red maples and conifer pines and black oaks and white elms – although learning to identify trees by their attributes would help us care for them (and is fun! says the birdwatcher). Rather, I mean that we could come to delight in the trees in our backyards or neighbourhood parks so much that we nickname them in the way we do our pets and even inanimate objects like our cars (Pearl) or our coffee makers (Old Faithful).

Naming the sycamore in my front yard would surely raise some eyebrows. The botanist Robin Wall Kimmerer notes, 'English doesn't give us many tools for incorporating respect for animacy. In English, you are either a human or a thing.' But the Bible gives us language for the breath of life in plants and animals. Listen to Job 12:

> But ask the animals, and they will teach you,
> Or the birds in the sky, and they will tell you;
> Or speak to the earth, and it will teach you,
> Or let the fish in the sea inform you.
> Which of all these does not know that the hand of the Lord has done this?
> In his hand is the life of every creature
> And the breath of all mankind.

Listening to creation is part of Job's pathway to wisdom. Later, God reminds Job that the sea and

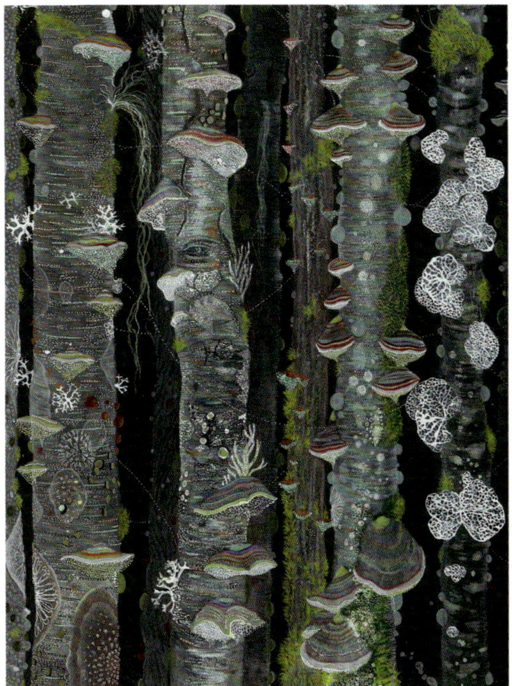

the stars and every living thing belong to him and are under his dominion. Once Job sees that he is but one small part of a vast, wild creation, he repents and is relieved of the distress from his human affairs.

If you are like me, perhaps you find it uninspiring to pursue a better relationship with the natural world under the banner of 'sustainability' or 'environmentalism.' Some of our efforts to protect creation, of course, must be scaled up; that can't be accomplished by one person or community. But it's hard to have a relationship with an *-ism*. A better place to start forging a relationship with the living world is by knowing it in our flesh and blood: by watching a mountain sunrise, tasting a freshly picked blackberry, smelling a pine forest, listening to the plaintive *hoos* of a great horned owl at dusk and touching the sturdy bark of the sycamore tree that towers over your flat. All are sustained by the Lord of life, and all are given for our earthly delight. It may not be long before the sycamore in my front yard becomes a Seymour.

Claire Burbridge, *The Nocturnal Life of Trees 2*, watercolour, pencil and ink, 2021 (detail).

The Riddle of Beauty in Nature

C S Lewis

We do not want merely to *see* beauty, though, God knows, even that is bounty enough. We want something else which can hardly be put into words – to be united with the beauty we see, to pass into it, to receive it into ourselves, to bathe in it, to become part of it. That is why we have peopled air and earth and water with gods and goddesses and nymphs and elves – that, though we cannot, yet these projections can, enjoy in themselves that beauty, grace and power of which Nature is the image. That is why the poets tell us such lovely falsehoods. They talk as if the west wind could really sweep into a human soul; but it can't. They tell us that 'beauty born of murmuring sound' will pass into a human face; but it won't. Or not yet.

For if we take the imagery of Scripture seriously, if we believe that God will one day *give* us the Morning Star and cause us to *put on* the splendour of the sun, then we may surmise that both the ancient myths and the modern poetry, so false as history, may be very near the truth as prophecy.

At present we are on the outside of the world, the wrong side of the door. We discern the freshness and purity of morning, but they do not make us fresh and pure. We cannot mingle with the splendours we see. But all the leaves of the New Testament are rustling with the rumour that it will not always be so. Someday, God willing, we shall get *in*.

C S Lewis, 'The Weight of Glory', in *The Weight of Glory: And Other Addresses* (HarperCollins, 2001), 42–3.

Gregory of Nyssa

Hope always draws the soul from the beauty which is seen to what is beyond, always kindles the desire for the hidden through what is constantly perceived. Therefore, the ardent lover of beauty, although receiving what is always visible as an image of what he desires, yet longs to be filled with the very stamp of the archetype. And the bold request which goes up the mountains of desire asks this: to empty the Beauty not in mirrors and reflections, but face to face.

Gregory of Nyssa, The Life of Moses, translated by Abraham J Malherbe and Everett Ferguson, *The Classics of Western Spirituality* (Paulist Press, 1978), 114–155.

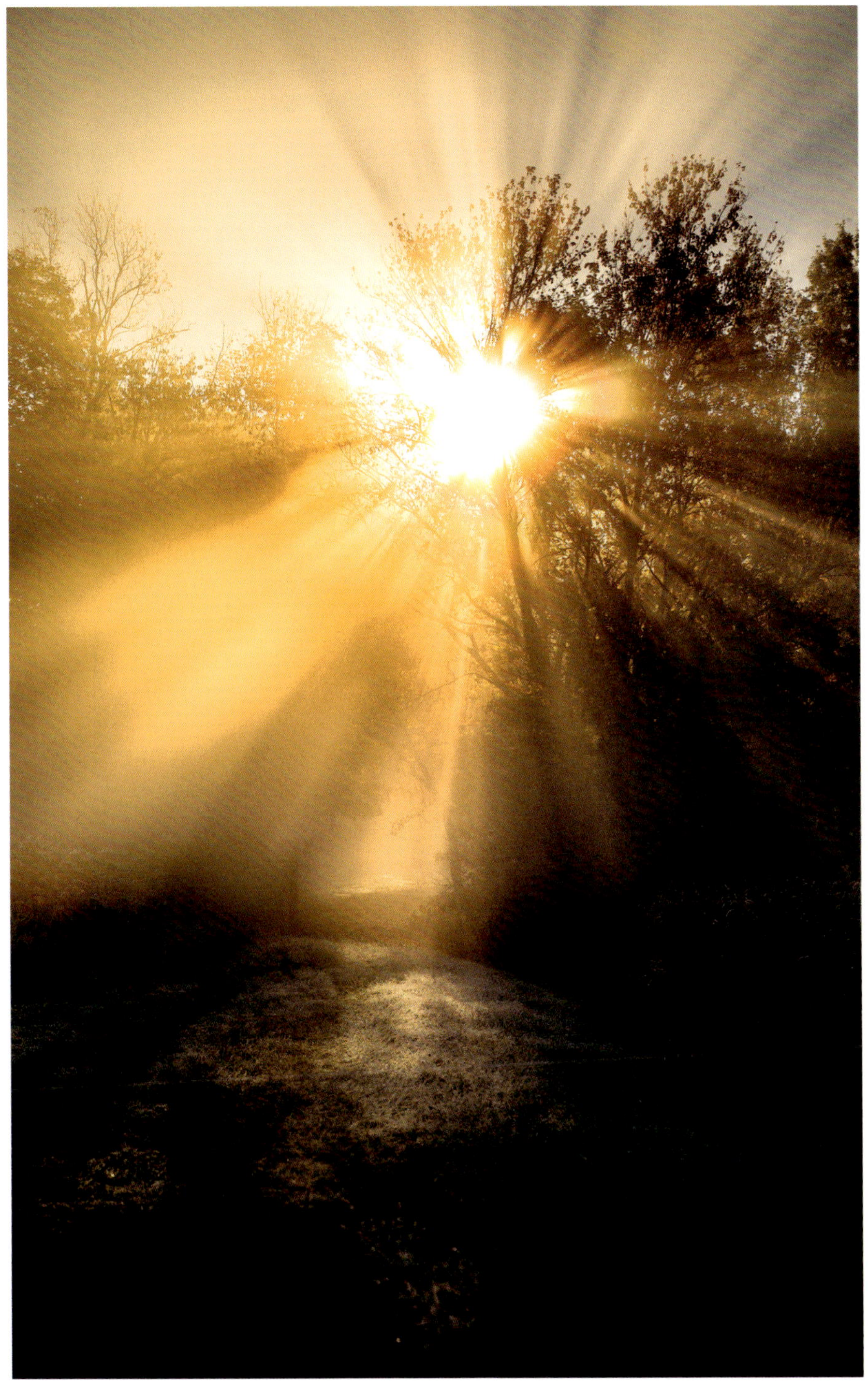

Photograph by David Zumpe.

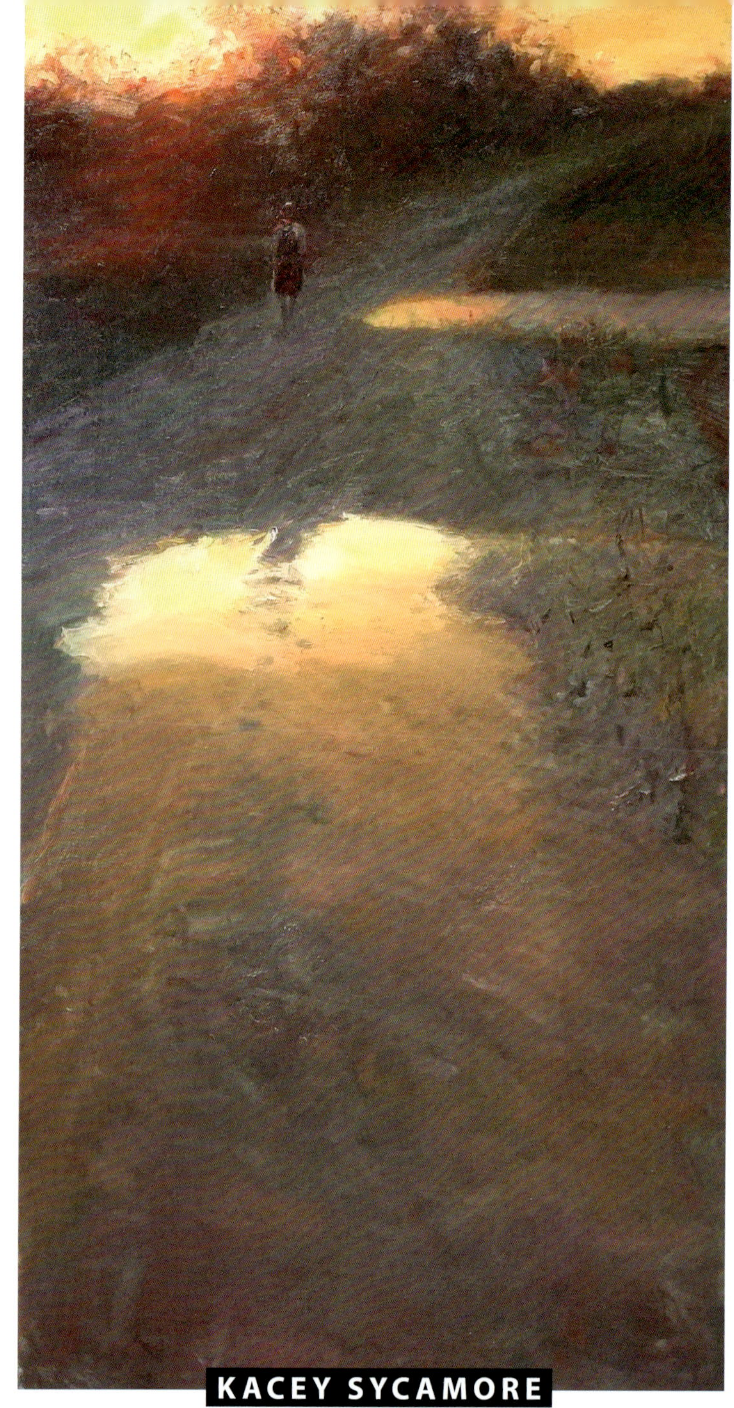

KACEY SYCAMORE

Beckoned by Beauty

I lost, then found, myself in a story much bigger and better than my own personal narrative.

GROWING UP, there was no better feeling than being immersed in a good story. When a wardrobe opened into Narnia or a letter delivered by an owl changed a little boy's life, I was swept away into a thrilling adventure. I can still remember my older sister's teasing as I emerged from my bedroom in tears after Dumbledore died.

In those moments reading, I experienced beauty. It had nothing to do with the way things looked. It was a journey of the heart out of myself and into some larger unity, a transcendent experience that left me with a deep sense of joy, hope and gratitude. I believe it was this experience that first expressed my unconscious longing to know myself as a child in the family of God.

But as I got older, these experiences of self-forgetting were few and far between. Most of the time, I was wretchedly self-conscious. I struggled to truly enter the fray of life and felt trapped inside the milieu of my own mind and emotions. By my mid-twenties, I was reasonably successful on paper, with a solid career, romantic relationships and all the trappings of modern autonomous life. But this polished image belied underlying pain, confusion and dissatisfaction. I often walked aimlessly around the city, yearning for my life to open up into something greater, like in one of those stories. I never imagined that there was One who saw all of those moments – and intended to offer the very beauty I loved.

A Response to Longing

In 2018, freshly single and drifting, I was sent by my California employer to a conference in Texas. There, during an idle moment, a young man from England introduced himself. It was a brief and friendly encounter, and I didn't think much of it. But when I met Ben again at an event later that day, hardly before I could realise it, our surface-skimming conversation had become a deep plunge into uncharted waters.

We were both 27, broken in different ways, but attuned to beauty, chasing the glimmers we'd encountered in music, books and fleeting moments of transcendence. Though we met as strangers from different parts of the world, it felt like we weren't really strangers at all, but two sides of the same coin, connected all along in a solid yet unseen way. I wasn't looking for marriage

We were both 27, broken in different ways, but attuned to beauty, chasing the glimmers we'd encountered in music, books and fleeting moments of transcendence.

or religion, and I certainly wasn't interested in 'Christianity', but this new connection unsettled what I thought I knew. While Ben, who was raised as an atheist, had come to believe in God and appreciated Christianity intellectually, I had cordoned off my heart from God. Raised marginally Catholic by divorced parents who didn't follow Jesus, and educated in liberal, secular settings, I considered religion deceptive, flimsy and unsophisticated.

I didn't think much at all about God, but I unconsciously hungered for that 'scent of a flower we have not found, the echo of a tune we have not heard, news from a country we have never yet visited', as C S Lewis so beautifully describes human longing. When Ben and I met, it was as if that longing in us had been responded to, and we were each given the completely unmerited gift of a partner. The slow realisation that seemingly out of the sky had fallen this relationship – where

Kacey Sycamore is a member of the Bruderhof and lives with her husband and three young children at Maple Ridge, a Bruderhof in New York's Hudson Valley.

Opposite: Charles Choi, *Going Home*, oil on canvas, 2018.

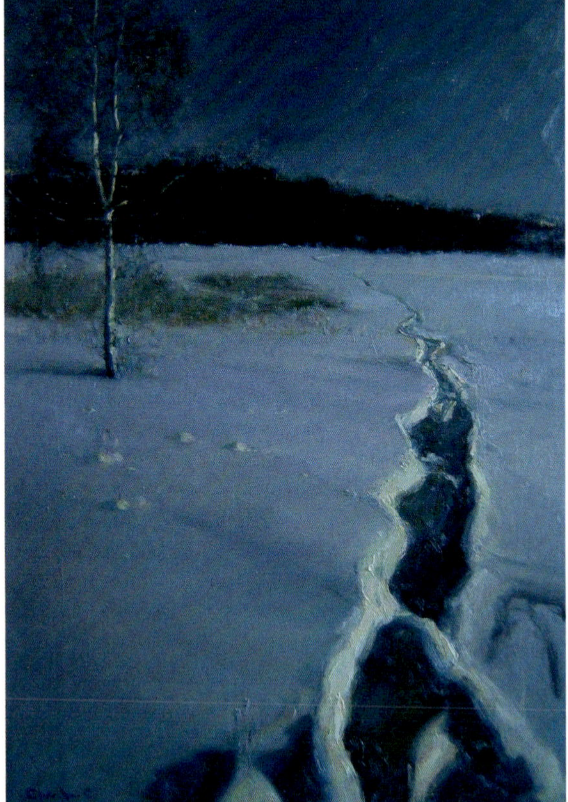

the real me could be seen and loved and called forth – overwhelmed me with awe and gratitude. I couldn't make sense of it within my existing worldview, and yet the evidence of some sort of intention and design at work was piling up.

Back at our respective homes, separated by an ocean, Ben texted me a verse that had once struck him after being handed a Bible on the streets of London. It was Romans 12:2, and it became the first verse consciously committed to my memory: 'Do not conform to the pattern of this world, but be transformed by the renewing of your mind. Then you will be able to test and approve what God's will is – his good, pleasing, and perfect will.' Unbeknownst to me, that transformation was beginning, the seeds planted for some time. God's will for us was good, pleasing – beautiful – but I still had no theological framework for understanding it.

A Divine Invitation

One morning not long after, a friend sent me a link to a podcast episode with no further comment. Titled 'The Inner Landscape of Beauty', it featured an interview with John O'Donohue, the late Irish philosopher, poet and priest. His voice, warm and lilting, spoke of beauty not as surface appeal but as an essential force that beckons us homeward, helping us heal old patterns and find new ground:

> Beauty isn't all about just nice loveliness, like. Beauty is about more rounded, substantial becoming... Beauty in that sense is about an emerging fullness, a greater sense of grace and elegance, a deeper sense of depth and also a kind of homecoming for the enriched memory of your unfolding life.

Enraptured by both the form and content of his words, I went on to discover *Anam Cara*, his bestselling book on ancient Celtic spirituality. As I read this book for the first time, teary-eyed and awestruck, sentence after sentence gave language and confirmation to what I was experiencing and opened the vista of my life out into eternity.

Anam cara is Gaelic for 'soul friend.' O'Donohue says that encountering this kind of deep soul connection mirrors the nature of God himself – who encounters us through Jesus and invites us to become fully alive through the flow of relationship. He writes:

> The *anam cara* is God's gift. Friendship is the nature of God. The Christian concept of God as Trinity is the most sublime articulation of otherness and intimacy, an eternal interflow of friendship. Jesus ... is the secret *anam cara* of every individual. In friendship with him, we enter the tender beauty and affection of the Trinity. In the embrace of this eternal friendship, we dare to be free.

It began to dawn on me that the love unfolding in my life wasn't just romantic – it was divine invitation. God, the hidden beauty behind all beauty, was beginning to show his face.

A Transformed Life

Swiss theologian Hans Urs von Balthasar describes beauty as a dynamic event, one that

Charles Choi, *Path*, oil on canvas, 2014.

requires a response. This is just how Ben and I encountered it, as marriage and newfound faith combined to set us on a new course together. If we were loved by a God who gave us our deepest longing as a completely free gift at a time when we were nothing but lost little sinners, what did that mean for our lives?

We attempted to discover just that, examining every aspect of how we had lived up until then and rebuilding based on the beautiful revelation of Jesus. We quit jobs, moved cities in search of community and grappled with our spiritual and psychological wounds. For a long time, it was hard to see outwardly whether we were lost or found. No one around us seemed to understand what we were going through. But keeping faith that we were being lovingly guided was enough to see us through the wilderness day by day.

When Covid hit, we were expecting our first child, living basically hand to mouth and still spiritually homeless – despite 'shopping churches', including Catholic, Orthodox and Reformed denominations. During this time, I stumbled upon an essay titled 'The Abyss of Beauty' by Ian Marcus Corbin in *Plough*.

> What a strange kind of animal we must be, to feel ourselves perched on the periphery of something, always only almost living. The thing in front of us, just a hair past our reach, seems ideal, if we could get to it. But can we? Does such intimacy exist? Are we delusional to hope so?

The essay explores how an apprehension of the beautiful can transform a life – or not – and how an individual responds to epiphany. I clicked through the website to the 'About Us' page and began to learn about the Bruderhof. At first, the Bruderhof way of life appeared foreign and drab. But when we looked past the exterior, we began to be moved by what we were seeing – things like the inclusion of elderly single people in families, natural and beautiful care at the end of life, a wholesome and safe children's community. We eagerly watched Laura from the Bruderhof answer questions on YouTube.

Then I found my way to the writings of Eberhard Arnold, the community's founder. Arnold explains the radical call of Jesus to a way of life – a way of being – that is completely contrary to the ways of the world. It is a life lived according to a sacrificial love that knows no boundaries. In this way only, the powers of evil and darkness are overcome through the gentle power of the spirit of God, which leads people to lay their lives down for their brothers and sisters.

> He who rose to life through the Spirit had a strength that exploded in an utterly new attitude to life: love to brothers and sisters and love to one's enemy, the divine justice of the coming kingdom. Through this Spirit, property was abolished in the early church. Material possessions were handed over to the ambassadors for the poor of the church. Through the presence and power of the Spirit and through faith in the Messiah, this band of followers became a brotherhood. (Eberhard Arnold, 'Introduction', *The Early Christians*, 1970)

One afternoon after reading Arnold in our California home, I woke my husband from a nap and said through tears, 'I think this is it.'

Beauty as the Form of Love

In the autumn of 2021, we sold the car we had just bought to finance a visit to the Bruderhof's Maple Ridge community in New York. We arrived to warm and kind people with strange accents and patterns of speech; we met schoolgirls in plain dresses and bare feet. We were hosted by a family with three children, with whom we had early-morning breakfasts, begun in song and prayer. In the evenings, we'd spend time with them and others, young and old alike, sharing about ourselves and our journey.

The people were genuine, peaceful, at home with themselves. In turn, I felt more at home

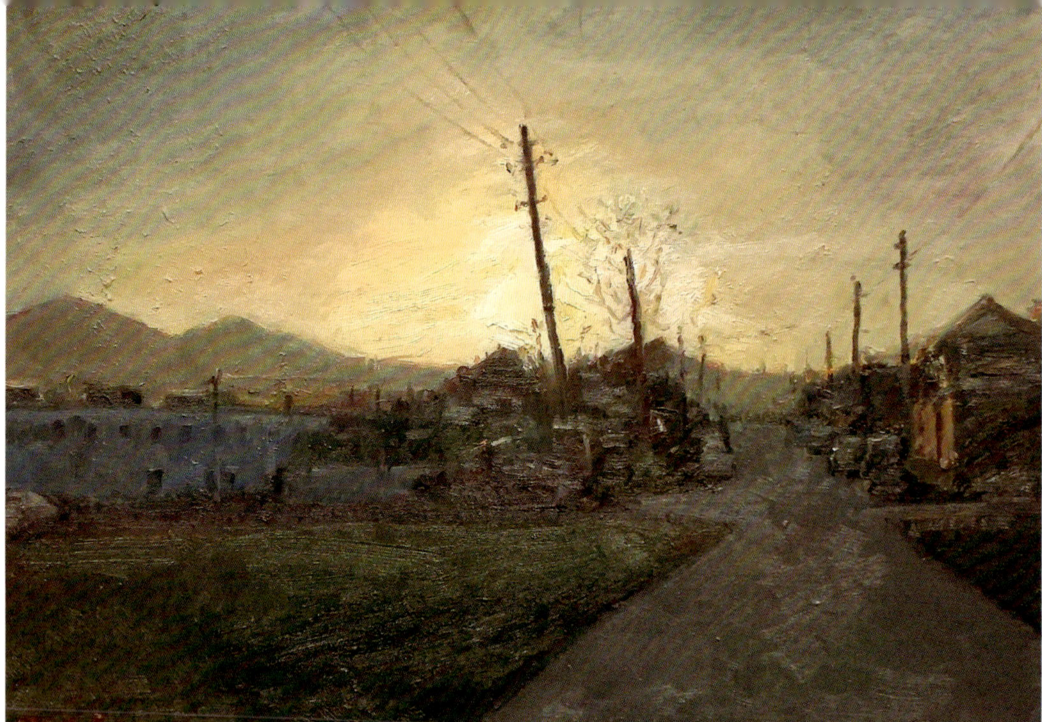

with myself than ever before. All this despite the fact that I was exhausted and overwhelmed, my nervous system locked in survival mode after spending the past year hustling to make ends meet and becoming a mother to a colicky baby girl.

During this first visit, God moved powerfully in our hearts. We were led, organically and quite by surprise, to unearth long-buried sins and to finally turn outward in trust to others who had already given their lives over to Jesus. Was this experience and way of life beautiful? Undoubtedly yes, but not glittering and attractive. It was beauty hidden in the surrender of self – a form shaped by love.

Participation in the Cross

If you had shown the old me a picture of myself now – in simple dress, no makeup, eyes shining – I wouldn't have known what to make of it. From the outside, there are stories one could tell about the transformation I've undergone: Was I radicalised by meeting my conservative husband? Choosing an alternative lifestyle to escape the world? Believing in a fantasy that helps me sleep better at night? But the real story is harder to photograph. It's inward. Ongoing.

It's true that joining this community has been like stepping into another world – not to escape the old one, but to find within it that the kingdom of God is truly at hand. Like the stories I loved as a child, this world insists that hope is stronger than despair, that love binds people together and that real beauty reflects an inner unity. This way of life isn't perfect – but through communal meals and shared work, suffering, celebration and quiet acts of love, I daily hear the echoes of eternity.

This beauty, as I now see it, is not about visual splendour, but about self-giving love. It's the experience of losing – and then finding – yourself in a story much bigger and better than your own personal narrative. This is a beauty that mirrors the ultimate beauty of Christ. Through offering friendship with Jesus, God didn't just answer my longing for beauty; he revealed the One who is beautiful. What I once experienced in storybooks – the friendship, the fight, the meaning – was like a light beckoning me to new life in him.

The gospel is not a fairytale. It is the truest story, and its beauty becomes flesh when we dare to live it out – imperfectly, together.

Charles Choi, *Small Village*, oil on canvas, 2016.

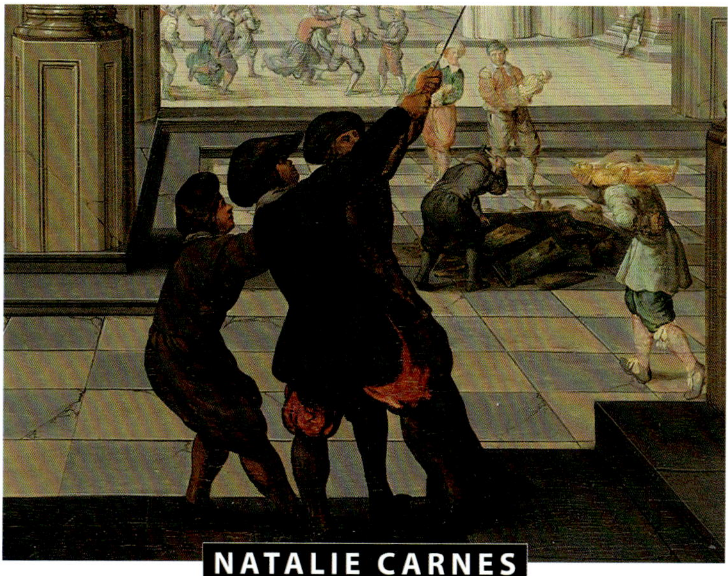

NATALIE CARNES

Icon or Idol?

Christianity has a love-hate relationship with sacred art.

THE CHURCH I ATTENDED during most of my childhood and adolescence was ugly – an unattractiveness that derived not from neglect but from intention. The carpet was an orange-brown that the chairs exactly duplicated. The white, windowless walls were bare except for a wooden cross hanging behind the pulpit. It was a young church, and as the years passed, some women tried to soften its harshness. They arranged greenery near the pulpit. They convinced the elders to paint the walls a light blue. Eventually, they successfully petitioned for new chairs, even new carpet. But throughout this brightening, no one dared to propose – no one even *thought* to propose – introducing visual art into the church's interior. No paintings, no sculptures, no stained glass windows were considered. This was, of course, a mode of faithfulness.

What my ugly church wanted to avoid was idolatry, a sin of unfaithfulness that runs throughout Christian history, sparking iconoclastic responses. It starts in scripture. When Moses sees the Israelites dancing around a golden calf, he smashes the tablets of the Ten Commandments and pulverises their idol; they have already broken the second commandment prohibiting graven images. Several generations later, longing to bring Israel back to a purity of worship, King Josiah makes a covenant with the Lord and levels the local shrines. Even Jesus has his iconoclastic moments. He overturns the money-changers' tables in the Temple, claiming they have turned a house of worship

---

Natalie Carnes is a constructive theologian and the author of several books, including Image and Presence: A Christological Reflection on Iconoclasm and Iconophilia *(Stanford University Press, 2017), and* Attunement: The Art and Politics of Feminist Theology *(Oxford University Press, 2024).*

Dirck van Delen, *Destruction of Icons in a Church,* oil on panel, 1630 (detail).

into a den of thieves, making money an idol like a golden calf. And he practised the iconoclasm of rule-breaking, healing and gleaning food on the Sabbath despite the Pharisees' interpretation of such actions as dishonouring the commandments. Isaiah even prophesies the Messiah's lack of beauty, declaring he has neither form nor comeliness that we should be drawn to him.

In post-biblical history, there were two famous periods of iconoclasm in Christianity: the Byzantine fight over images in the 8th and 9th centuries and the image-breaking of the Reformation era in the 16th and 17th centuries. But Christian iconoclasm is not confined to these two moments. It runs throughout the tradition. Certain strands of desert monasticism worried about how images might infect the imagination. Evagrius Ponticus, for example, forbade even mental images in prayer lest they delude a person about the God who surpasses all imaginings. In the Middle Ages, Bernard of Clairvaux argued that abbey churches should use simple rather than precious materials for their liturgical items and that such churches should not be unduly adorned. John Calvin's argument that the heart is a factory of idols provoked Christians across nations and centuries to strip their churches of images and art, and inspired the Puritans to wariness towards any aesthetic investments. In the past decade, some churches, together with many other types of public buildings and spaces, have experienced a new spate of iconoclasm as they reckoned with the racist legacies of their monuments. At my current academic home of Duke, the school removed a statue of Robert E Lee from the chapel in 2017. Where he once stood, there is now an empty niche between President Thomas Jefferson and poet Sidney Lanier.

As the diversity of these examples suggests, iconoclasm can express a range of different impulses. Sometimes iconoclasm attempts to intervene in the worship of a false god, like Moses demolishing the golden calf. Sometimes iconoclasm responds to misrepresentations of the true God or corruptions in our worship of that God, like Jesus in the temple or King Josiah attacking the high places. Sometimes, as in Bernard of Clairvaux's writing, iconoclasm wants to redirect our attention – to the God who transcends all human-made art, for example, or towards our brothers and sisters in need. Sometimes iconoclasm expresses a worry about sensual indulgence. And sometimes, iconoclasm wants to proclaim God's omnipresence, the way God cannot be contained by any particular image, statue or sacred place. This concern to preserve God's transcendence inspired much of the furious removal of images from worshipping spaces during the Reformation. 'If you're God, then save yourself, but if you're man, then bleed', iconoclasts jeer while wrenching a crucifix from a church in Basel. The public performance of the image's impotence is an anti-idolatry gesture meant to insist that God cannot be contained by artifacts.

Iconoclasm can have shared purposes with images; images can want what iconoclasts also want. An image might invite us to purify our hearts for worship – to redirect our attention to the God who is not defined by worldly wealth and hierarchy, or to our brother or sister in need. In his reimagining of the Holy Family's flight through Egypt as that of present-day immigrants seeking refuge and in his 2020 pietà of a Black Madonna and Child entitled 'Mama', the artist Kelly Lattimore wants, in his icons, to draw viewers' attention to Christ's presence in marginalised communities. In various images, he presents Christ in the homeless: the nativity amidst the rubble of Gaza, the Holy Family in a tent city. His work is not without controversy. A group of students at The Catholic University of America petitioned to have 'Mama' removed from the law school chapel where it hung, calling it 'disrespectful and sacrilegious.' Before the university responded, the icon was stolen.

Who is the iconoclast here? The ones arguing that Lattimore's art ought to be removed? Lattimore, for challenging conventional imaginations

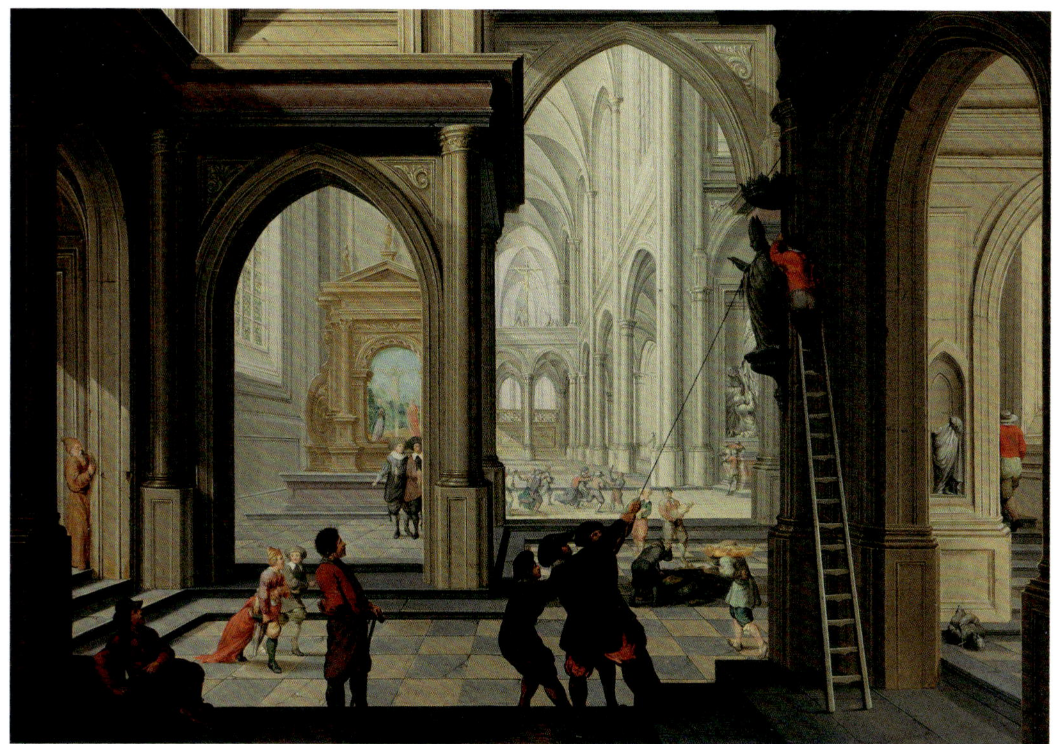

about a religious image? What does it mean that both camps want to see viewers' attention directed to Christ? The fidelity sought by image-makers and iconoclasts is bound together in complex ways. Sometimes the iconoclast redirects attention from blasphemy, like Moses smashing the golden calf or Duke Chapel removing Robert E Lee from its statuary. But sometimes the iconoclast herself blasphemes by mistaking holiness or the critique of blasphemy for blasphemy itself. Perhaps we might see those attacking Lattimore's images in that way. The struggle to be faithful can be marked with sin and error, and in their mutual struggles, the image-lover and the image-breaker can be closer than they may seem.

The interiors of the churches where I have chosen to worship as an adult contrast starkly with the church of my youth. Images have, in the intervening years, become an important part of my spiritual life, and beauty is for me an important sign of divine presence. Yet I still find something to admire in the ugly church I once called home. Its austerity embodied hope for an undistracted form of worship, that the faithful might inhabit a singularity of devotion. Beauty and images are, I think, good things, but even good things – especially good things – can become idols for us. The very things that draw us to God can become the things that distract us, absorbing our attention and adoration for themselves rather than directing us on to the Lord.

My iconoclastic church was alive to that danger, vigilantly guarding against anything that might come between us and the Most High. I take my history in that community with me into the beautiful, image-laden worship spaces of the churches I now enter. Carrying with me the memory of the single wooden cross on those otherwise bare walls rising from an expanse of orange-brown carpet, I ask how, amidst my current life with images, I can honour this struggle for holy attention.

Dirck van Delen, *Destruction of Icons in a Church*, oil on panel, 1630. This painting depicts *Beeldenstorm*, or 'attack on the images or statues', a wave of iconoclasm in the summer of 1566 in which Protestants destroyed altarpieces, statues and sacred vessels in countless churches throughout the Netherlands.

Believing in the Last Judgement

During two papal conclaves, I sat in contemplation below Michelangelo's masterpiece.

CHRISTOPH SCHÖNBORN

Michelangelo's enormous *The Last Judgement* in the Sistine Chapel in the Vatican is undoubtedly one of the most famous paintings in art history. During the two conclaves I was able to attend (2005 and 2013), I had time to contemplate it. Christ, the judge of the world, is at the centre. To his right, the saved ascend to heaven; to his left, the damned are dragged down to hell by devils. Countless visitors to the Vatican Museums stand amazed before this masterpiece every day. Do they believe that it will really be like this one day, heaven and hell? Do I believe – not theoretically but quite soberly – that one day it will be decided for me too: eternal happiness or eternal damnation? Did Michelangelo himself believe what he depicted? Among those damned to hell, he included cardinals of his time. Was this malice on the part of the artist towards the powerful figures of the church?

Fifteen hundred years earlier, someone asked Jesus, 'Lord, will only a few people be saved?' What answer did he expect Jesus to give – generalities about the relationship between heaven and hell? Augustine, the great teacher of the church, seems to have seriously believed that only a few people will actually be saved and that consequently, the vast majority will be lost forever. His view hung like a dark cloud over Christianity for a long time. In our day it seems to have lifted. Today, the confidence that the Rhinelanders sing about seems to prevail: 'We will all, all go to heaven because we are so good.' Jesus' words are not a joke. He does not give a general answer, no statistics about heaven and hell. He addresses everyone personally: 'Strive with all your might to enter through the narrow gate.' His prediction is harsh and painful: many will not succeed! This leaves all of us, if we entertain the thought at all, with the question: Will I succeed? And: What must I do to make it through the narrow gate?

I must admit that I find it difficult to accept eternal damnation. Nevertheless, I take Jesus' clear words about heaven and hell seriously. They are not an invention of Michelangelo. One thought helps me: there are courts on earth. Serious crimes are punished with life imprisonment. My actions have consequences, both good and bad. Fraud is punished, as is murder, with greater or lesser penalties. If I believe in eternal life, why should my actions only have consequences in this life? Jesus speaks of a final

---

Christoph Cardinal Schönborn, OP, is a friar and theologian, and served as the Cardinal Archbishop of Vienna from 1995 until his retirement in 2025.

Image from Wikipedia (public domain).

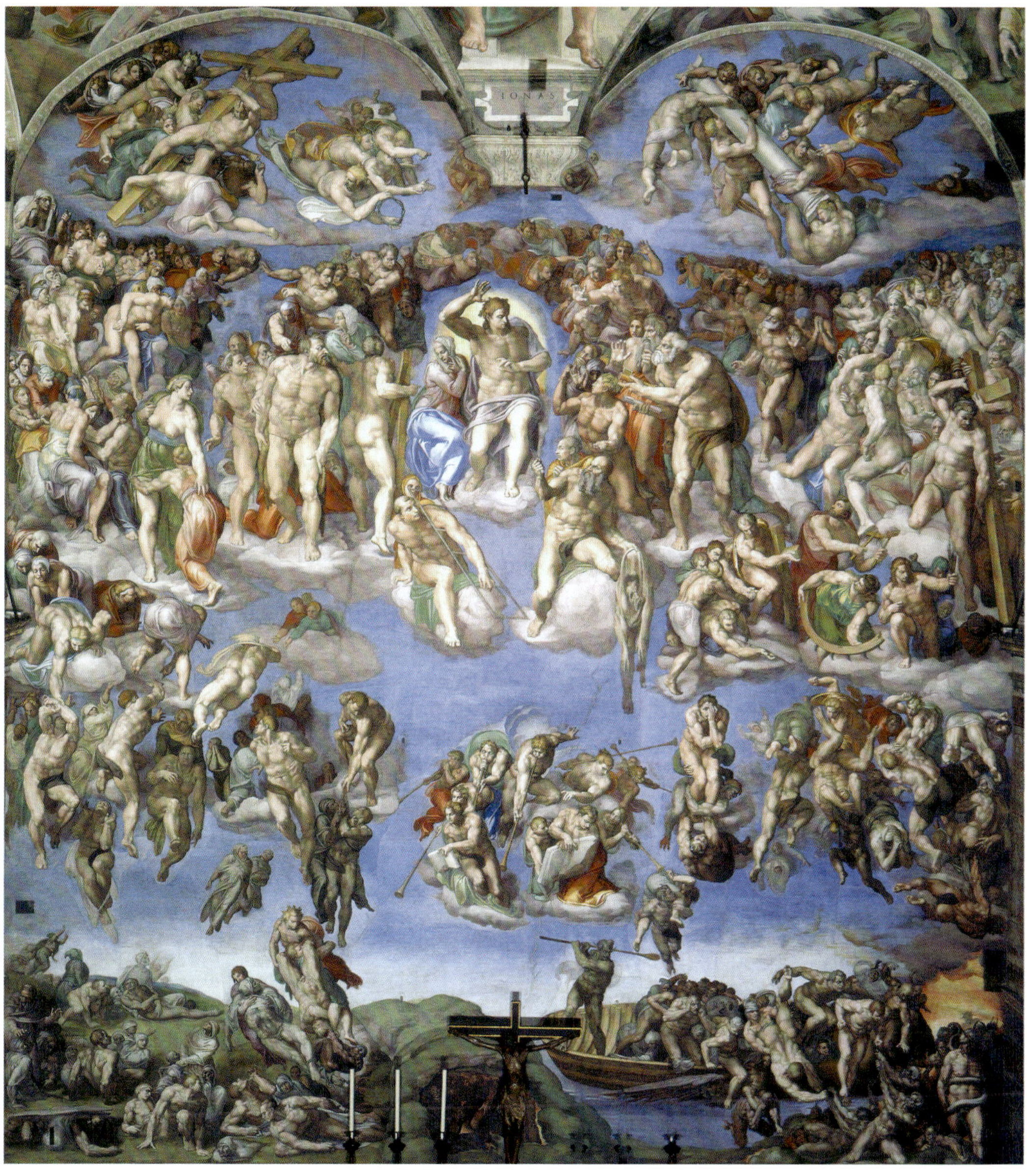

closing of the door. There is such a thing as 'too late', not only when we miss a train, but also if we die without having made amends for what we have done wrong. It can torment us for a long time if someone dies before we have asked them for forgiveness. We have missed our chance forever. Jesus makes it clear that our eternity is decided here and now. If so much depends on us, will only very few be saved? Does it depend on whether we make life heaven or hell for each other here on earth? Once, the disciples asked Jesus in alarm, 'Who then can be saved?' Jesus' answer is our only hope: 'With man this is impossible, but with God all things are possible.'

Michelangelo, *The Last Judgement*, fresco, 1536–1541.

The Art of the Beautiful

Sergei Bulgakov

'God saw everything that he had made: and, behold, it was most beautiful' (Gen. 1:31). God is good; he is goodness itself. God is true; he is truth itself. God is glorious, and his glory is beauty itself. Beauty is an objective principle in the world, revealing to us the divine glory. The divine source of objective beauty is also the source of the human creation of beauty, that is, of art. God created man in his image, granting to this image three gifts: a will directed towards the good, the gift of reason and wisdom and the gift of aesthetic appreciation. Man is meant to be the wisdom of the world, just because he participates in the Logos; he is also meant to be the artist of the world, because he can imbue it with beauty.

Man must become not only a good and faithful worker in the world; he must not only 'dress and keep it' (Gen. 2:15), as he was commanded in paradise, but he must also become its artist; he must render it beautiful. Because he has been created in the image of God, he is called to create. Things are transfigured and made luminous by beauty; they become the revelation of their own abstract meaning. And this revelation through beauty of the things of earth is the work of art. The world, as it has been given to us, has remained as it were covered by an outward shell through which art penetrates, as if foreseeing the coming transfiguration of the world. Man has been called to be a demiurge, not only to contemplate the beauty of the world, but also to express it. Does this not speak of a new service of the church, one that has not yet been fully revealed in the heart of man and in his history: the service of realising the work of human participation in the transfiguration of the world?

Sergei Bulgakov, in *The Time of the Spirit: Readings Through the Christian Year* (St Vladimir Seminary Press, 1984), 11. Used by permission.

Iris Murdoch

Great art teaches us how real things can be looked at and loved without being seized and used, without being appropriated into the greedy organism of the self. This exercise of detachment is difficult and valuable whether the thing contemplated is a human being or the root of a tree or the vibration of a colour or a sound. Unsentimental contemplation of nature exhibits the same quality of detachment: selfish concerns vanish, nothing exists except the things which are seen.

Beauty is that which attracts this particular sort of unselfish attention.

Iris Murdoch, *The Sovereignty of the Good* (Routledge, 2014), 62–63. Used by permission.

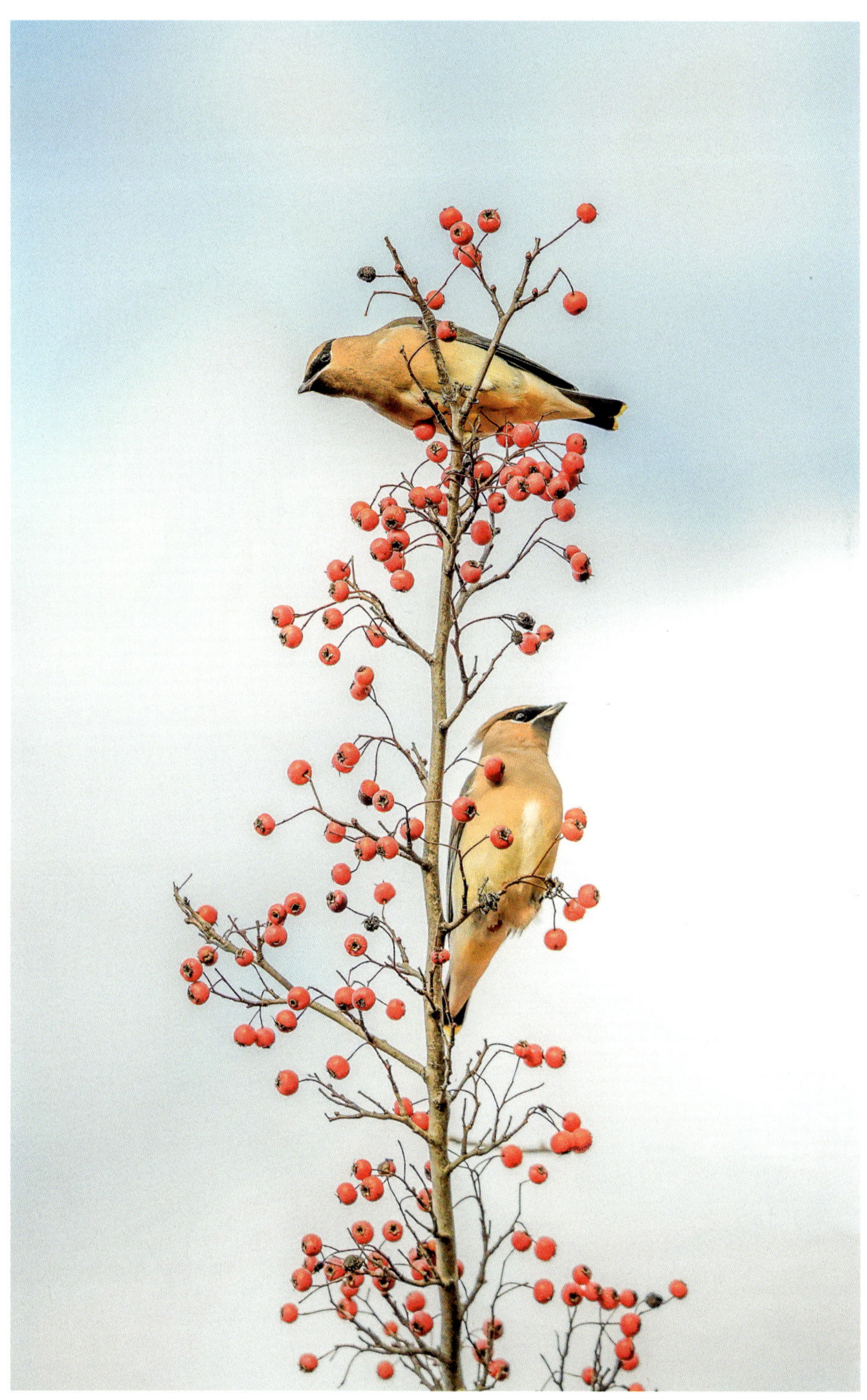

Photograph by David Zumpe.

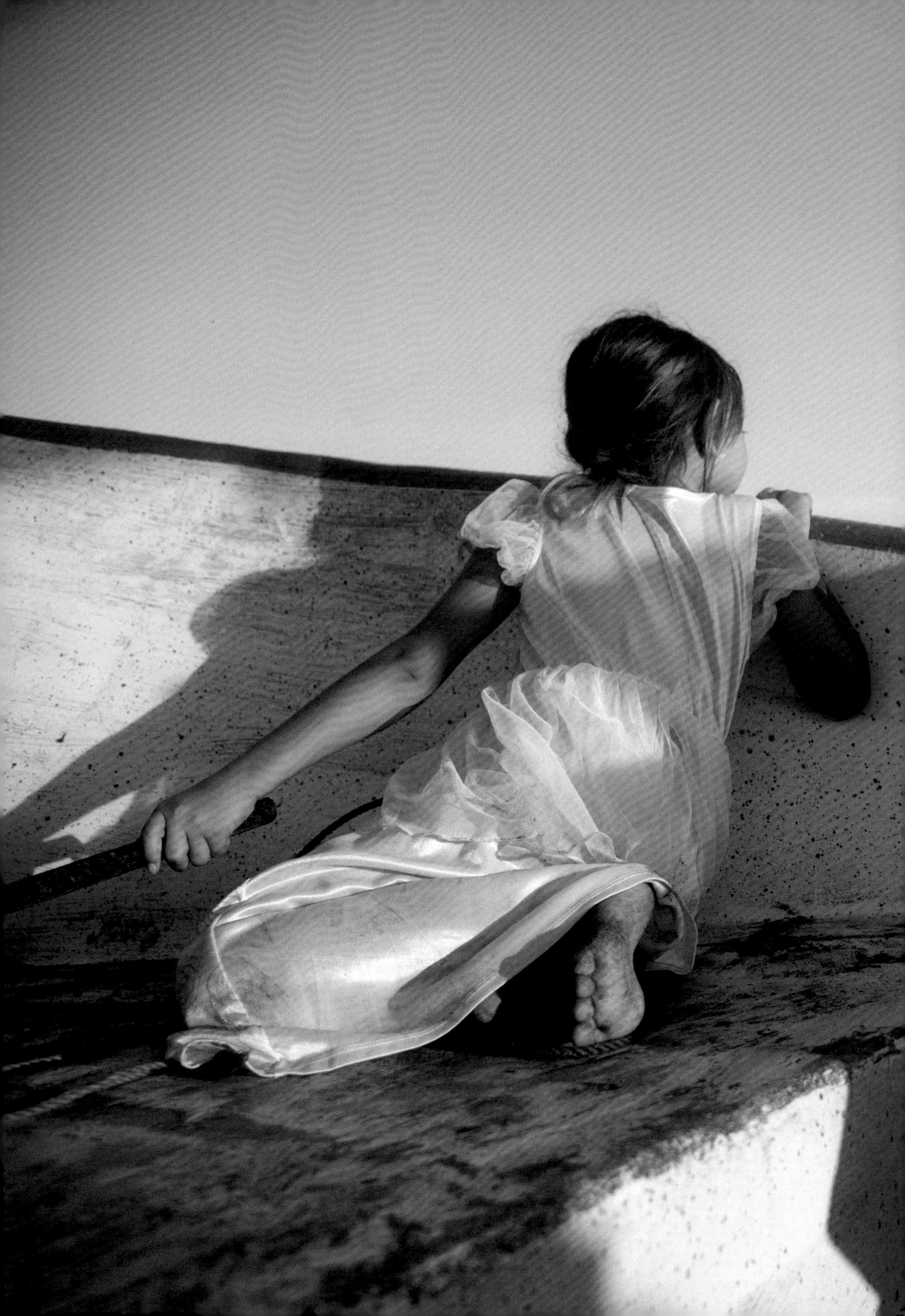

Luna of Tasajera

On a windswept island far from the gangs and prisons,
I saw the future of El Salvador.

PHOTOS AND TEXT BY PHILIP HOLSINGER

What do I look for when I photograph a story? I look at a man's hands. And a child's shoes, if she has any. Their hands and shoes will tell you what even they have never yet dared to say.

You have to find the words no one is saying. There's a lot of noise and shouting: politicians and celebrities, press conferences and protests, grand openings and new products, preachers and travelling carnivals – not to mention bombs and earthquakes. But the quiet are quiet with their words – words that come ever so slowly, if at all. They're not speaking to anyone because they don't even know that they have anything to say.

Find the quiet person. And find a way to listen to his life. But be warned, this way will not give you quick answers, and it will require something from you too. You must be patient and have dinner and sit for a while. Because the quiet man has not yet learned what he is expected to say, he may say nothing. He may tell you about his wedding day 40 years ago, or about the day his father died and he felt completely alone in the world. He may tell you his feet hurt and his hands ache. You will be tempted to overlook these things. Don't overlook them because they will tell you who he is. And in him you will begin to see his nation.

Take this photograph of the hands of the old cowboy of Arambala in the northeast mountains. Look at what the earth has written on his body. He is a book that, if you take the time, you can read. It will be the story of his life. And because he is Salvadoran, it will be a book about El Salvador. Maybe not the whole story, but the essence.

There are things you will be tempted to avoid in your story – embarrassing things or horrible things. Some people believe the poor are embarrassing and want to avoid showing them. Others exploit the poor, using them as mere illustrations, or worse, to make a statement about their own indignation. We should not shy away from the truth, but we should also not indulge our indignation. As a general rule I find it's better to withhold images that

---

Philip Holsinger is an American photographer and writer who lives in Nashville, Tennessee. His work has been featured on ABC and CBS and in Time *magazine.*

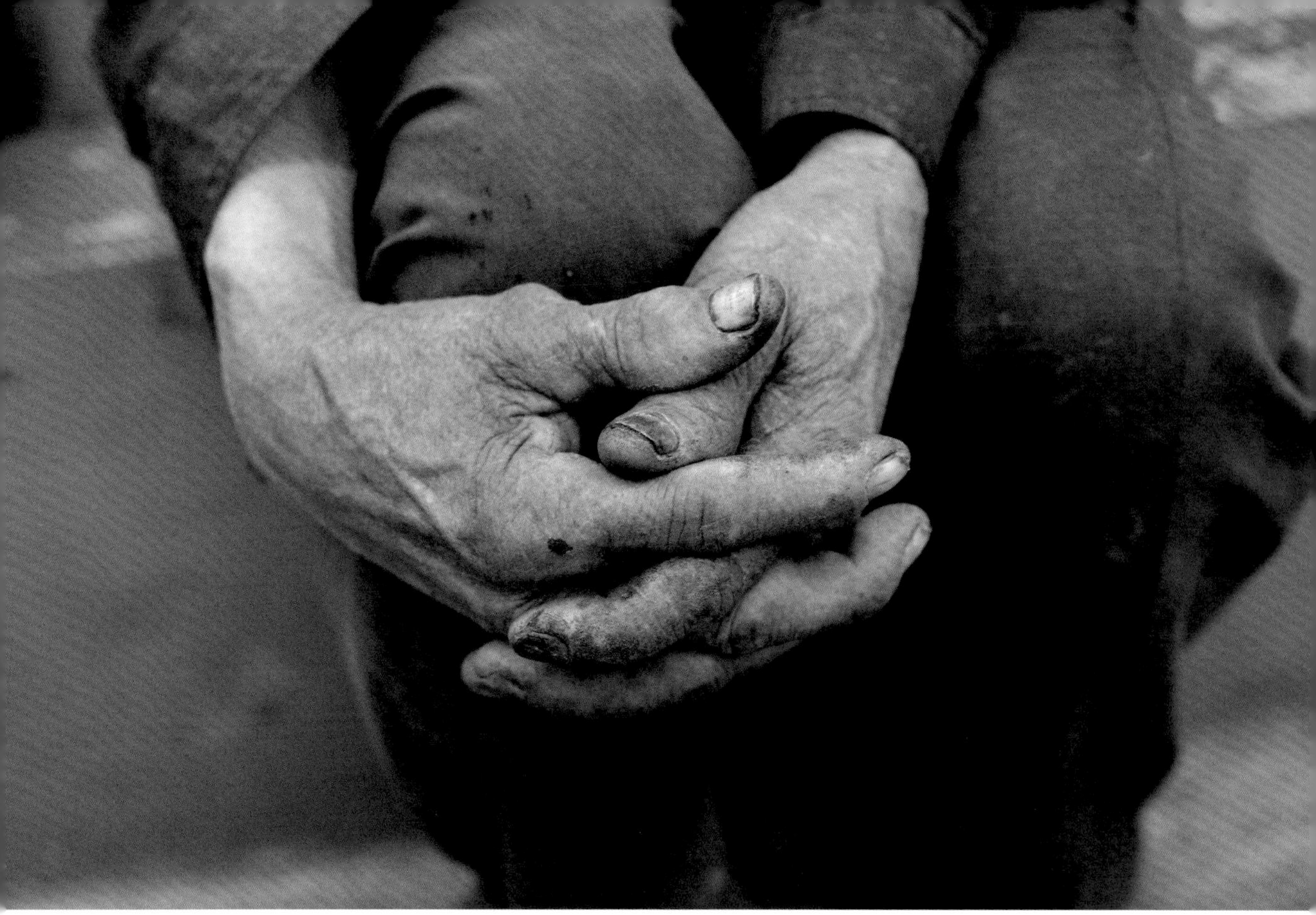

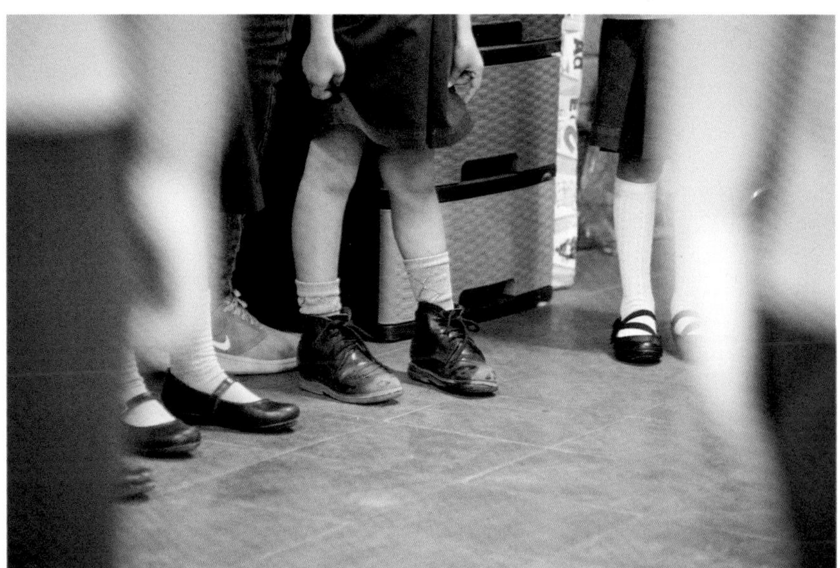

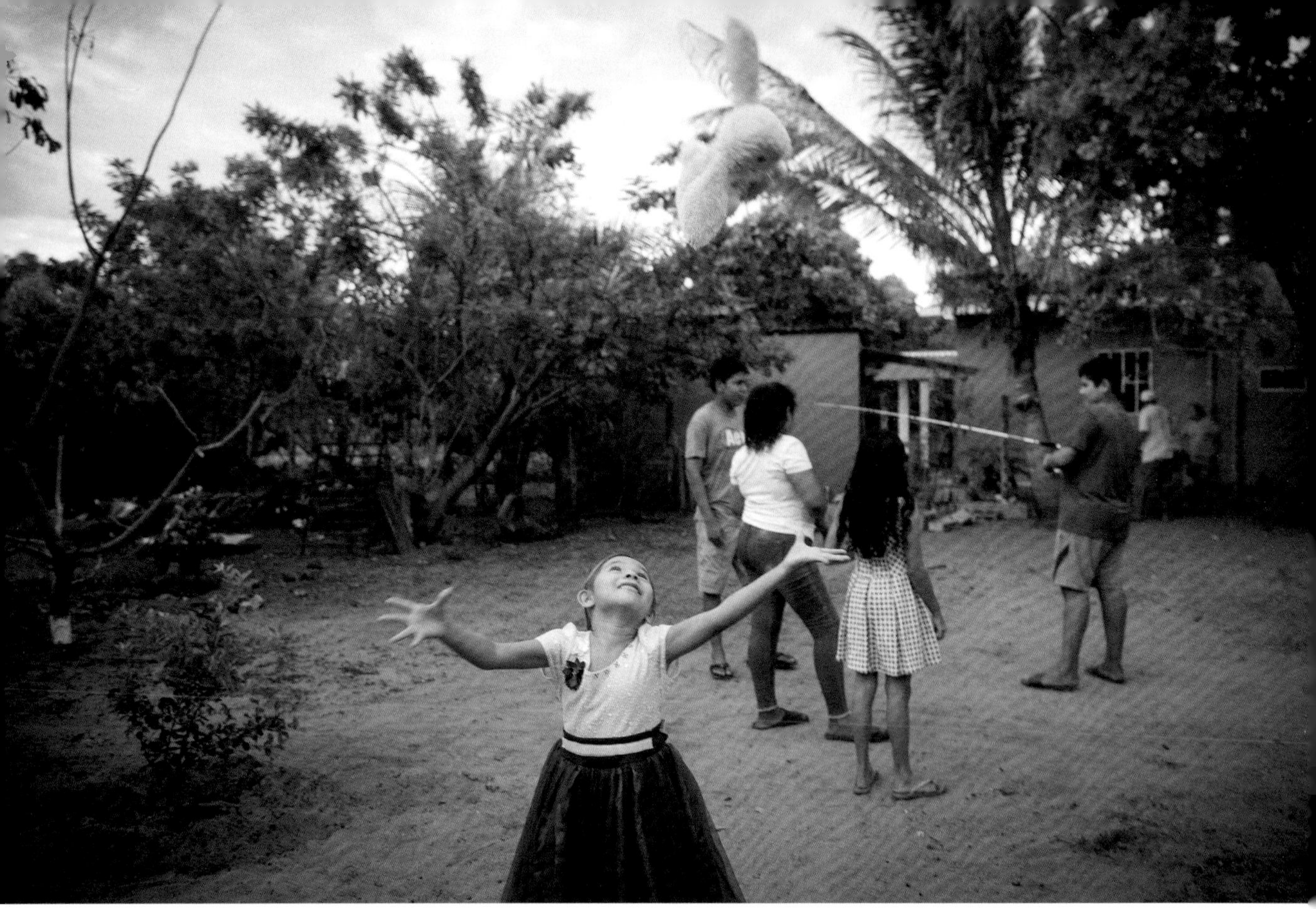

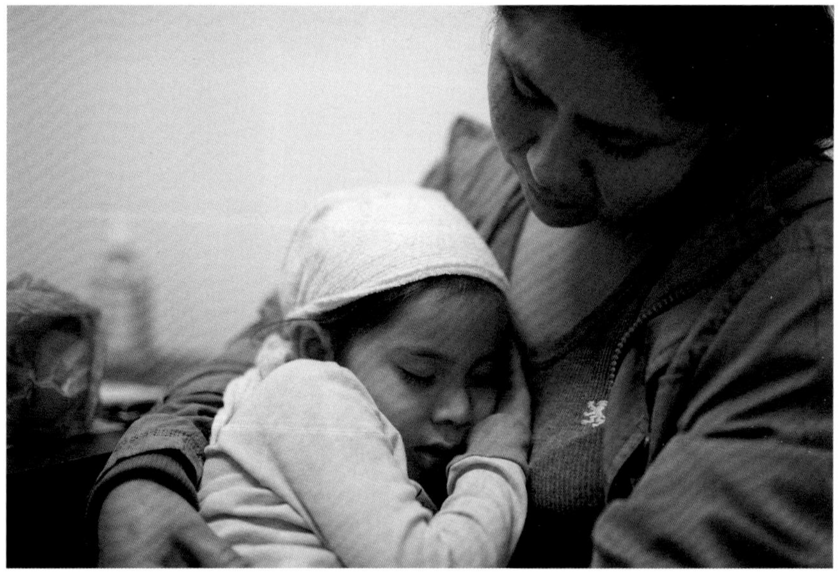

unnecessarily hurt people. But some hard things must be shown. You must not shy away from showing dirt roads and poverty, but don't fall into the activist's trap of hiding people's smiles.

Not only is dignity evident in dirty fingernails, so is kindness. Things close to the earth express the earth's patience. One thing, personally, that has surprised me in El Salvador has been people's patience.

AFTER THE HORRORS, the visits to the killing sites and the prisons, the young journalist travelling with me seemed to lose her words. We were walking towards our truck after an exhausting day in the prisons and I wanted to say, 'I cannot tell you I know what I am talking about, but I can tell you what I know.'

I know the hands and shoes are the language. I know that when I stood before the killing tree I internalised the pain. But I also know that I too often thrill to the hunt. I know I take a terrible pride in every time I have been shot at – as if a bullet missing me has somehow made me brave. I know the world is full of pain. But the air we breathe isn't painful – it is a wonder.

Before the young journalist departed, I took her to the remote island of fishermen and cashew farmers, Tasajera. I wanted her to meet the little girl Luna. I met Luna during my first expedition when her mother brought her into the government clinic at midnight. Luna was suffering a dangerous asthma attack. I was there investigating the veracity of the government's social projects, such as this remote clinic. And because my method is to simply move in and wait, I was there at that clinic the night when Luna arrived.

Social projects quickly receded from view as my reporting turned to the government's war on gangs, but over the course of a year I kept returning to the island to see my friend David, the fisherman, and Luna and her family. Over time, I recorded a deep picture of Luna's life: at school, playing princess and with her father at the wild, remote beach. This island is a wild place and the beach is not a beach for beachcombers; it is the edge of the earth, difficult to reach because no houses exist on the ocean side of the island – the weather is too difficult. One side of the island is dark and quiet against a channel of black water and mangroves. The other side is the moon. And Luna loves it, though she only gets to go with her father when he has time.

On this visit we climbed in David's boat with Luna and her family and putt-putted our way around the island channel, through the mysterious mangroves, to the remote end of the island, where the waves break over a spit of sand.

When we landed it was Luna, barefoot and in her Disney princess dress, who first leapt from the bow of the boat onto the spit and up to the beachhead and the sea. She ran and flailed like a maniac, flinging black volcanic sand, shouting songs at the sky as if none of us were there and she was communicating with something bigger than us all. Her wonder became my wonder. And I saw that the young journalist, too, was moved by the spectacle of a little girl who appeared to choreograph the sea.

When we were back in the boat and had been quiet a while, the young journalist turned and asked me, low and discreet, 'I appreciate that you brought me here, but what does Luna have to do with the story of El Salvador?'

Her question stung me, and I felt a little silly because I didn't have a ready answer. But then I knew the answer: Luna is like the sand. She is like the sea and the mangroves with their aquatic roots holding black, sun-drenched branches. She is the waters of the ocean. She is a black stone uncovered by a smashing wave. These are things without opinions, ideas or judgements. There are no headlines in the trees. Among the pelicans there is no war. Luna collects the warmth of a daylight star; sea salt decorates her skin. Like a stone in the sun, Luna does not judge, nor fear the day's end.

Luna is El Salvador without guile. Luna is what El Salvador would be without politics and business interests and all the things we falsely label 'progress.' Luna is not an illustration; she is the reality. If you want to know what El Salvador could become, you only need to look at what Luna is.

We were silent in the deafening wind. I lifted my camera and shot a frame of Luna in the prow with one hand holding her body against the wood and one hand on an anchor. And I thought how alike Luna and that old anchor are – fastened to the roots of things down deep where no one can see.

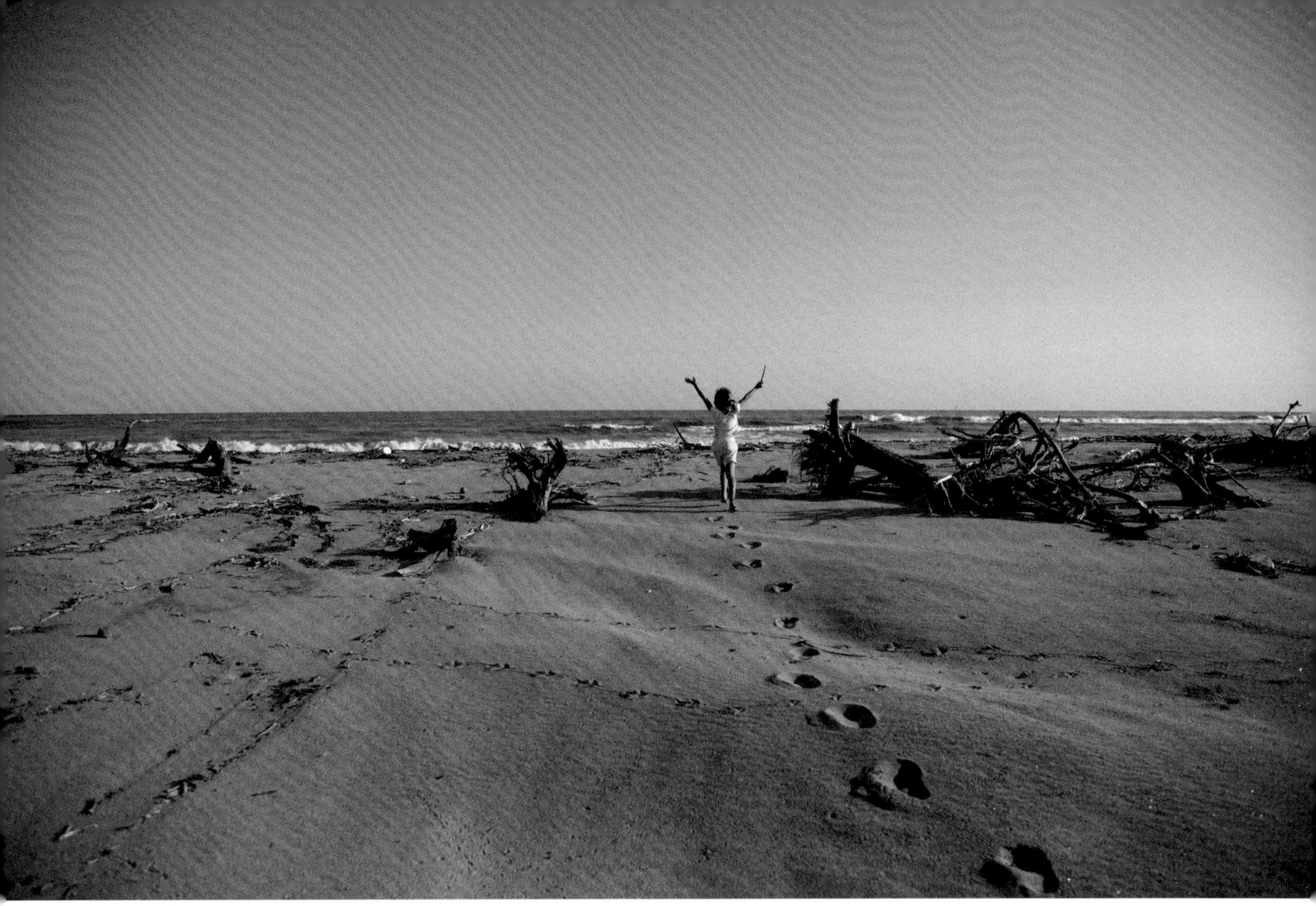

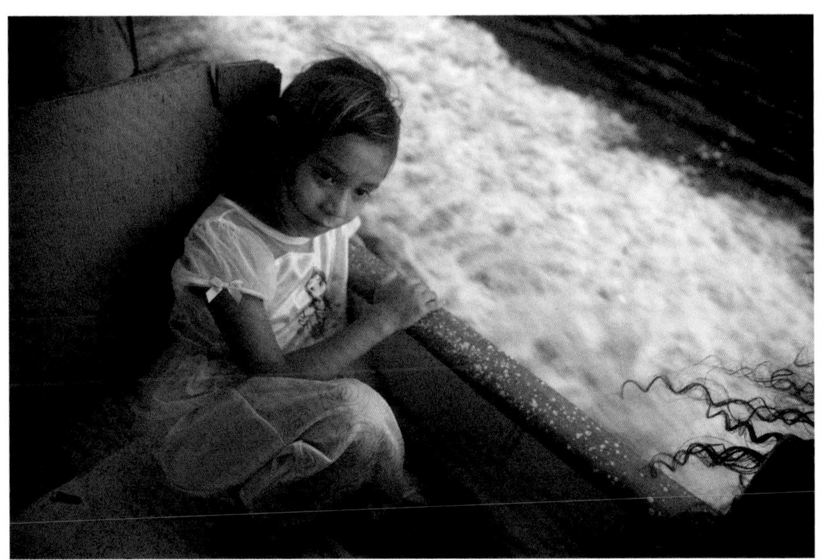

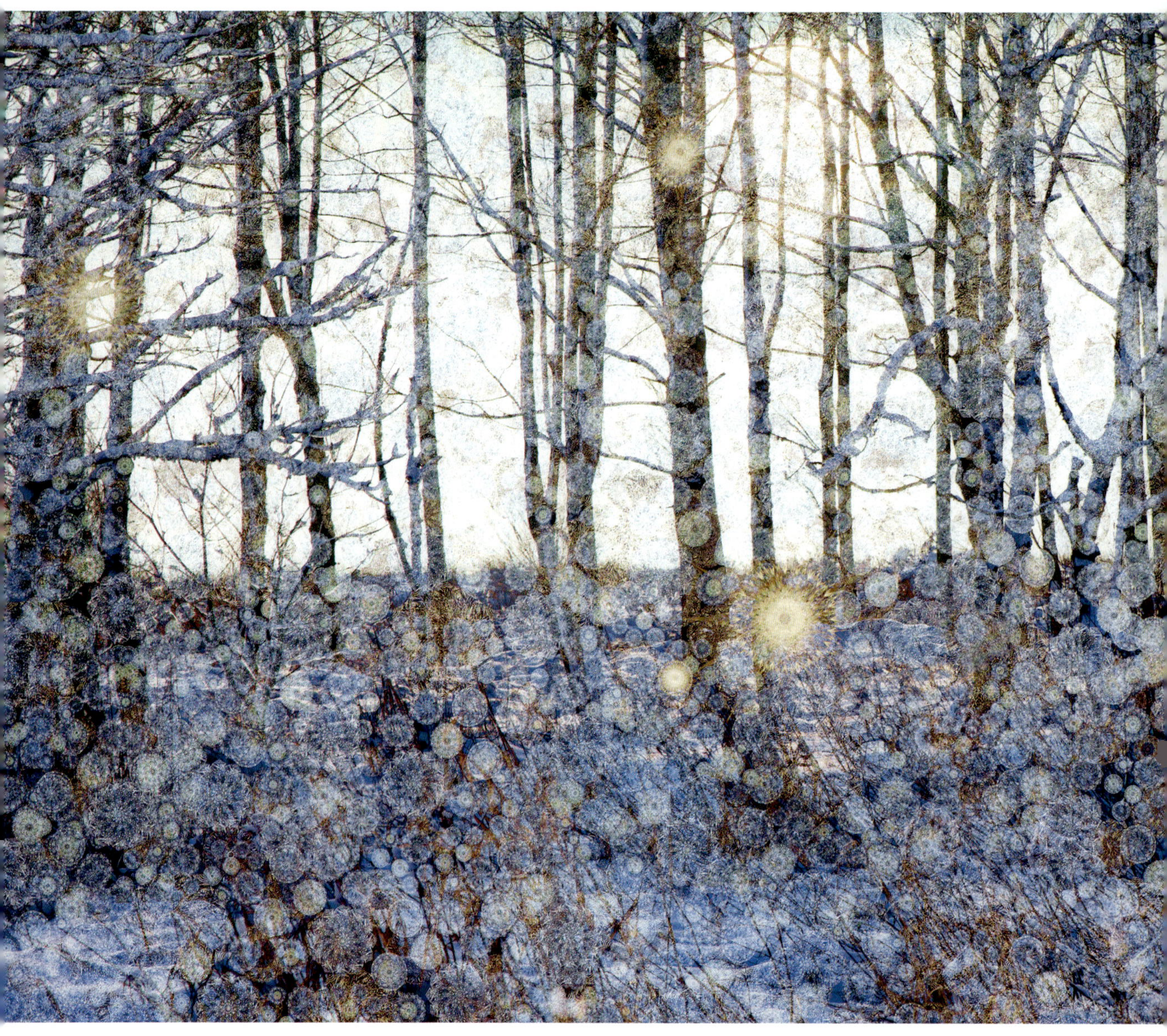

Children of Terabithia

What is there of beauty in losing an unborn baby?

CAITRIN KEIPER

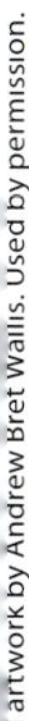

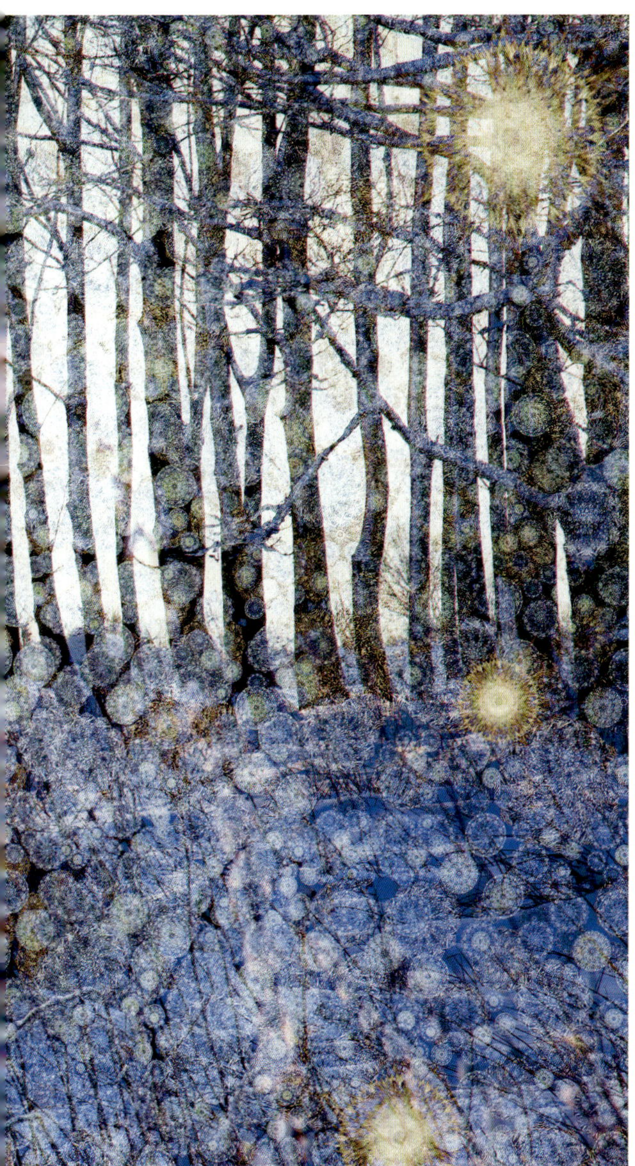

All artwork by Andrew Bret Wallis. Used by permission.

We hear the heart rate at 85 bpm. This is close to what mine is, normal for an adult, but it isn't right for a seven-week embryo's, whose heart rate should be double that. We all hope for our children to race ahead of us, dream up and do things we never could; in a sense, these early rapid heart rates signify their readiness to do that, to grow and become someone of their own. But this baby isn't going to.

As I wait for a doctor to come tell me What It All Means, what I already know, my mind wanders to the trail of boogers that an older child has left on the wall at home, up the stairs and down the hall, and the corresponding trail of post-it notes that someone else has put up to point out where they all are. Who would have ever thought to do something so gross and ridiculous? Not me, that's who; it could only be another person, once a fragile embryo himself, now on his own pathway through the world (a pathway apparently marked by accusatory post-it notes), driven by his own ideas and doing things his mom would never dream of. I reflect on what an incandescent miracle it is for anybody to live long enough and develop the self-determination to leave trails of boogers on the wall.

The doctor says we have a few weeks to see how things go. I resolve that if this is all the life on earth this baby is ever going to have, we are going to count every moment and *live it to the max*. One child has a jiujitsu tournament, and we all go in force to cheer him on, pumping it up with fight songs ('Went the distance, now I'm not gonna stop / Just a man and his will to survive…' *Survive, fighter baby! Go the distance!*). Another child turns four and a half and is convinced, from the bottom of her sparkly heart, that this is as deserving of a party as an actual birthday. Is she wrong? No, she is not. So we make cupcakes, cover the house in balloons and celebrate yet another miracle. *This is your family. You are part of this.*

I desperately want to convey to this baby, struggling to develop and keep that heart going, how much he or she is loved, supported, cherished, not alone. But how can I communicate this? I can talk and sing, but the hearing won't develop for another several weeks. I can sort of poke around

---

Caitrin Keiper is editor-at-large of Plough *and a senior editor of* The New Atlantis. *She lives in Virginia USA.*

Andrew Bret Wallis, *Winter Dawn*, mixed media, 2012.

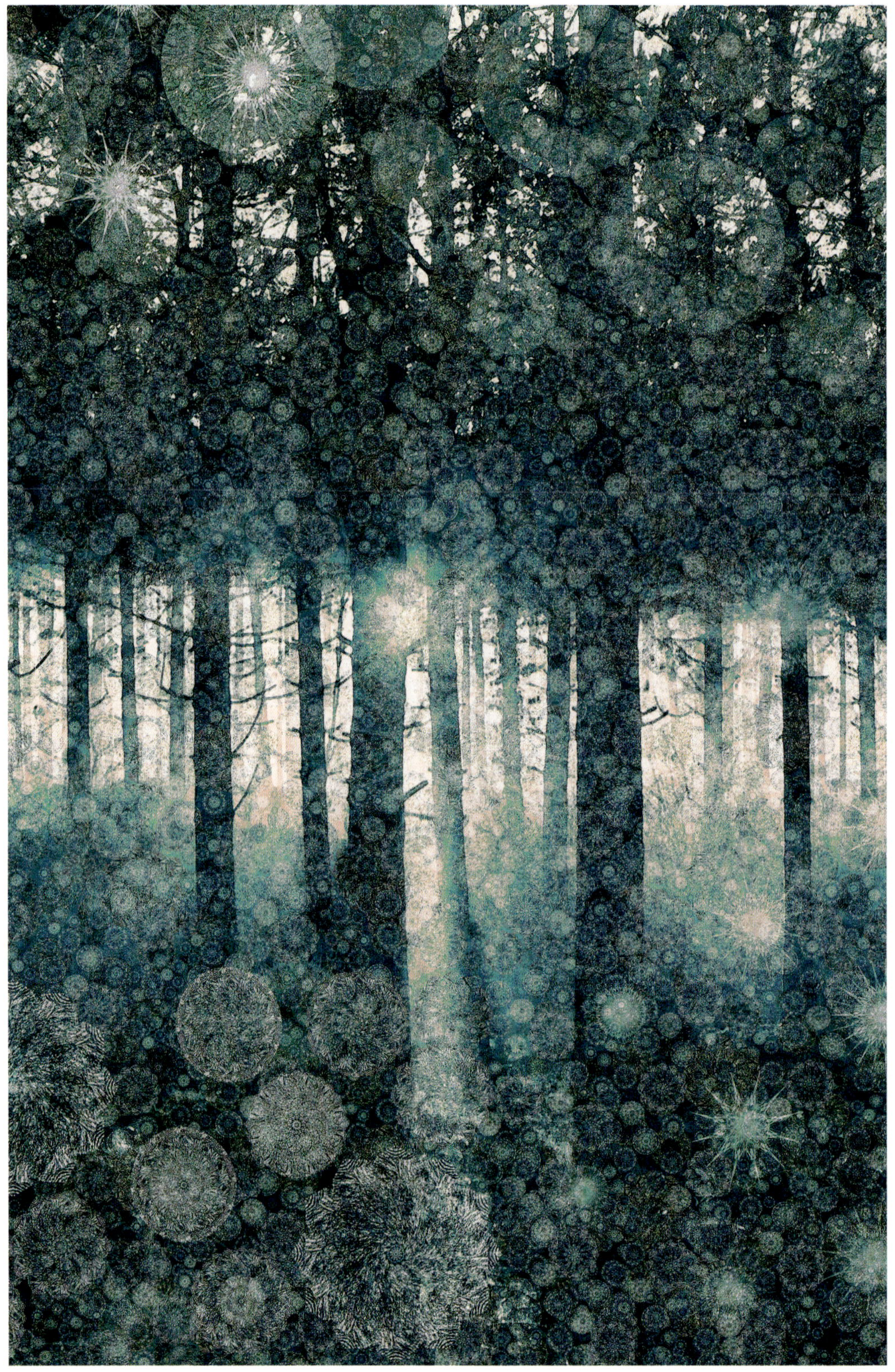

Andrew Bret Wallis, *Enchanted Forest*, mixed media, 2012.

from the outside like a greeting, but this does not say what I want it to: *I, your mom, am with you, I am here*. In the end, it seems the only way to express this is to do what I'm already doing – just *be* home and sustenance, just *be love*, just *be*.

At some point I wonder if God might feel the same way for us, wishing to express a love we don't yet have the capacity to recognise. 'Oh Jerusalem', says Jesus, 'How often have I longed to gather your children together, as a hen gathers her chicks under her wings' (Matt. 23:37). Even when we don't know it, we are enveloped all the same.

One thing the baby and I do together almost every day is go for a walk in the forest. The trees lifting to the sky remind me of Terabithia, the secret country dreamed up by two children in Katherine Paterson's 1977 Newbery-winning novel. Ten-year-old Jesse is trapped in what already seems like a drab, misunderstood existence when a new kid moves in next door. 'The person had jaggedy hair cut close to its face and wore one of those blue undershirtlike tops with faded jeans cut off above the knees. He couldn't honestly tell whether it was a girl or boy.' Leslie – 'one of those dumb names that could go either way', Jess thinks, though he senses she's a girl – is determined to make friends with him, as much as he tries to brush her off. But when he finally lets her in, more than one world opens up to him.

Every afternoon, they swing across the dried-up creek bed at the border of the woods and become king and queen of Terabithia, 'here where the dogwood and redbud played hide and seek among the oaks and evergreens, and the sun flung itself in golden streams through the trees to splash warmly at their feet.' There, they build a castle stronghold, fight invaders and explore their realm. Jess is wary of the deeper forest, 'dark places where it was almost like being underwater', which he feels are haunted, but Leslie explains it is a sacred place that 'even the rulers of Terabithia come into … only at times of greatest sorrow or of greatest joy.'

Even outside Terabithia's enchanted borders, where his older sister picks on him for his '*girl* friend' and his father is never not disappointed in him and everyone is small-minded and no one has enough to make ends meet, Jess and Leslie take on new adventures in a way that Jess had never known before. When an older girl bullies his little sister May Belle, they take great pleasure in cooking up a scheme to get back at her. But when they catch that same bully weeping over circumstances even crueller and more powerful than herself, they find themselves, to their own amazement, coming to her rescue.

Then the rain begins. The dry creek bed turns to swollen rapids. Jess and Leslie go into the sacred grove and pray to overcome the 'spell of some evil, unknown force' the rain portends. Jess is filled with dread while Leslie, as ever, seems to live without fear. One morning, she tries crossing into Terabithia alone, but falls on a rock and drowns.

In his grief, Jess feels that Leslie 'had tricked him. She had made him leave his old self behind and come into her world, and then before he was really at home in it but too late to go back, she had left him stranded there – like an astronaut wandering about on the moon. Alone.'

By the time of the next ultrasound, the little life has slipped away. I deliver my dead baby, name her (?) Leslie, and bury her in a tiny blanket stitched with a Celtic knot, a symbol of forever.

The next day it rains, hard and cold and unrelenting. Although I know her spirit is long gone, I can't bear to think of her body, now for the first time apart from me, all alone under the freezing wet earth.

Before there was Terabithia, there was music class – one half-hour, once a week, when Jess and the kids of Lark Creek Elementary would take flight. Gathering on the worn-out rug, they let the chords ripple over them, and sang of 'a land bright and clear / And the time's coming near / When we'll live in this land / You and me, hand in hand.' With the teacher strumming the guitar, 'people began to join in, quietly at first to match her mood, but as the song built up at the end, their voices did as well, so that by the time they got to the final "Free to be you and me", the whole school could hear them.' Even the kids who pretended it was beneath them couldn't help but be swept up in the spell.

When I was their age, I went to a choral camp where I learned, or thought I learned, a version of 'For the Beauty of the Earth' that was totally distinct from the familiar hymn. It was soaring and aethereal and lifted me on wings I didn't know I had. But after the summer was over, I couldn't recall any strain of the new melody or the name of the arranger or any other unique detail, and had no idea how to find it again. My feeble attempts to search for it only brought up the ubiquitous original – and after some time, I started to doubt whether the song I thought I remembered had ever actually existed, or had somehow been a dream.

Years went by. I grew up. One All Souls' Day, I was profoundly moved to hear John Rutter's *Requiem* performed at church. I tracked down the recording of it, as well as every other work by that composer I could get my hands on. The *Requiem* was what I returned to the most, the sonorous dread from the depths raised up into a wail, and then – mercy. A peace bathed in eternal light.

The rest of his music sat quietly on my computer until one day, on a whim, I set my iTunes library to total random play while I puttered around getting ready to go out. Suddenly, there it was. The song from a decade ago that I had ceased to believe in. I froze across the room, staring agape at the laptop. 'For the beauty of the earth', sang John Rutter's Cambridge Singers, 'for the beauty of the skies; for the love which from our birth over and around us lies.' (A mother might amend that love begins before our birth, but I digress.)

Light and untroubled, so unlike the *Requiem* in tone, it yet offered the same hope: that what seems to be lost or even nonexistent might not be so, in the end.

Miscarriage is a loss that many have experienced, a loss felt most in what might have been. In the commonness of its occurrence, it seems to take its sad place in the order of things.

But the death of a child is shocking. It seems to cut against the very fabric of reality that such a thing should somehow be allowed to happen.

Bridge to Terabithia grew out of such a devastating loss. When Katherine Paterson's son David was eight years old, his best friend, Lisa, was struck and killed by lightning. Paterson said in a 2009 interview for the audio edition that she wrote the book to 'try to make sense out of a tragedy that didn't make sense.'

What sense is there to make in that? Isn't it almost offensive to even try?

Certainly, *Bridge* has often been protested or 'banned' here and there because 'death isn't an appropriate subject' for children, Paterson has explained. 'No, it isn't', she agrees, 'but it happens.'

After David lost Lisa, he blacked out so much of the experience that he couldn't even remember what she looked like. Decades later, as an adult, he saw a picture of her and was gobsmacked to realise that she looked just like one of his own children's friends, a girl whose face had always fascinated him though he had never made the connection why. Her presence is also felt in the way that any number of people who never knew the real Lisa have felt an uncanny kinship with Leslie.

With respect, I don't think Paterson did make sense of the tragedy. What she did do, strangely enough, is make something beautiful. This itself does not make sense – what is there of beauty in an event like this, and why would anybody want to read about it? – and yet it *is* sublimely beautiful,

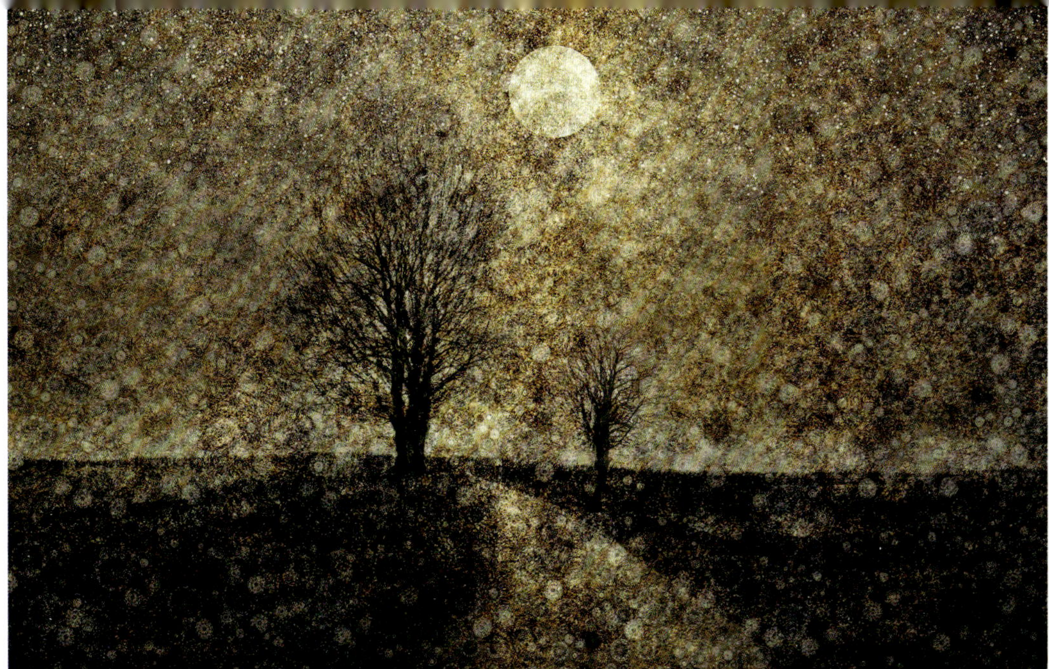

in a way that points to – what? 'Banned' as it is, the book is also beloved in a way that people struggle to articulate, often gesturing towards the magic of the few pages spent in Terabithia, the world within a world. But, as Jess comes to believe, the real significance flows outward.

> It was Leslie who had taken him from the cow pasture into Terabithia and turned him into a king. He had thought that was it. Wasn't king the best you could be? Now it occurred to him that perhaps Terabithia was like a castle where you came to be knighted. After you stayed for a while and grew strong you had to move on. For hadn't Leslie, even in Terabithia, tried to push back the walls of his mind and make him see beyond to the shining world – huge and terrible and beautiful and very fragile? (Handle with care – everything – even the predators.)
>
> Now it was time for him to move out. She wasn't there, so he must go for both of them. It was up to him to pay back to the world in beauty and caring what Leslie had loaned him in vision and strength.

Jess takes his sister May Belle, who has only ever wanted him to love and include her, and puts flowers in her hair. He builds a bridge across the creek bed he and Leslie used to swing over and ushers her across. '*Shhh*', he says to May Belle. 'Look.'

'Where?'

'Can't you see 'um?' he whispers. 'All the Terabithians standing on tiptoe to see you.'

'*Me?*'

'*Shhh*, yes. There's a rumour going around that the beautiful girl arriving today might be the queen they've been waiting for.'

My own Leslie, traveller to the undiscovered country, has indeed gone far beyond me and what I know. But the love she brought into being remains, needing to be shared somehow.

In the world she left behind, huge and terrible and shining, there are intimations, echoes, clues of a peace that passes all understanding. They're not always there when you want them. There is no resolution to the mystery. They don't erase the grief. But they have something to say.

A story that bridges truth and fiction, life and death. A strain of music blown in from some other plane. The irreducible beauty of a life that ever existed at all. A gaze up through the solemn trees into the wide open sky, seeking contact with the love that's all around.

Andrew Bret Wallis, *Sun Glow*, mixed media, 2019.

The Paradox of Beauty

Pope Benedict XVI

CAN THE BEAUTIFUL BE GENUINE, or, in the end, is it only an illusion? Isn't reality perhaps basically evil? The fear that in the end it is not the arrow of the beautiful that leads us to the truth, but that falsehood, all that is ugly and vulgar, may constitute the true 'reality' has at all times caused people anguish. At present this has been expressed in the assertion that after Auschwitz it was no longer possible to write poetry; after Auschwitz it is no longer possible to speak of a God who is good. People wondered: Where was God when the gas chambers were operating? This objection, which seemed reasonable enough before Auschwitz when one realised all the atrocities of history, shows that in any case a purely harmonious concept of beauty is not enough. It cannot stand up to the confrontation with the gravity of the questioning about God, truth and beauty. Apollo, who for Plato's Socrates was 'the God' and the guarantor of unruffled beauty as 'the truly divine' is absolutely no longer sufficient.

In this way, we return to the paradox of being able to say of Christ: *'You are the fairest of the children of men'* (Psalm 45:2) and: *'He had no beauty, no majesty to draw our eyes, no grace to make us delight in him'* (Isa. 53:2). In the Passion of Christ, the experience of the beautiful has received new depth and new realism. The One who is beauty itself let himself be slapped in the face, spat upon, crowned with thorns. However, in his face that is so disfigured, there appears the genuine, extreme beauty: the beauty of love that goes *'to the very end'*; for this reason it is revealed as greater than falsehood and violence.

Is there anyone who does not know Dostoyevsky's often quoted sentence: 'Beauty will save the world'? However, people usually forget that Dostoyevsky is referring here to the redeeming beauty of Christ. We must learn to see Him. If we are struck by the arrow of his paradoxical beauty, then we will truly know him, and know him not only because we have heard others speak about him. Then we will have found the beauty of Truth, of the Truth that redeems.

Selections from Pope Benedict XVI, 'The Feeling of Things, the Contemplation of Beauty', 2002. Lightly abridged.

Augustine of Hippo

TOO LATE HAVE I LOVED YOU, O Beauty so ancient and so new, too late I have loved you! Behold, you were within me, while I was outside: it was there that I sought you, and, a deformed creature, rushed headlong upon these things of beauty which you have made. You were with me, but I was not with you. They kept me far from you, those fair things which, if they were not in you, would not exist at all. You have called to me, and have cried out, and have shattered my deafness. You have blazed forth with light, and have shone upon me, and you have put my blindness to flight! You have sent forth fragrance, and I have drawn in my breath, and I pant after you. I have tasted you, and I hunger and thirst after you. You have touched me, and I have burned for your peace.

Augustine, *The Confessions of Saint Augustine*, translated by John K Ryan (Image Classics, 1960), 220. Used by permission.

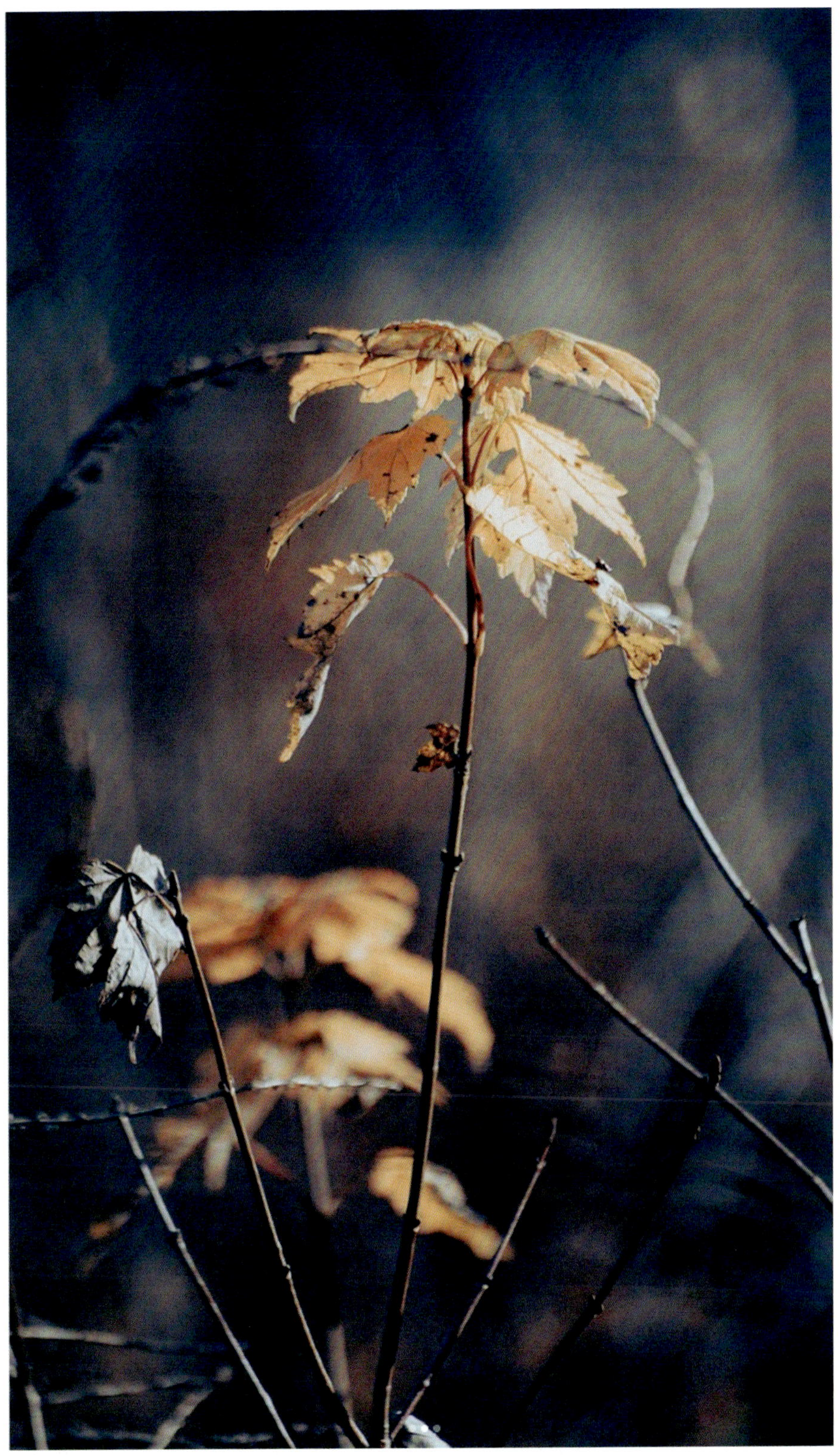

Photograph by David Zumpe.

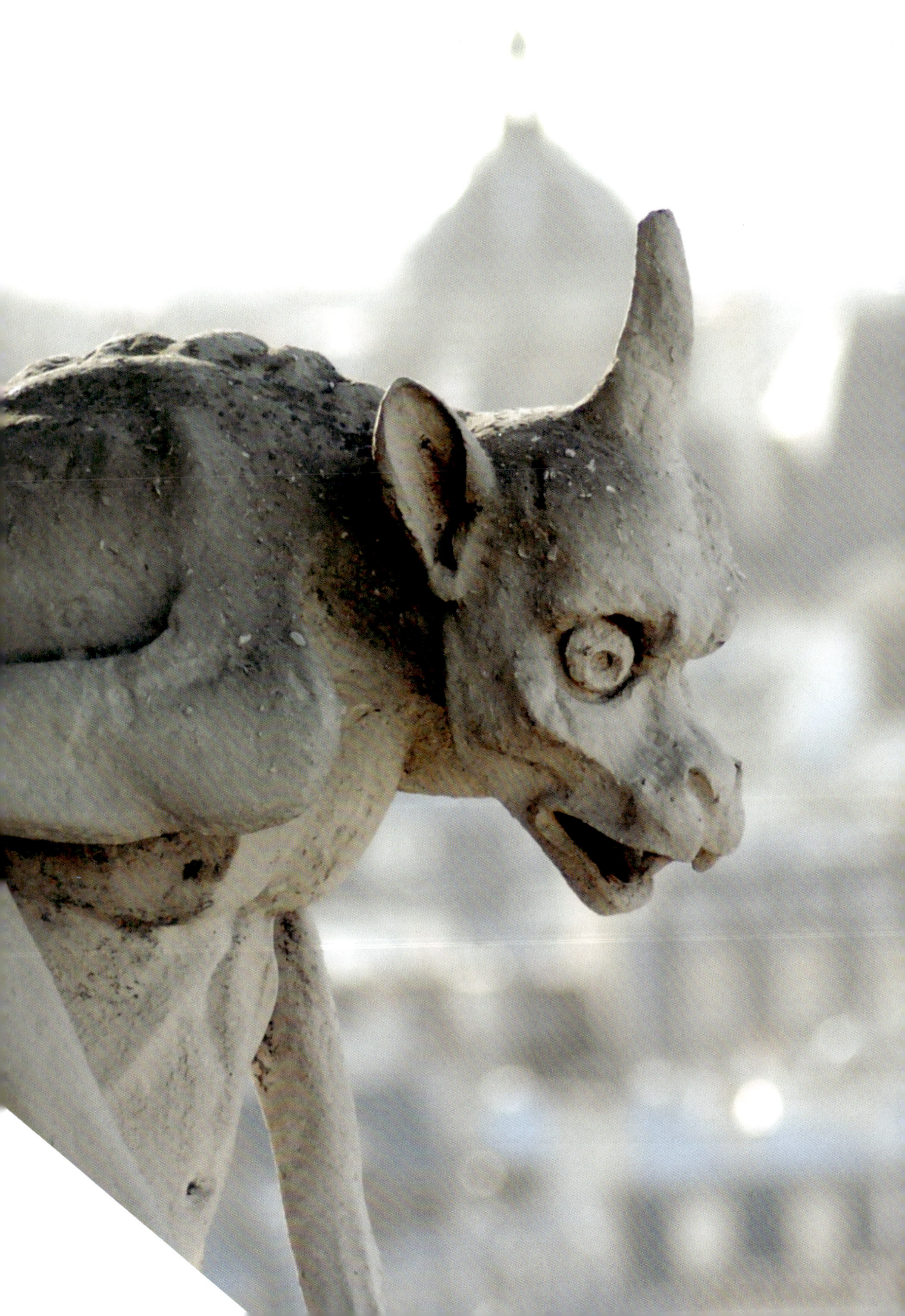

Those Hideous Stewards of Beauty

The grotesques on Notre-Dame Cathedral have a unique perspective.

SERGIO BERMUDEZ

'why was I not made of stone like thee?'
—Quasimodo in Victor Hugo's *The Hunchback of Notre-Dame*

I MOVED TO PARIS three years ago. My French is still bad, but I have grown familiar with this city. It is strange to call a place home that is so romanticised in the minds of so many. When I first arrived, I did not know what to expect, but I, like so many others, had read of Paris from different eras. So it was a bit surreal, when I first saw Notre-Dame, to witness the rebuilding of it instead of the timeless imagery I had seen in films, video games and even the animated Disney feature, *The Hunchback of Notre Dame*. On those first visits, I was greeted with scaffolding, a large metal barrier blocking the front façade, and cranes towering over the church towers. The front of the church peeked out from behind it, looking impressive, but almost as a memory of what it once was, and a promise of what it might become again. That was a few years ago; since then, I have walked by it many times, noting the changes each time. Initially I watched very carefully, noting each minor shift, feeling like I alone was able to witness the transformation in whole.

It has recently been 'finished' and the barriers have been removed. Replacing them are large lines of people waiting to visit. Along the sides and towards the back are still a few cranes, providing a means to finish the 'minor' details that need to be resolved, but for all intents and purposes, the church has been rebuilt. It was strange, for me, to finally enter this church after so many months of seeing it closed.

My first visit was attending Mass. Not the inaugural Mass, but a regular Sunday service. I was struggling to follow the French readings and homily. But Mass is Mass, so it was familiar all the same. I focused on trying to understand the service, but kept losing that battle to the people shuffling along the sides photographing the architecture and the ushers trying in vain to keep them moving along and outside the rope to respect the divine. Two Italian women, when the usher was not looking, ducked under the ropes, sat next to us and took some selfies before shuffling off with the rest of the tourists.

On some level, I understand. Inside the great church there is a sense of grandeur, of great beauty, history and stories older than our parents and their parents. To be a part of that, even for a moment, is incredibly appealing. After witnessing the interior, I had to reconsider the exterior. The white stone, the vaulted arches, the spires, all these elements we assign to a style of architecture we call 'the Gothic.' All pointing up towards heaven. And, of course, there are the gargoyles.

Along the church at the edges of our perception as we walk by are creatures, grinning, snarling growling, contemplating our existence, staring at us, observing our movements. They may not be the first thing a person notices, but they are always there in our minds and perceptions. They have become synonymous with Notre-Dame and the concept of Gothic architecture itself.

They stand in contrast with the majesty and beauty of the cathedral, and deliberately so. Notably, Saint Bernard of Clairvaux was not a fan. He wrote, 'What is the meaning of these unclean monkeys, these strange savage lions and monsters? To what purpose are here placed these creatures, half beast, half man or these spotted tigers?'

In one sense the purpose is straightforward. 'Gargoyle' stems from the French word *gargouille,* which translates to 'throat or gullet.' Some have said the word is meant to mimic the gurgling sound they make when the water pours forth. In other words, the original responsibility of the gargoyle was to prevent rain from accumulating in pools on the roof, thereby reducing water damage. Many churches still possess gargoyles that function this way. However, some do not. Although we still refer to these snarling, laughing creatures as gargoyles, the technical name for them is 'grotesques.' There is no definitive answer to Saint Bernard's question. We do not know why these creatures were placed there.

Some say they exist as a reminder of the evils of the world (hence their facing outward from the church); in Barcelona I was told one of the gargoyles even points to where a brothel used to be in the old city. Others say they exist as 'preachers in stone' designed to teach the illiterate of the ugliness of sin and that true beauty is found in God alone. The contrast of the grotesques occupying the same space as the divine appealed to Victor Hugo, who would write his famous novel

---

Sergio Bermudez is a freelance writer who lives in Paris.

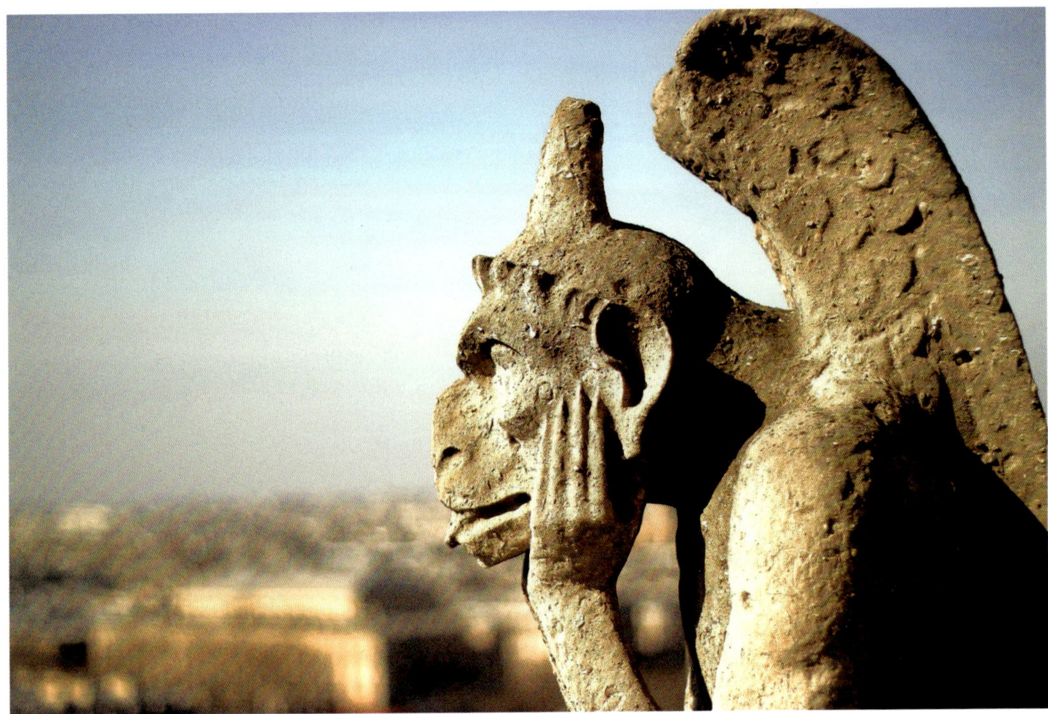

Photograph by Justin Mier on Flickr. Used by permission.

about the church that watches all, and a lonely bellringer who longed to be a part of Parisian life.

Victor Hugo was fascinated with the grotesques. For him, their value was not just in their being 'preachers in stone' for the uneducated. He argued that their ugliness and their horrifying faces were what made them valuable. Only by witnessing and walking under their terrible grins and fearsome gaze can we truly appreciate the beauty and divinity of the sublime.

THE WORD 'GROTESQUE' has had many definitions over the years, initially referring to ornamentation that was more supernatural and imaginative as a flourish. (This was common in the Renaissance.) The term evolved and was used somewhat pejoratively to label these flourishes as something absurd and uncouth. There is a common thread through all this. It is a term used to discuss distorted, hybrid things. Later definitions included ugliness as another primary aspect of this term.

Years before he would write *The Hunchback of Notre-Dame*, Hugo wrote a play about Oliver Cromwell. The play is very long and features an immense cast, and as a result has been underperformed. What makes the play notable, however, is the preface, where Hugo writes what could be considered a manifesto for the entire Romantic movement. In the preface, Hugo discusses and emphasises the importance of the grotesque and how it relates to the sublime.

> The universal beauty which the ancients solemnly laid upon everything is not without monotony; the same impression repeated again and again may prove fatiguing at last. Sublime upon sublime scarcely presents a contrast, and we need a little rest from everything, even the beautiful. On the other hand, the grotesque seems to be a halting-place, a mean term, a starting-point whence one rises towards the beautiful with a fresher and keener perception.

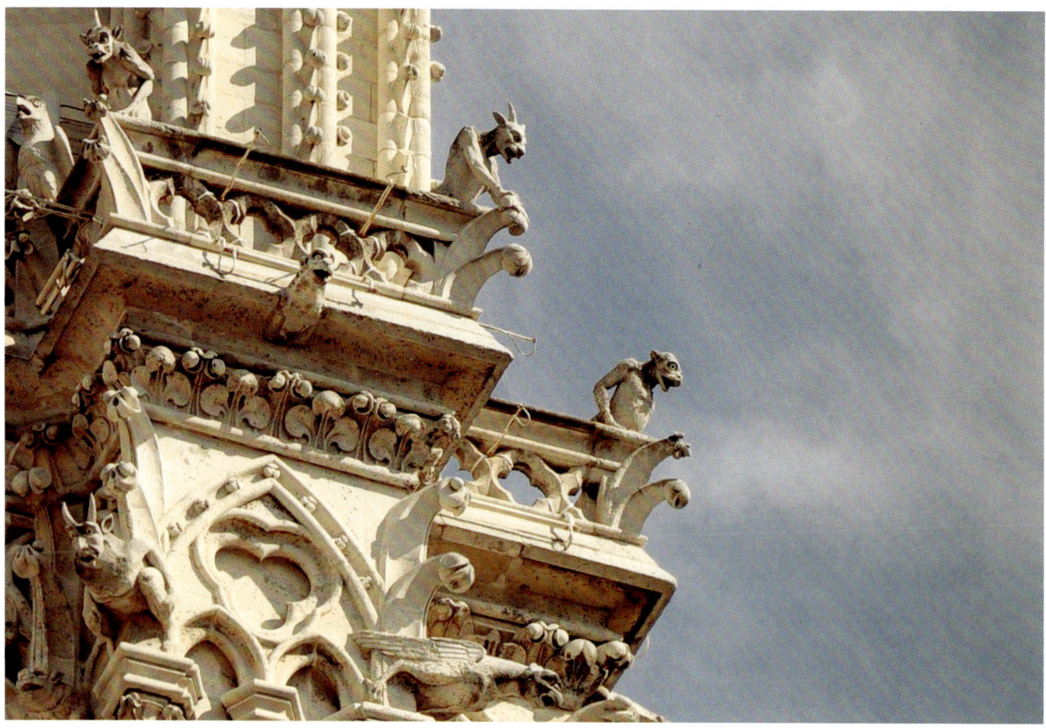

Photograph by Ajith on Flickr. Used by permission.

Years later, Hugo published his story of a lonely hunchback living atop the great cathedral with the grotesques as his only companions. In the present, the importance of the grotesques remains as they gaze upon the city, observing the rich, the poor and everyone in between going about their business. Their grins might be taken as a type of sardonic judgement, but there is another way to see it. From their lofty perch, the grotesques look down and see themselves in us. The ugliness we carry, both that within us and that imposed upon us by a world of judgements. And they understand these things do not define us. Just as they do not define them.

We do not like to imagine ourselves as monsters or ugly twisted things, but this is the nature of sin, and none of us is spared from its influence. We are all subject to the warping distortions it imposes on our minds and souls. Only through this understanding can we even hope to embrace the possibility of a form without ugliness. Hugo writes, 'What we call the ugly, on the contrary, is a detail of a great whole which eludes us, and which is in harmony, not with man but with all creation.'

Maybe it is my love of monsters, but I wish to see the world as the grotesques do. They do not seek out the ugly as we do. They do not examine themselves in the mirror. They do not lament their body shape. They do not bemoan the state of their clothes or nitpick flaws. They also do not impose this on others. Instead, their gaze is turned outward, towards creation. There is something serene and beautiful about this. They do not need to look within the church. We do. They see a beauty in the world that we cannot.

I am new to Paris, but have come to know and love the city as a resident. The people within the church and without, the visitors and the natives, are all grotesques. Beyond the ancient churches, you might encounter a woman singing opera for some change, or a man asleep in his own piss in the Métro. These are all the same, and it can be argued that their existence is in harmony, and if that understanding fails to be grasped, it is easier (but harder on the ego) to realise that fault lies within us rather than in them. Yes, some of these encounters are more ideal than others. I will not say which ones are preferable, but I will say that it is only through all these encounters that true beauty can be realised.

Beauty is not a matter of taste, nor is it a matter of aesthetics. It is a means by which we attempt to grasp at the sublime. It is a textured reality that exists in a feverish dream that was previously only understood by madmen and poets. Art, like humanity, cannot recreate or capture the sublime. However, what it can do is remind us that within us is the spark of divinity.

The only way to see this is to see it as a grotesque does. If one cannot adopt this outlook, then one must acknowledge, even begrudgingly, its necessity. The contrast of our everyday lives is what provides us with the inspiration to improve, to create, to love, even if there are times when it is difficult and we would rather not.

I want to return to the hypothetical man sleeping on the Métro I mentioned earlier. (I have witnessed real men doing this, but out of dignity and respect, let us imagine a hypothetical man.) Perhaps, in that moment, in the corner of a subway car, filling the rest of the car with a nauseating smell, he has found peace and possibly even joy that he cannot find in his waking hours? We will never know what this imaginary, but real in theory, man dreams or why he is sleeping in a subway car. But as we move away from the puddle of his efforts that glides across the floor, fearful of being made a participant in his decisions, we can spare a moment to contemplate the beauty of a person who has found a fleeting moment of peace, and even wish him well before changing cars at the next stop. In this way, we can see him as a grotesque might.

No one can blame us for recoiling or looking away. But after that initial recoil, some reflection is required. The contrast of a man in need finding peace for a moment and our discomfort presents an opportunity to contemplate beauty. Standing there (or sitting, if you are lucky enough to find a seat on the Métro), maybe it is our failure to see as the grotesques do that causes us to look away. Our own distortion bars us from appreciating the artisan that is God, and marvelling at his works even when we cannot fully understand their place or situation in the grand design.

If we are questioning beauty, there is also a question about what precisely is ugly here. We do not know this imagined man's situation. There might be a desire to create a narrative of an otherwise saintly man who has fallen on hard times, but maintains his virtue despite the physical lapse of control. There would be many who would witness this and conjure up an image of this as an assault on upright society, those who wear fine clothes and can control their bladders. Such narratives exist about many in our society, urine or no urine. That which is different from us can be distorted to embody all sorts of fears or even potential threats to our persons, our children and our loved ones. There are many who do this.

If beauty is to be true and good, then it must be for everyone. It must be difficult or complicated or coarse or hard to perceive. It must be worth struggling for. And it must exist in all of us, regardless of our initial reactions. If we cannot see this, the fault is in ourselves. We have failed to take the central lesson from those 'preachers in stone.'

It is difficult, and it takes time and patience, and it may very well turn out that the grotesques of Notre-Dame will change before I do, but to see Paris, to see all of creation as a grotesque does, feels like a noble endeavour. As my teachers lean over the edges of the cathedral, protecting the church by drenching this complicated earth in water from the heavens, perhaps they are not reminding me of the sins outside of the faith, but the ones within. As I pass by that famous church on the Seine, I contemplate this, looking up into the Paris rain.

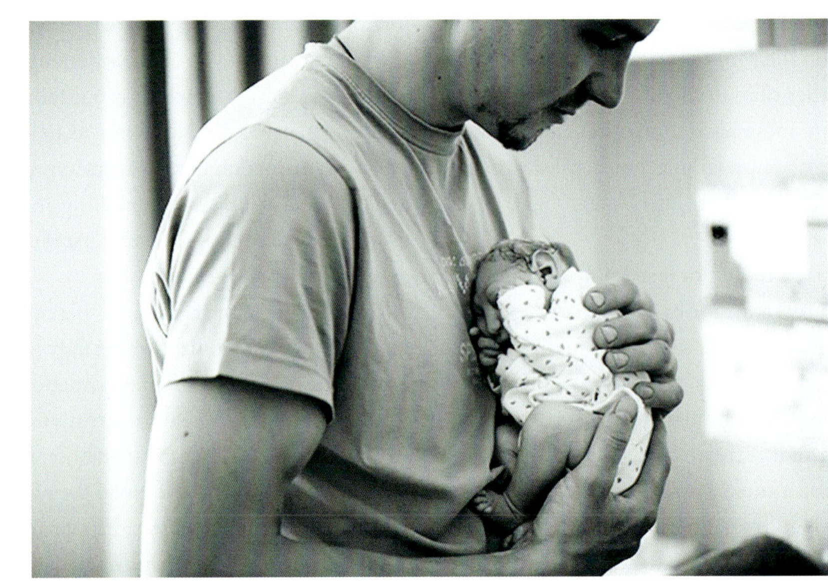

When Life Begins with Death

In Vienna, a hospital offers palliative care to babies with debilitating or life-threatening diagnoses.

VERONIKA KABAS

Sometimes, life is just starting when you have to let go of it. That's the unavoidable reality that confronted Doris and Johannes when they were expecting their first child. 'It doesn't look good', Johannes remembers his wife telling him on the phone – and suddenly their entire world came to a halt. It was 23 December 2020. Their baby's life, though it had only just begun, was already falling apart. Doris's gynecologist advised her to terminate the pregnancy immediately, pending the confirmation of his suspicions by amniocentesis.

A few weeks later, the results were in: Doris and Johannes's child had '13q deletion syndrome' – a rare genetic disorder with a minimal life expectancy. The anxious father's gaze happened to fall on further information in the report: 'female chromosome set.' When they asked the doctor if the baby was a girl, he responded with a curt 'yes', and once again urgently recommended terminating the pregnancy. That way, he told them, they could start focusing right away on having a healthy child. 'Of course you can decide for yourselves', he went on, 'but 90% of the couples in your situation would terminate the pregnancy today.' His advice was

Johannes holds his newborn daughter, Anna, 2021.

clear. So was Doris and Johannes's certainty that they would not be following it.

Through a 'life protection agency', as pro-life associations are commonly known in Austria, the young couple learned of a possible alternative. Since 2020, Vienna's St Josef Hospital has been offering perinatal palliative care. Here, couples like them who wish to welcome a child with debilitating or life-threatening diagnoses are supported in realising their dreams.

With almost 4,000 births a year, St Josef is one of the largest maternity clinics in Austria, and daily life is characterised by happy new beginnings. In the midst of it, though, is a safe space for those whose path is different. Here, a different sort of care and healing takes place, with quiet acceptance and holistic care.

Sister Teresa Schlackl, chief ethics officer at St Josef, describes it as a 'beautiful and difficult task.' Of course, the news of a life-threatening or fatal diagnosis is always difficult for anyone. Your world collapses. But the decisive difference at St Josef is how this reality is approached and dealt with. For Schlackl, a Salvatorian nun, it is clear that every life has equal value, whether it lasts a second or 98 years. But in her experience, most people have difficulty believing this, which makes comforting them difficult. 'In such situations, I have to learn the meaning of simply standing by.'

As she explains, the focus is not on prolonging life at any cost, but on the question: How can we treat the child with as much dignity and love as possible? Together with the family, a path is planned: from personal counselling and a carefully coordinated birth plan to medical and emotional care and sensitive support in saying goodbye. Families are accompanied from the beginning to the end of the process – and beyond. Parents are allowed to experience every emotion: fear and grief, but also the love and joy of every precious moment spent together with their child.

Initially, parents bring their fears and hopes to paediatrician Dr Andrea Schiller, a member of the interdisciplinary team. 'At first, they hope that the baby isn't sick after all. Then they are preoccupied with worries and fears, such as: What will our baby look like? Will it suffer? Will it be in pain? What will it be like when it dies?'

Dr Schiller is always happy to share a couple's optimism – she does not feel it is her place to take away anyone's hope. However, she also sees it as her job to help them take a close look at the situation at hand: 'Thankfully, we work very closely with the gynecologists, and that way, we can all be together during ultrasound examinations and see, for example, that a baby is much too small, or that it has no lungs or no kidneys. That makes it easier to comprehend what is going on.'

DORIS AND JOHANNES were one of the first couples to take advantage of St Josef's programme. After those harrowing conversations with their gynecologist, they felt relief at being finally accepted for who they were – the parents of a severely disabled child whose life they wished to honour and welcome. Anna was born on 27 June 2021. 'We were even feeling positive by the time we drove to the hospital for the birth', recalls Johannes.

Because Anna's brain did not develop normally, due to the genetic defect, no one could tell her parents exactly what would happen at her birth. Nor could anyone predict whether and how the biological processes that occur in a healthy baby after birth would transpire in her particular case. Would her brainstem be too deformed to control her breathing? Would her nervous system be able to coordinate vital processes?

As it turned out, Anna managed everything herself, 'with hardly any help', Johannes adds,

---

Veronika Kabas is a graphic designer and social worker specialising in art therapy. She lives in Vienna.

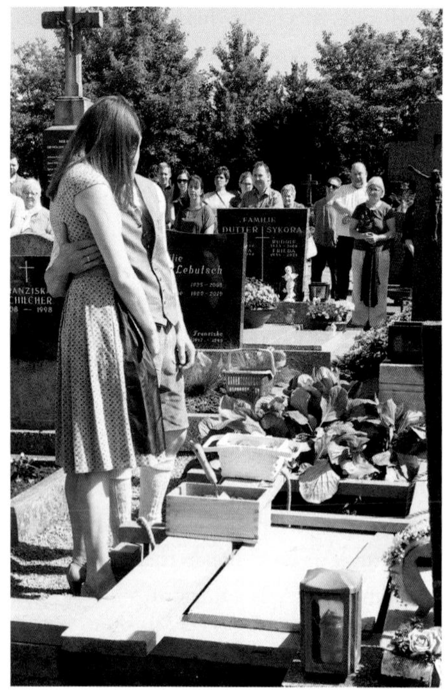

Doris and Johannes say goodbye to their daughter, 2022.

smiling as he talks about the birth. 'Considering that we didn't know if she would even survive delivery – if it would be her death – it was incredibly beautiful.' As he speaks, there is something in his eyes of that special sparkle fathers have when they boast about their children's achievements. And though she only weighed a delicate 1.38 kilos, she quickly began to nurse and show strong signs of life. A week later, the new parents were able to take their daughter home – another overwhelming moment.

Even at St Josef, little Anna stands out. Most children of parents who opt for palliative care die while still in the ward. 'In most cases, the fact is that the baby is terminally ill; or it was an ectopic pregnancy and can't survive. That can seem unbelievable to a mother who feels the baby in her belly moving', Dr Schiller says. And so she always tries to guide parents to live as fully as possible in the present moment – in the here and now. If a woman is seven months pregnant, Dr Schiller allows everything to be fine, even just for that moment. Let it be a moment for joy, love and gratitude.

The point of no return is the birth. 'Up to that point, you can hope', says Sister Teresa. In an oncology ward, she notes, people have a very different attitude towards death: they look it in the eye. At birth, naturally, they don't expect it. But none of that matters for this nun. For her, it is standing together at the beginning and the end of life that counts. Beyond all the medical interventions and clinical support, it is simply being there for people that is so infinitely precious. Dr. Schiller agrees. 'At the moment when life comes to an end, it's about being there. In my experience, mothers in particular are simply glad that someone is there. It's not about saying anything. It's about being there and simply going through it together. Simply enduring the death of a child, as sad as it is.'

Meanwhile, there is the option of having a photo taken by a professional photographer. Farewell rituals are tailored to the wishes of individual families. A child might be baptised or blessed. Parents are encouraged to do 'normal' things like washing, bathing, dressing and holding their child. All this allows parents to remain close – right there with their child – as his or her life is drawing to a close. 'It's about letting them participate in what's happening – letting them understand, in the deepest way', Dr Schiller says.

Then, they suddenly notice that the baby is growing cold; the little body changes. As hard as that moment is, Dr Schiller says, it is important, because it gives parents a healthier way to grieve – that is, it leaves them with something concrete that can be worked through. Saying goodbye is easier to cope with when you have had a relationship with the dying child – because the relationship is what ultimately remains.

In the early morning of 13 May 2022, just six weeks shy of her first birthday, little Anna passed away. A few days later, her extended family took leave of her. 'We would have loved to experience so much more with Anna', her parents admit. 'The beautiful thing about our story is that for us, there are no unanswered questions. Anna's story has a beginning, a middle and an end.'

Johannes is convinced that if they had followed their gynecologist's advice and terminated the pregnancy, he and Doris would have been left with a host of unanswered questions. 'Even if you disregard ethical and religious aspects, or personal convictions, this is a valid reason to decide in favour of giving birth', he says.

As part of St Josef's perinatal palliative care programme, parents are encouraged to take advantage of counselling with psychologists and pastors, if they wish, after the death of a child. Two months after the birth, they are invited to a follow-up meeting, and every year a memorial service is held. Sister Teresa gets goose bumps when she describes the atmosphere in the chapel – the sense of community that arises from shared experience in a place where there is room for conversation and exchange. 'That is always our concern, after all: the healing of the whole person. Life may be short, but our humanity goes on.'

It is also about creating a place of remembrance for the parents and sharing memories. 'We – the staff here – are often the only ones with whom the parents have shared the presence of their child. We are the only other witnesses to the fact that the baby was really there.'

In a culture where dying is given little space in public life, there is a particularly strong taboo around the death of unborn and newborn children. After all, birth is marketed with rose-coloured glasses as an event of pure joy. But as the staff at St Josef knows, the reality is more complex. It is simply a fact that a pregnancy can be highly problematic. This is why the programme at St Josef was initiated: because healthcare professionals saw the need and were determined to address it rather than look the other way.

Perinatal palliative care is not so much about a wing or a ward of St Josef as an approach to care. In fact, it is a comprehensive programme that is supported by the entire hospital and takes place in multifaceted ways. Nurses, midwives, paediatricians and gynecologists sit down together at the same table from the very beginning. Pastoral counsellors and psychologists are also involved at an early stage. Case managers help parents with administrative matters such as filling out forms. If parents take a child home to die, a mobile child-care service is contacted and instructed on how to provide support.

All in all, the programme illustrates the myriad possibilities that arise when institutions and committed people make a joint effort together – when interdisciplinary co-operation becomes part of the hospital culture, and flexibility and personal needs and convictions are supported by leadership. Sister Teresa explains, 'Two things are needed: first, the institution that says, "We are going to offer this kind of care"; and second, the employees who say, '"We are going to support this." Because it is very intensive work, and it demands a lot.'

So far, five or six couples have taken advantage of the service each year. For Sister Teresa, that is not enough. 'Our goal is to make the service better known. It should not just be a silent option, but a visible and recommended alternative. Women and families should be enabled to choose this path.'

When Anna was three months old, the family went back to the hospital where Doris had her initial examinations: she and Johannes had made an appointment with the head of the gynecology department. 'We made a checklist with suggestions for the staff – how to deal with a diagnosis of severe disability.' Among other things, the list suggested contacting the perinatal palliative care team at St Josef. 'Who knows what they will actually do?' says Johannes. 'But at least we know they have the hospital's information flyer on hand.'

Shortly after Anna's death, Johannes began telling her story to others. At first, he found it extremely difficult, but it seemed too important not to share. 'Maybe someone who has experienced something similar will stumble across it. Maybe I can help even just one person to overcome some of their fear.' He remembers that at the beginning, he and Doris kept asking themselves, 'Why is this happening to us?' Later, over the course of the pregnancy, there were other conversations – especially after they began to realise that they were not alone. During the six long months between diagnosis and birth, it helped them to read and hear about other couples whose children were confronted with a similar fate – to be informed and thus encouraged. By the time Anna arrived, in spite of all the uncertainties, they had gained a strong sense of confidence.

Anna's story is not a tragic secret. Rather, it is a quiet reminder of how vulnerable – and therefore how precious – every life is.

Deciding to accept a child despite the prediction of a limited or minimal lifespan means accepting life as it comes. Life cannot be planned; it cannot be controlled; it is not always fair – but it is valuable in all its aspects. When we learn to stop fighting death, but to face it – with mindfulness and dignity – our view of life also changes.

Johannes wants parents to remember that there is never a guarantee of having a healthy baby. 'Love for another human being – in our case, love for our own child – cannot be dependent on that person's health or outlook.' The fact that abortion was presented as the obvious best way out of their difficult situation still upsets him to this day. To him, it's an indication of how society treats people with disabilities. 'Where are we supposed to draw the line when we begin judging someone as worthy of living – or not?' he wonders.

Dr Schiller adds, 'Personally, I believe that every life is valuable, which is why I think it is absolutely important that we offer this option. But ultimately it is the woman – the mother – who has to walk through it. There are many for whom this is the right thing to do, and who are grateful to accept our offer of support. But sometimes there are those who say, "I just can't do it."'

Johannes, too, is clear-eyed about this, and notes that in Anna's case, the final decision lay with his wife. 'I am infinitely grateful to Doris for her motherly love, and unendingly happy that she wanted to let Anna live. It's the greatest, most precious gift she could ever give me.'

Today Doris and Johannes have a second child, Marlene. When asked about her older sister, the two-and-a-half-year-old responds with 'Anna!' as if it were the most natural thing in the world. For her, Anna's story is not a tragic secret. Nor is it one for her parents. Rather, it is a quiet reminder of how vulnerable – and therefore how precious – every life is. Beyond that, it is a reminder that as humans, our fragility is not a weakness, but rather a great strength that can call forth the ability to love – even when we have to let go.

This article first appeared in Plough's *German edition as 'Wo Leben mit Tod beginnt', 14 October 2025. Translated by Chris Zimmerman.*

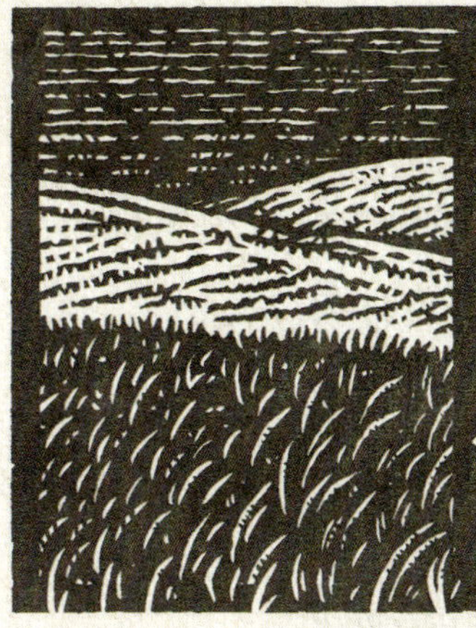
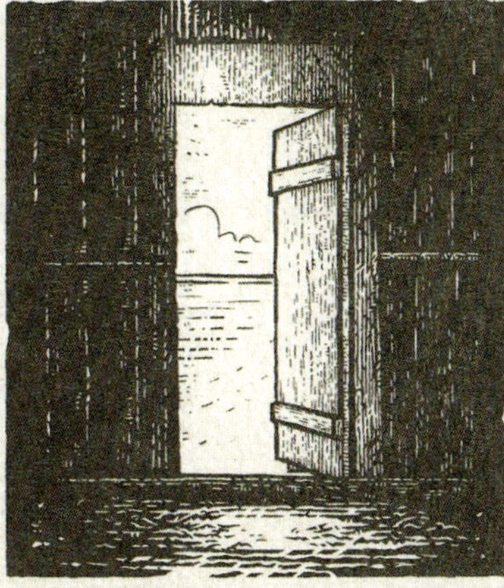
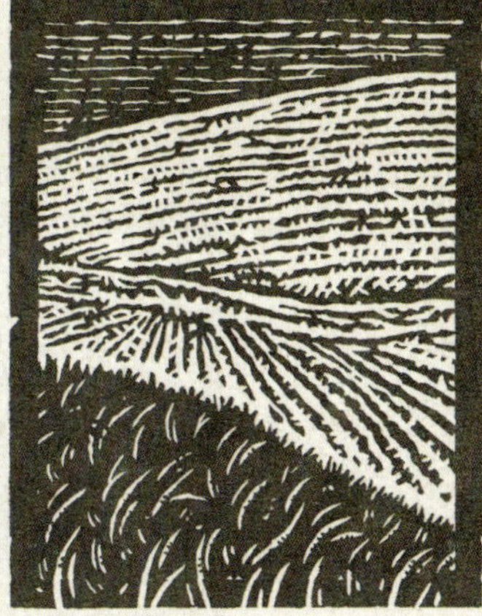

The Partition Thins

In six new poems, Wendell Berry approaches a threshold.

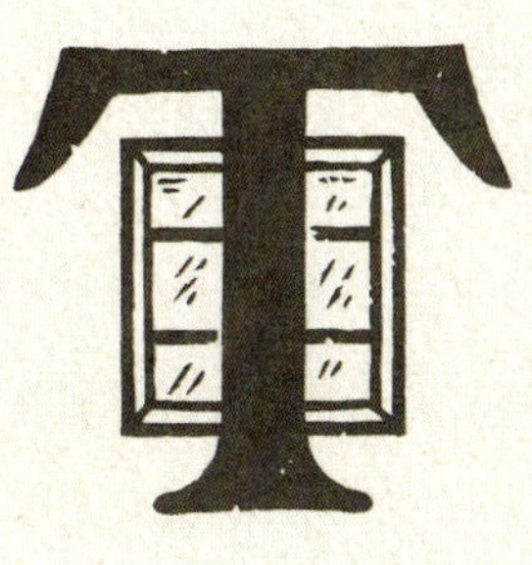

HE WORD 'VERSE' has an agricultural past: it comes from the Latin word for 'furrowing' or 'turning up the soil.' Language, then, is a field ready for the plough; a poem is the careful turning up of that field. A poem must break up the dry outer crush of assumptions to expose the fertile soil underneath.

Wendell Berry, whose poems we are honoured to feature here, is a well-known essayist and novelist, a life-long farmer and a great champion of the particular and human against impersonal, mechanised social and economic forces. He is also a masterful poet. For over 60 years, Berry has turned to verse to explore the rhythms and patterns that make up human life.

In this series of poems, the guiding concerns of Berry's life merge. Here ploughing (and not just in a metaphorical sense – remember, Berry actually ploughs actual fields) turns up the field of memory and gives us a glimpse of the beauty that comes when we love a place and its people particularly and deeply.

The poems stand in relationship with each other. The fields of one poem become fertile soil for a meditation on language in the next, which in turn yields a prophetic vision in which 'On the other side of the partition / the dead are living.'

The inevitable but startling unfolding of the poems and their interrelated themes is more than an imaginative discovery; it is a moral one. Throughout these poems, the speaker explores his changing relationship to the world he has loved with all his might. He discovers that even though he cannot stop time or keep the fields and land and the people he loves, he need not despair. Here is the final great turning of these poems: a turning away, at the last, from the things of this world only to discover that the things he has loved have been kept safe, 'more alive, more essentially themselves', on the other side of death. Perhaps, these poems suggest, death itself is simply another turning of the soil. —*Jane Clark Scharl*

All artwork by Stephen Crotts.

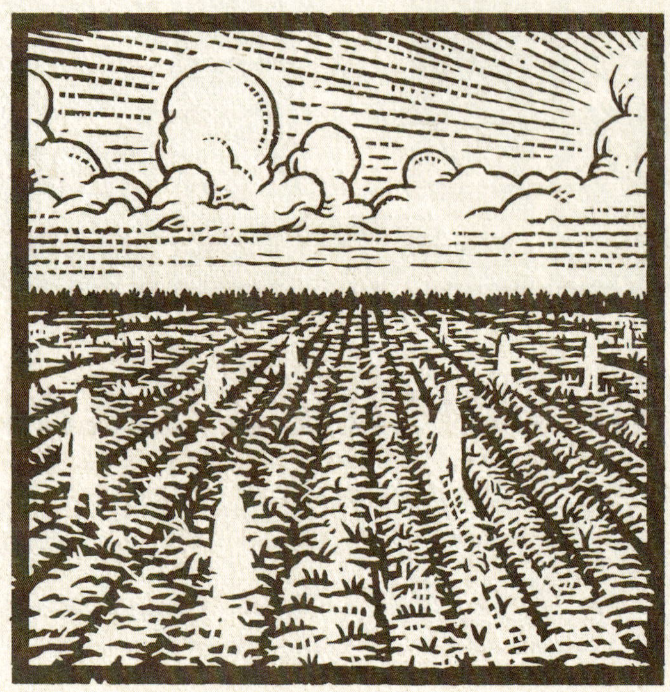

I had a dream half awake
that led into the company of the dead who
were alive still in the fields
we worked together, now purified
of our loss of one another.

WENDELL BERRY

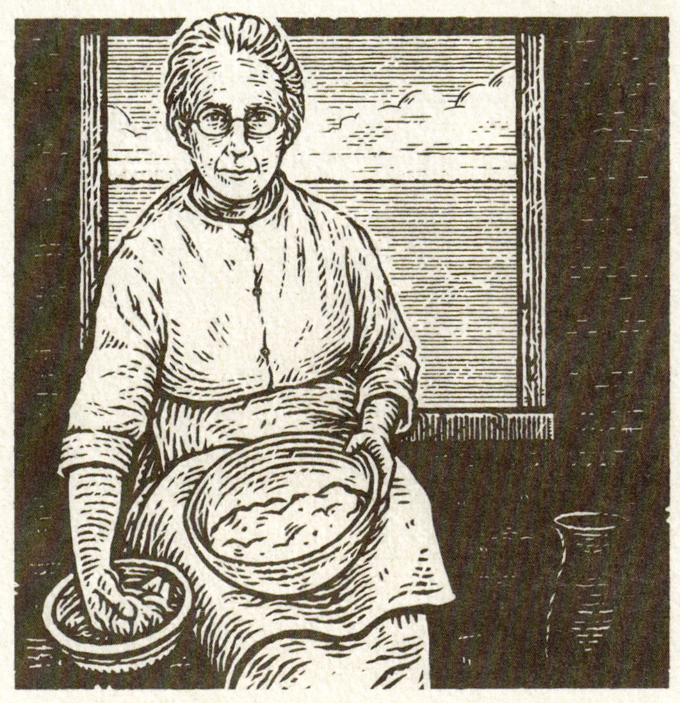

No more as if I picture them
lighted mid-breath on a black page,
now the dead pass out of time.
The ones I loved are present to me
as living souls, and I to them,
as once in time we used to be
without my even guessing so.
Don't comfort me. Against age and time,
by missing them I keep them with me.

WENDELL BERRY

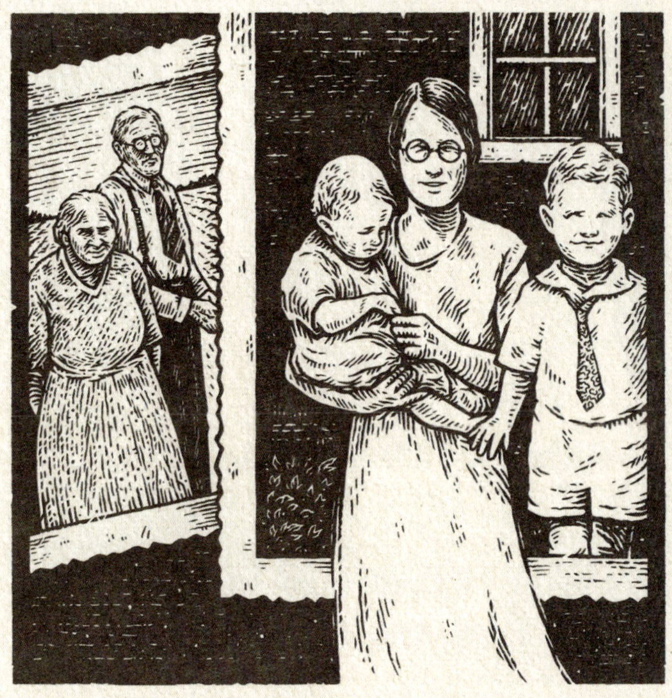

Now they're coming closer,
those I've known forever.
We were here together
who in this world's great Other
have never been apart.

WENDELL BERRY

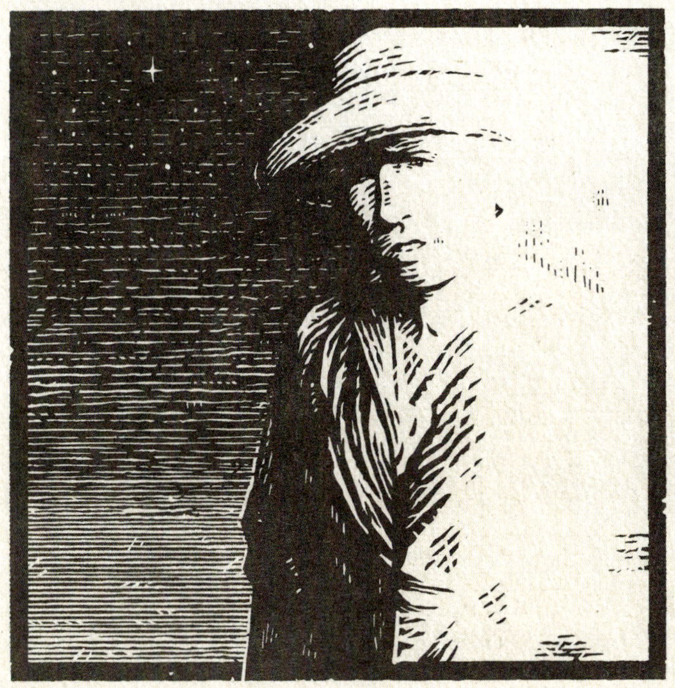

Only when you have the language for it
can you imagine it. Only when you can imagine it
can you know that it is real:
the angel alight with glory walking
among the shepherds half asleep in their watching.

WENDELL BERRY

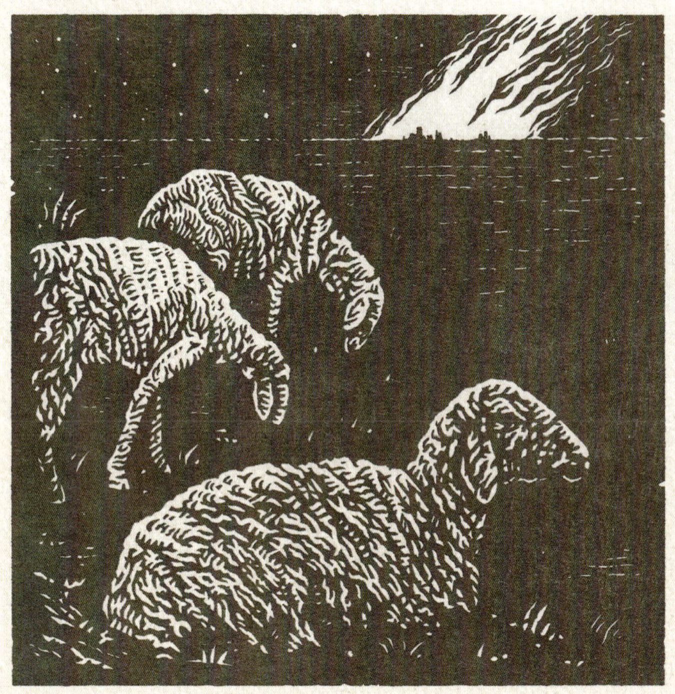

The empire of money, war, and fire
cuts across the land.

There are in the same country
shepherds watching their flocks.

WENDELL BERRY

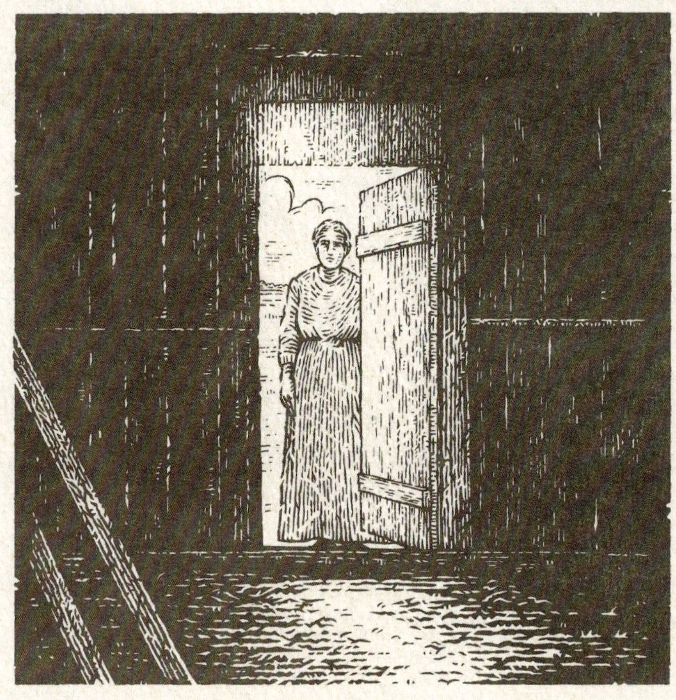

The partition thins between this world and the world to come, or the next or the other world. On the other side of the partition the dead are living. As one grows older some of the dead grow more alive, more essentially themselves. One loves them more. As the next world grows more distinct, this one becomes, not more vague, but more strange.

WENDELL BERRY

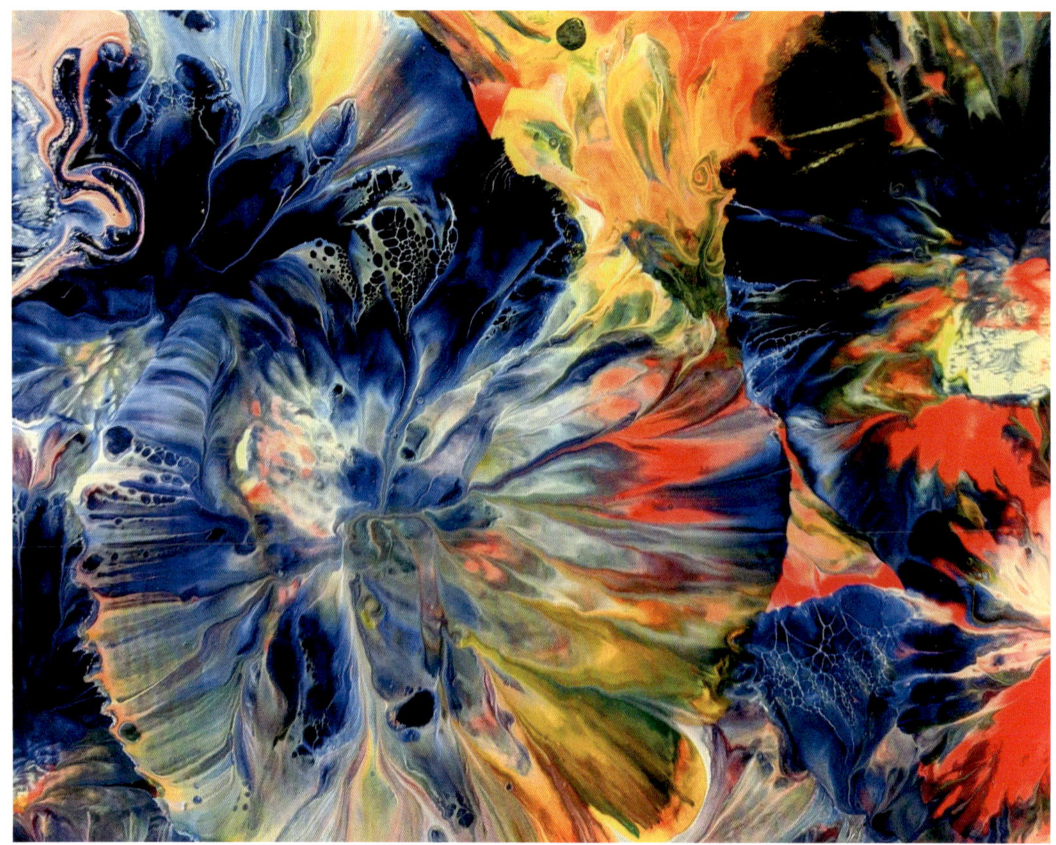

Crafting Beauty

We asked a poet, a visual artist and a musician to tell us what role beauty plays in their work.

Poetry: Beauty Is an Accusation

Steven Toussaint

'Beauty *is* an accusation', wrote Ezra Pound in a 1909 essay about Walt Whitman. This line had managed to elude me until one of my students pointed it out during a recent tutorial. I found myself nodding vigorously, intrigued by the gratuitous italics, assenting to the idea without really knowing why.

After all, the more intuitive definition of beauty would be something like the one offered by Thomas Aquinas: *Pulchrum est quod visum placet*, or 'Beauty is that which pleases when seen.' This seems right, if a little banal. The experience of beauty is the satisfaction taken in something complete, well-formed and radiant, not the satisfaction demanded by an aggrieved plaintiff and exacted at 20 paces. If beauty *is* an accusation,

Bokani, *Marigold*, acrylic on canvas, 2020 (detail).

who is the accused and who is the accuser?

But such ambiguity does not, for me, diminish the force of Pound's definition. If anything, my faith has primed me to be unsettled by the forms beauty takes. I have been taught that the beauty of God – which is to say, *beauty itself* – is only truly revealed in the way Jesus bears himself under trial, judgement, humiliation and execution. This was clear to me even as a child, shuffling between the stations of the cross on Fridays during Lent. On the other hand, the whole point of the Passion narrative is that Jesus, spotless victim, was *falsely* accused by the one whom scripture calls 'the slanderer', and Satan, notoriously beautiful, speaks through our mouths.

There is a piece of Passiontide performance art situated at this exact moment of inversion between accuser and accused. I first heard the *Improperia*, or 'Reproaches', sung during the Good Friday liturgy at Little St Mary's in Cambridge seven years ago. I remember joining the slow procession up the aisle to kiss the foot of the cross, while the choir, antiphonally positioned in stalls on either side, interrogated us as the voice of Christ: 'O my people, what have I done to you? How have I offended you? Answer me.'

My experience of beauty that day, though wedded materially to John Sanders's musical setting, the shrouded statues in the gloomy 14th-century church, and the great, dark crucifix looming, cannot be separated from the words of accusation at its heart. If this is what beauty *is*, it is threatening rather than consoling, and particular rather than universal. Each of us will have to answer Christ in a different way.

So far, my experience of the 'Reproaches' is the closest analogy I have found for what it feels like to write a poem. Most of the time, I am swept up in the inertial drag of my words, surrendering to the constant temptation of reaching into the ragbag of practised flourishes that I rely on to avoid the genuine agony of trying to find the single most fitting way to resolve a poem, given the form it has occasioned for itself. Every poet has their own vanities and cheats, and I am still discovering mine.

I don't know if I have ever written a beautiful poem, but I have read many. And when I am writing, it is those voices I hear demanding to be answered. When I let their accusations stand and find a way to reckon with the bullshit and bad faith with which so much of my linguistic life is conducted, I would not say I find the writing pleasurable, but it does feel like justice.

Visual Art: Beauty Is a Free Spirit

Bokani

My studio in East London has large north-facing windows. It's in this context, bathed in light, that I create with stained glass paint on mirrors. My intention is to bring the viewer into the artwork, jolting them out of the passivity of a spectator by confronting them with themselves rendered through vibrant distortions. I typically choose materials based on what I want to say and to whom. For an exhibition at the National Gallery in Zimbabwe, I chose reed mats – found in every home there, familiar to the audience, and ripe for subversion – presenting a different yet recognisable type of reflection.

I rarely go in with an imagined or drawn sketch, preferring to respond to the material, light, colour and resonance within. In this way, the painting itself begins its work in my imagination. I have not so much pulled the work out of the ether as I have made myself available to receive its emergence. As John O'Donohue says, 'Beauty is a free spirit and will not be trapped within the grid of intentionality.'

Steven Toussaint *is a poet and philosophical theologian based in Cambridge UK and the author of several books.* ***Bokani*** *is a Zimbabwean-born artist living in London.* ***Joanna Gill*** *is a Scottish composer who lives and works in London.*

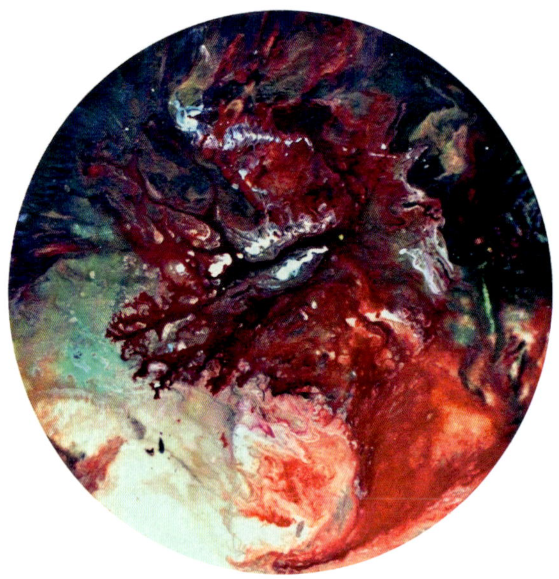

Once I have the material or object to paint, I begin by pouring colour onto the surface. My process involves a lot of experimentation. I typically paint on horizontal surfaces, and I try not to manipulate the paint with a brush, preferring to let gravity do most of the work, occasionally shifting colours around with a partially inflated balloon. By moving the paint, I am on a search, an inquiry made more compelling because I don't know what I am longing for. You could say I leave a lot of room for grace. When I think I have found it, I leave the painting to dry, looking forward to being surprised by the finished piece upon returning to the studio.

Some in the art world disparage beauty. Interest in beauty and her conspirators – light and colour – have often been dismissed as unsophisticated, naive or unserious. John O'Donohue makes a strong case for resisting beauty's detractors in his introduction to *Divine Beauty: The Invisible Embrace*. He writes, 'Because our present habit of mind is governed by the calculus of consumerism and busyness, we are less and less frequently available to the exuberance of beauty.' For me, the work is to make myself available to the pouring forth.

John O'Donohue is one of a handful of writers, including bell hooks and Audre Lorde, whose words ricochet off the walls in my studio, interplaying with the background music of sweeping opera or amapiano. As I join this maelstrom, I can lose myself in the painting; the veil between now and not-now, here and not-here, the material and immaterial, falls away. I feel most free in that time when I am at one with it all. The resulting painting seems to appear fully formed in an instant, even after hours of work. This collapse of time and order lends a wildness to my work which I protect fiercely from market forces that require repeatable formats. My regular return to the studio is a journey of discovery sometimes tinctured by surprise and delight, most recently at the golden hour, as my mirror paintings throw around rainbow refractions.

Music: Beauty Is Eternal

Joanna Gill

Music has an innate power to evoke and create emotion. The first time I heard *O magnum mysterium*, a choral piece by the American composer Morten Lauridsen, I was completely moved to tears. Around three minutes in, the choir sings a phrase that leads to a clustered chord of three adjacent notes. This effect creates a suspension, which is then beautifully resolved into a chord that feels more familiar and comfortable. To me, it sounded heavenly; a glimpse of a place where true peace and harmony lie.

The definition of beauty can mean many different things to different people. Thoughts, feelings and perceptions about beauty are unique to the individual, but I believe that creating beautiful music offers a new path to the divine and can be used as a tool to connect to a higher purpose and meaning.

Theologian R T Kendall once said, 'Artists have a vocation to reimagine and re-express the beauty

Bokani, *Celestial Desert*, acrylic on canvas, 2018.

of God to lift our sights and change our vision of reality, which is often not even considered.' True beauty can happen in any moment of sadness, happiness, failure, success, elation or weariness. It is in these places that the arts can draw out a fresh meaning, open dark rooms and allow the light to come in.

On Christmas Day in 2010, my first nephew, Oliver, died of cancer just shy of six months old. I remember experiencing a new level of grief that I had never known before and felt unable to put into words. I sensed a nudge to portray my feelings through music. I took the words my sister-in-law had spoken of her son, 'a beautiful baby boy', and I began to put them to music, which slowly evolved into a new composition: 'Safe in the arms of He.' I arranged the lyrics in a contrapuntal fashion, layering the voices over one another in a repetitive manner, offering stillness and peace. The music flows through suspensions and resolutions that highlight the pain, then completes with a major chord presenting a feeling of hope. For me, this composition wasn't only about expressing grief; it became an exploration into finding light in a place of darkness, finding beauty in a place of pain and allowing what feels like death to become hope for new life – thus creating a place where pain is not the end, and beauty is eternal.

I believe my vocation as a composer is to create music that brings a touch of that eternal beauty, something that can be glimpsed in this lifetime – not just for a moment of escapism, but to point to hope of the overflowing beauty that is to come in the new heaven.

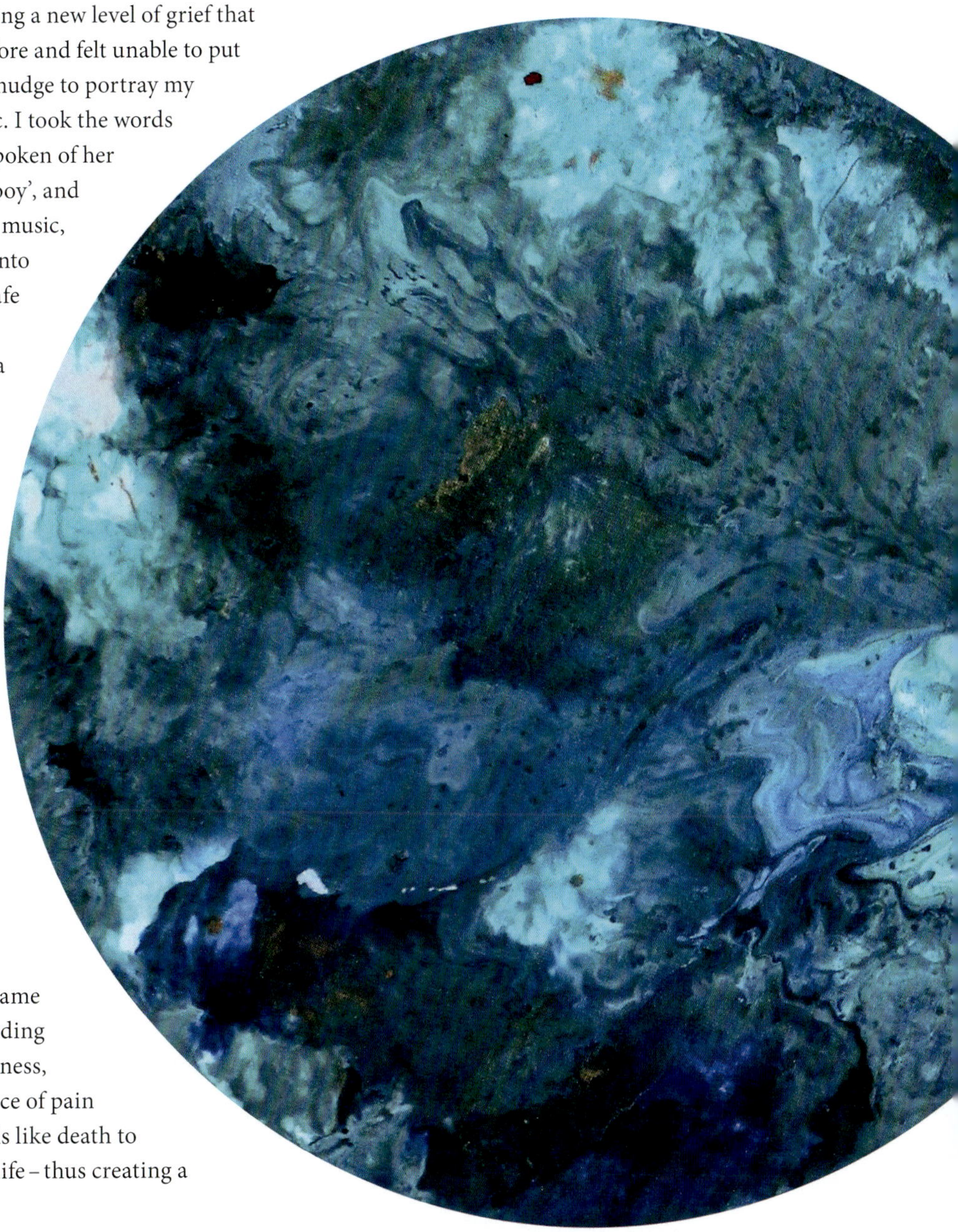

Bokani, *Aquarii II*, acrylic on canvas, 2018.

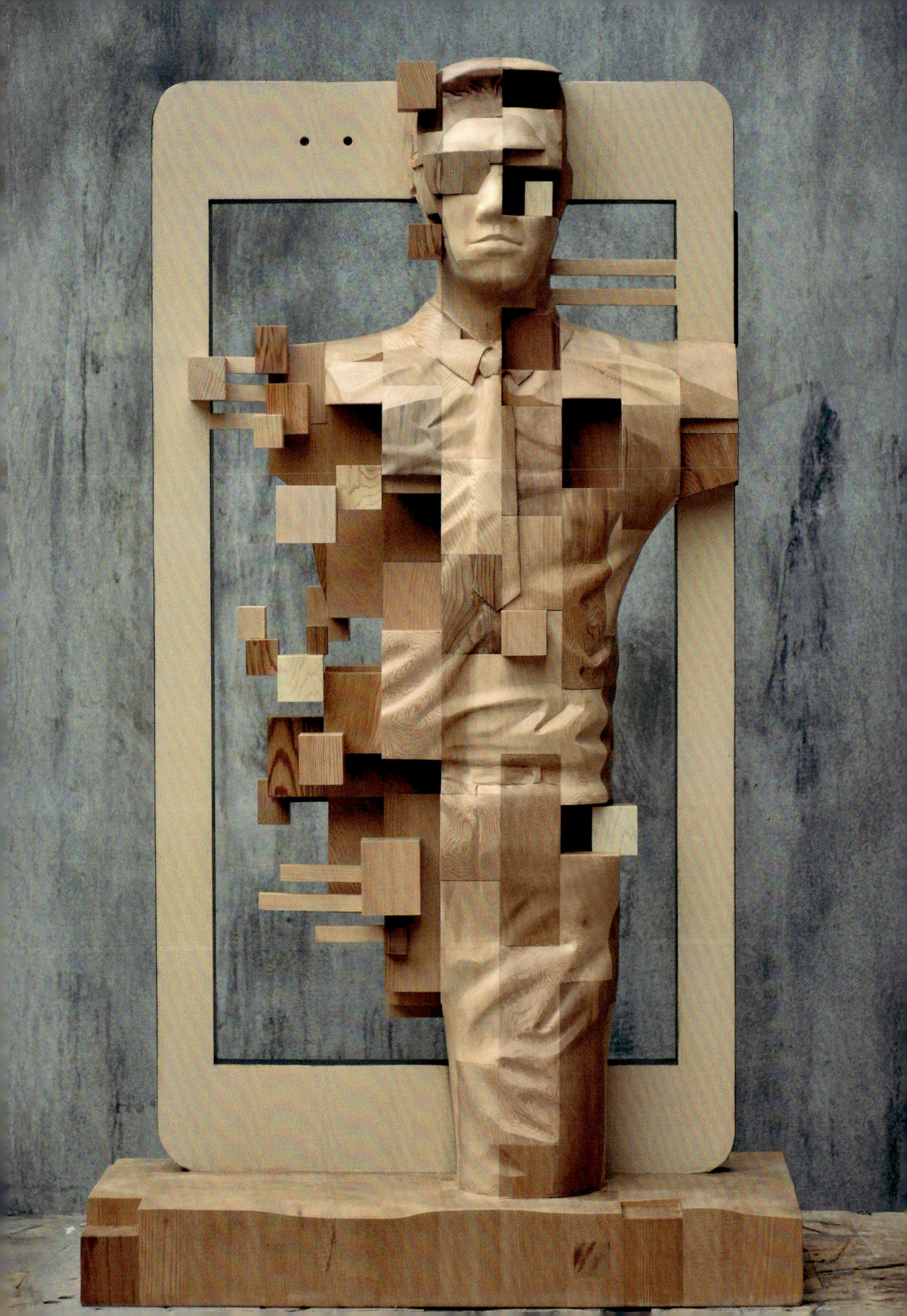

Six Ways to Resist the Machine

The technological mindset is corrupting our souls. It's time to fight.

PAUL KINGSNORTH

This article is based on a talk sponsored by Plough and the Abigail Adams Institute on 1 October 2025 at Harvard University, to mark the release of Kingsnorth's new book, Against the Machine: On the Unmaking of Humanity *(Thesis, 2025).*

IT IS THE YEAR 2025. We are 213 years out from the invention of the first commercial steam engine. It is 155 years since the construction of the first modern factory, 140 years since the invention of the commercial motor car, 122 years since the first manned flight and 115 years since the invention of the neon light. We are 67 years on from the coming of the microchip. It is 65 years since the first contraceptive pill went on sale, 60 years since the first atomic bomb exploded, 56 years since man walked on the moon and a mere 18 years since the invention of the iPhone.

Paul Kingsnorth is a writer living in Ireland.

Han Hsu Tung, *i-Fashion*, Western red cedar, 2019.

It's been an eventful two centuries. In this same time period, the earth's human population has grown from one billion to over eight billion, the earth's climate has begun to shift, half of the planet's forests have been destroyed and the sixth mass extinction in history has begun. The lifestyle of the whole of humanity has been transformed, for better or for worse, by the vast technological and commercial forces that these developments, and many more, have unleashed. Now we stand on the brink of another development: one which has received endless hype and not a little hysteria, whether positive or negative. This is the development of artificial intelligence. If it lives up to even half of the hype that is currently swirling around it, it may be more transformative than anything else.

Maybe all of this explains why our times seem so unstable. We can all sense the craziness in the air, the feeling of our moorings being cut one by one. It feels hard sometimes just to stay upright as we live through what feels like a threefold earthquake: a global ecological breakdown, the cultural disintegration of the West and the rise of networked technologies of control and surveillance which daily have us tighter in their grip. The powers of the world sometimes seem to be merging: corporate power, state power, institutional power, ideological power, the power of the oligarchs who built and control the internet, the power of the network itself. Some days it can feel as if we are living inside the plot of a piece of 20th-century dystopian sci-fi. The twist is that this time Agent Smith is the hero, while Neo has been dismissed as a far-right conspiracy theorist.

What is at the root of all this – and how might we navigate it?

We are trapped within this Machine, whose momentum is always forward and which will not stop until it has transformed the world.

The American historian and cultural critic Lewis Mumford, in his massive study *The Myth of the Machine,* published in two volumes between 1967 and 1970, attempts to chronicle the rise and triumph of the system of power and technology which now increasingly entwines us all. He calls this system 'the megamachine.' In the first pages of volume one, he explains what he means by this:

> The last century, we all realise, has witnessed a radical transformation in the entire human environment, largely as a result of the impact of the mathematical and physical sciences upon technology... Never since the Pyramid Age have such vast physical changes been consummated in so short a time. All these changes have, in turn, produced alterations in the human personality, while still more radical transformations, if this process continue unabated and uncorrected, loom ahead.

Mumford's 'megamachine' manifests today as an intersection of money power, state power and increasingly coercive and manipulative technologies, which constitute an ongoing war against roots and against limits. Mumford predicted that this structure would allow 'the dominant minority [to] create a uniform, all-enveloping, super-planetary structure, designed for automatic operation. Instead of functioning actively as an autonomous personality, man will become a passive, purposeless, machine-conditioned animal whose proper functions, as technicians now interpret man's role, will either be fed into the machine or strictly limited and controlled for the benefit of depersonalised, collective organisations.'

This, I believe, is where we mainly find ourselves today. We are trapped within this Machine, whose momentum is always forward and which will not stop until it has transformed the world. To do that, it must raze or transmute many older and less measurable things: rooted human communities, wild nature, human nature, human freedom, beauty, religious faith and the many deeper values that we all adhere to in some way or another but find difficult to describe or even to defend. Its modus operandi is the abolition of all borders, boundaries, categories, essences and truths: the uprooting of all previous ways of living in the name of pure individualism and perfect subjectivity. Its endgame is the replacement of nature with technology, in order to facilitate total human control over a totally human world.

It's often suggested that when we moved from Christendom via the Enlightenment into our current age, whatever we might call it, we desacralised or 'disenchanted' our culture: that we became pure materialists. For its proponents, this process was a move towards 'reason' and away from 'superstition.' For opponents, it represented a slide into decadence and moral dissolution. The best-known proponent of this notion first introduced it in 1917, and for some it has been one reason for that collapse. 'The fate of our times', writes Max Weber, 'is characterised by rationalisation and intellectualisation and, above all, by the disenchantment of the world.'

This 'disenchantment thesis', as we might call it, has been influential for over a century now. But is it really true? Historian Eugene McCarraher has taken issue with it. In his book *The Enchantments of Mammon*, he argues that modernity did not in fact dispense with the West's sacred order, leaving only a desiccated materialism in its place. 'Since the 17th century', he writes, 'much modern history has provided good reasons to show that "disenchantment" is more of a fable, a mythology that conceals the persistence of enchantment in "secular" disguise.'

If McCarraher is right, we have not junked a sacred order for a profane one. We have instead enthroned a new god and disguised its worship as the disenchanted pursuit of purely material gain. We have dressed up a technological force as our new idol and sovereign: what I am here calling the Machine. We are still living, in other words, in a religious time. We just have a new god.

My book *Against the Machine* attempts to paint a picture of this new deity. I have tried to explain how this process happened, how it is manifesting now and what we might do about it. We are living today on the verge of what may be an age of intelligent machines. More than one thinker on the matter can be heard suggesting that the so-called 'singularity' – the moment at which machine intelligence surpasses ours, and our creations slip from our grasp – is a mere 15 years away. It is, then, more urgent than ever to understand what is going on – and what we can do about it.

It's this question that I want to focus on here: what we can do. Or, more accurately, how we might live through this radically transformative time. I'm going to offer six proposals of my own. They are, needless to say, hardly comprehensive. They are simply one man's attempt to work out how to survive the age of the Machine. You may have your own ideas, and they may be better.

To do that, it must raze or transmute many older and less measurable things: wild nature, human nature, human freedom, beauty and faith.

1. Become Indigenous

What the Machine wants to do above all is to make us rootless, placeless and homeless. In a Machine culture, we are to be 'digital nomads', browsing in a borderless world as consumers; as individuals, torn away from communities, from history, from nature. This is greatly damaging in many ways. But what is the alternative?

The Irish philosopher-mystic John Moriarty, whom I write about in my book, came to believe that what the Irish and the Europeans and all the modern people need in the age of the Machine is to access their own version of what Australian Aboriginals call *Altjeringa*: dreamtime. Taking this for the title of his best-known book, Moriarty produced a text that is in itself a strange kind of dream: in his words an *aisling*, an old Gaelic term meaning dream-vision. He laid out his dream like this:

> The hope is that, however ethnically various it might be, there is a European Dreamtime... It is sometimes the case, isn't it, that individuals are healed as they are at present only as a consequence of being healed as they were in their past. As with individuals, so, sometimes, with a whole people... Our past we will always have with us. Our past we must always re-realise. And to do this we need people who can live in our cultural Dreamtime, people who go walkabout, creatively, within the old myths, people who go walkabout into the unknown.

What Moriarty is seeking throughout *Dreamtime*, and in all of his other work too, is access to his own aboriginality; a way of learning how to belong to the earth again in the age of the Machine. How to be a creature; how to be a human. How to inhabit our stories, and to be connected to natural reality rather than technological fakery or ideological vapours.

Words like 'indigenous' tend to make people twitchy in the West today, unless we're talking about tribal people in some safely far-off place. Downstream of the Holocaust, we are still highly sensitive to notions of rootedness, land and belonging. And we should certainly keep our ears pricked up in this regard; we should avoid making idols of nations or cultures and not be naive about where such narratives can lead. But we should remember too that all human beings have, in the words of another modern mystic, Simone Weil, a 'need for roots.'

Moriarty explicitly repudiated, as we all should, any 'racial or sectarian ground' for his notion of a modern Dreamtime. He is looking to an earth-wide story which is told everywhere in a local dialect. This kind of aboriginality – this deep belonging to place and the cultures that spring from it – is, he says, our human inheritance. It is also a radical rebellion against the Machine.

In my book I attempt to pin this down with a formula, which I call 'the Four Ps':

1. **The Past.** Where a culture comes from, its history and ancestry.

2. **People.** Who a culture is. A sense of being 'a people.'

3. **Place.** Where a culture is. Nature in its local and particular manifestation.

4. **Prayer.** Where a culture is going. Its religious tradition, which relates it to God or the gods.

Maybe cultures can survive without one or more of these elements. In fact, some measurably do. Nomadic cultures, for example, do not have a permanent link to a particular place, but are no less culturally or spiritually rich for it. Still, if you remove more than one element from this list, your chance of sustaining a cultural story through time is slim. You will make yourself prey to a Machine culture that wants above all for you to be a consumer, browsing in the endless digital forest.

2. Build a New Counterculture

Back in the sixties, as the last of the old world crumbled, the marginal energies that had been building for nearly a century exploded into a revolution that still shapes us. The Man, the system, became the enemy. Strictures, limits, boundaries, norms, old ways: all would go. Free love, wild music, the end of the family, the end of all the old repressions and secrets and lies. The eclipse of religion by 'spirituality.' The New Age. Aquarius rising. We had been hemmed in for too long.

People of my generation, the children of the boomers, grew up in the wake of this. We never got to experience Haight-Ashbury or Swinging London, but we got to see the backwash: the broken homes, the new drug culture, the abortions, the pop charts, the mockery of all authority, the easy sex and booze, the loosening of the rules, the strange sense that anything was permitted yet nothing was centred or lasting.

The counterculture had, in its own way, taken aim at the Machine, at mammon, at the military-industrial complex, but it had stood on the ground of extreme personal liberation, and that ground turned out to be too swampy to hold. It took two decades for the hippies to become yuppies; three for the simple lifers to become Silicon Valley billionaires; four for 'imagine there's no countries' to become the policy of the WEF and the WTO. Now everything is hanging out everywhere. The counterculture has become the culture, and everyone is having a bad trip, man.

Radical individualism in all areas, from sex to spirituality, is the essence of the culture now, and this radical individualism does not obstruct the Machine; rather, it fuels it. We therefore need, perhaps, a new counterculture, to run counter to the values of the Machine. But what should it look like?

It would have to avoid making the same mistakes. So it would not reject the past; it would not try to blank slate its way towards some notional utopia. It would remember that every time this has been tried it has simply broken more of our bounds, uprooted us further and greased the path of the Machine. Instead, a new counterculture would have to be rooted in the eternal things. It would need its feet on the ground and its face pointed towards that Dreamtime. It would express what Moriarty called 'our aboriginal desire to be in league with the earth.' It would need to embrace not a rebellious individualism but what in my book I call a 'reactionary radicalism': a rejection of Machine values based on an embrace instead of the eternal things. Its core would be those four Ps: people, place, prayer and the past.

What if we don't try to go back to anything? And what if we also slough off the idea of 'saving the world?' What if we reject all the utopias and frown at all the gadgets and the grand plans;

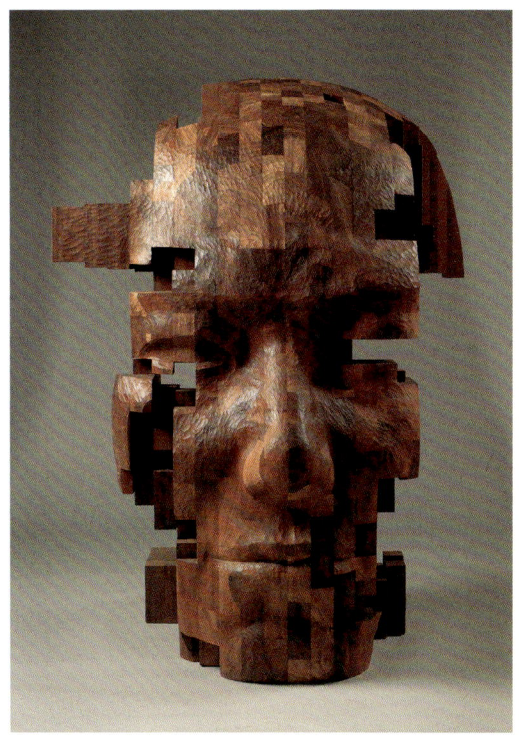

Han Hsu Tung, *Head no 2*, African padauk, 2013.

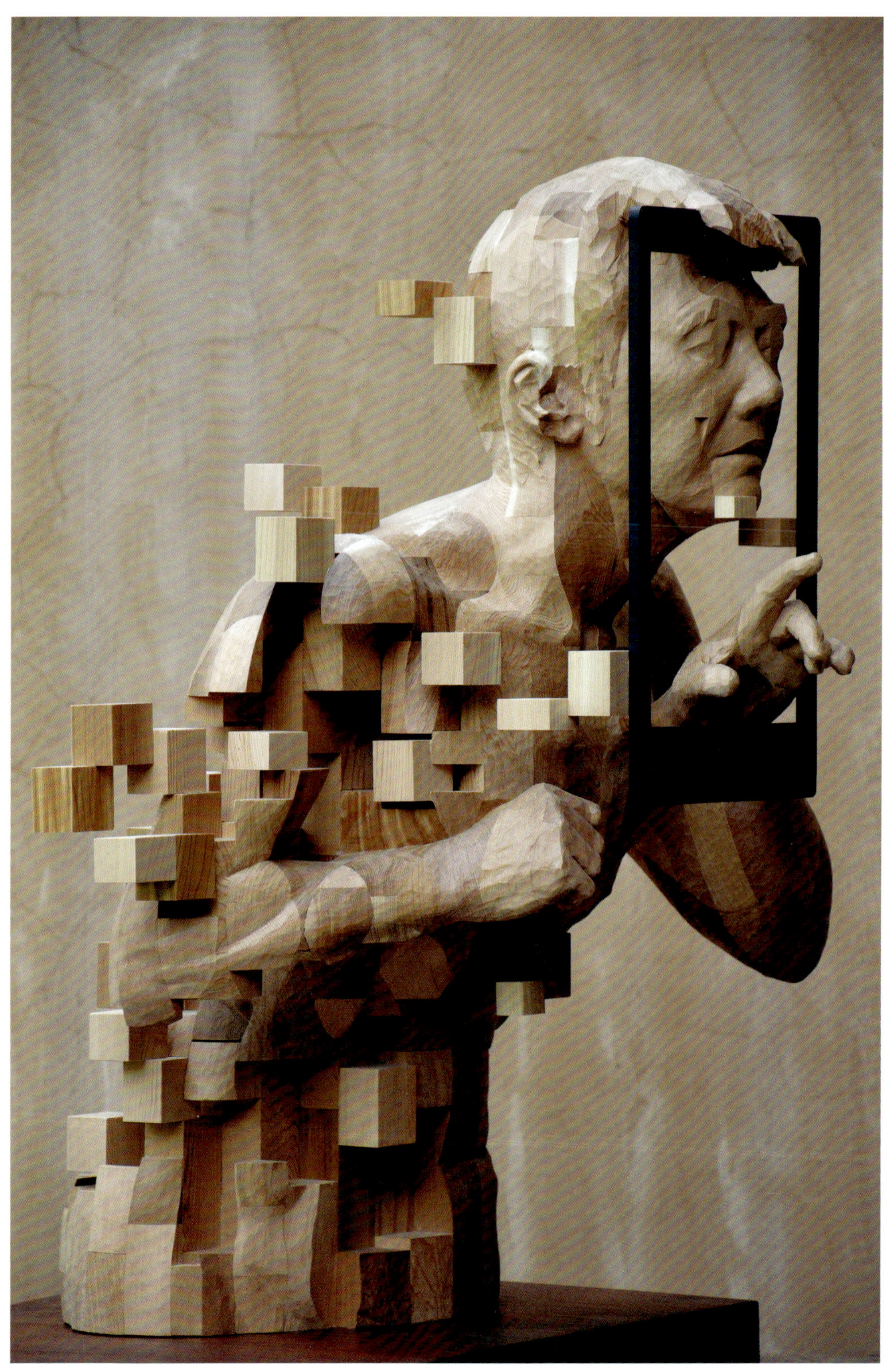

Han Hsu Tung, *Where is the 'Like'*, Western red cedar, 2017.

what if we take off our shoes and get our feet back properly on the ground?

'But *how?*' you may ask. I can't answer the question for you because I don't know you. But I have worked through this for long enough to understand that if we start from where we are, things will ripple out. If we don't have an endgame – 'saving the world', say – then everything gets easier. The earth still turns. There are churches. Prayer works. Nature gives and takes. The sunset is astonishing. There is poverty and death and injustice. There are miracles, and there is some strange, saving love. It's all still here.

Maybe the question is what we turn our attention to. And how.

3. Construct Monasteries

I live in Ireland. Once, in a dark age a very long time ago, the Irish built monasteries. As the pagan armies flooded through the West in the wake of Rome's collapse, burning books and people, slaughtering priests and kidnapping villagers, the monks kept the manuscripts safe, and the teachings. In his book *How the Irish Saved Civilisation,* the historian Thomas Cahill makes the bold claim that without the Irish monks keeping these treasures safe, Christianity may never have recovered in Europe. The world would have been a very different place.

But the monks did keep those teachings safe. They kept the Gospels and other old manuscripts hidden. They kept the craft of writing alive. Then, later, they emptied themselves and went out to the margins, to offer up those teachings to the barbarian kings. It was a ridiculous idea. As ridiculous as sending two halflings to throw a ring into a volcano under the nose of the dark lord. It was madness. But it worked. The pagans became Christians. Sometimes, the ridiculous ideas are the only ones worth having.

We live in a time of collapse again. Little we once took for granted is likely to survive this century. Perhaps, then, it is a time of monasteries again – of real ones, but also of metaphorical or personal ones. We could ask ourselves what we can keep safe, what we can preserve and protect from the rising tide of digital breakdown. How can we preserve human values in an inhuman time?

4. Become a Barbarian

This point may sound like it contradicts the last one! But bear with me.

In his book *The Art of Not Being Governed,* the historian James C Scott offers up what he calls 'an anarchist history of upland Southeast Asia.' Scott's aim is to rewrite the standard story of historical progress as it applies to the region. The 'hill tribes' and 'barbarians' living outside civilisation's walls, he says, are neither 'left behind' by progress, nor the 'remnants' of earlier 'backward' cultures; they are, in fact, escapees:

> Not very long ago ... self-governing peoples were the great majority of humankind. Today they are seen from the valley kingdoms as 'our living ancestors', 'what we were like before we discovered wet-rice cultivation, Buddhism and civilisation.' On the contrary, I argue that hill peoples are best understood as runaway, fugitive, maroon communities who have, over the course of two millennia, been fleeing the oppression of state-making projects in the valleys – slavery, conscription, taxes, corvée labour, epidemics and warfare. Most of the areas in which they reside might aptly be called shatter zones or zones of refuge.

What is happening here could even be said to be communities building their own versions of monasteries, to protect their cultures against top-down state intrusion. Certainly, states have always aimed their guns at these people.

In ancient China, says Scott, the state distinguished between two different kinds of barbarian outsider: the raw (*sheng*) and the cooked (*shu*). A 12th-century document detailing the relationship of the Li people with the Chinese state speaks of the 'cooked Li' as those who have submitted to state authority and the 'raw Li' as those who 'live in the mountain caves and are not punished by us or do not supply corvée labour.' But while the raw Li were clearly enemies of the state, the cooked Li were not exactly friends either. They occupied a liminal space: state officials 'suspected them of outward conformity while "slyly" co-operating with the "raw" Li.' The raw barbarians lived outside the walls, and the cooked lived within, but neither were really to be trusted.

What we have here, then, is two equally applicable approaches for people who refuse to have their lives shaped by the Machine. Some of us, perhaps, could live like raw barbarians. I know people who live in off-grid cabins, for example, and don't work for money. America, with its vast area, offers more opportunities for raw living than Western Europe.

But for most of us, being cooked barbarians is the best we can do. We can live within the Machine's walls, as we are mostly now required to do, but we don't have to accept its values. We can grow our own food, throw away our smartphones or whatever else seems to be a small friction against the Machine. And we can talk to others who feel the same. We can keep the human spirit alive, below the radar. Maybe it is the best we can do.

It is getting harder and harder to find anywhere to hide from the Machine. But humans are creative. We can always find our liminal spaces – raw or cooked – and there are countless practical ways in which cultural refusal can manifest in our everyday lives. Nothing is easy; everything is compromised. But building anew, building in parallel, retreating to create, being awkward and out of shape and hard to grasp, finding your allies and building your zone of cultural refusal, whether in a mountain community or in your urban home: What else is there?

We can live within the Machine's walls, as we are mostly now required to do, but we don't have to accept its values. We can keep the human spirit alive, below the radar. Maybe it is the best we can do.

5. Practise Technological Ascesis

What I call 'the Machine' is not simply a euphemism for technology. Technologies – and especially digital technologies – are simply the outward manifestation of a *way of seeing* that treats humans like cogwheels or microchips, and the earth itself as a giant mechanism, to be taken apart and put back together in a new shape.

The end point of this way of seeing is famously described by C S Lewis: 'Human nature will be the last part of nature to fall to man, and the battle will then be won, but we won't know precisely who has won it.'

The digital revolution, though, is increasingly coming to look like a spiritual crisis. As we attempt to build intelligent machines that will lead, in the eyes of their utopian builders, to the end of death and the conquest of the universe, we find ourselves back in the Garden of Eden, eating the apple daily, attempting to become 'as gods, knowing good and evil.'

If this is a spiritual crisis, then a spiritual response is needed. That response, I would suggest, should involve the practice of technological ascesis. The Greek word *askesis* translates simply as 'exercise.' Asceticism, therefore, is a series of spiritual exercises designed to take us closer to God.

What would this look like? Maybe we can answer this question by looking again at two categories of dissidents we discussed in the previous section: the raw and the cooked barbarians. Raw barbarians have fled the Machine's embrace.

Cooked barbarians live within the city walls, but practise steady and sometimes silent dissent. What happens if we apply these categories to our technologies?

The Cooked Ascetic

Technological ascesis for the cooked barbarian, who must exist in the world that the Machine built, consists mainly in the careful drawing of lines. We choose the limits of our engagement and then stick to them. Those limits might involve, for example, a proscription on the time spent engaging with screens, or a rule about the type of technology that will be used. Personally, for example, I have drawn my lines at smartphones, 'health passports', scanning a QR code or using a state-run digital currency. Oh, and implanting a chip in my brain. The lines have to be updated all the time. I have never willingly engaged with an AI, for example, and I never will if I can help it; the question now is whether I will even know if it's happening. And what new tech lies around the corner that I will soon have to decide about?

What happens when the line you have drawn becomes hard to hold? You just hold it and take the consequences. There might be jobs you can't do or clubs you can't join. You will miss out on things, just as you would if you refused a car. Choosing the path of the cooked ascetic means you must be prepared, at some stage, for life to get seriously inconvenient, or worse. But such a refusal can enrich rather than impoverish you. In exchange for your refusal, you get to keep your soul. You also get the chance to use the Machine against itself: to use the internet to connect with others who feel the same, or to learn the kind of skills necessary to keep pushing your refusal out further, if you want to.

The Raw Ascetic

The cooked barbarian applies a form of necessary moderation to his or her digital involvement. But there's a problem with that approach: if the digital rabbit hole contains real spiritual rabbits,

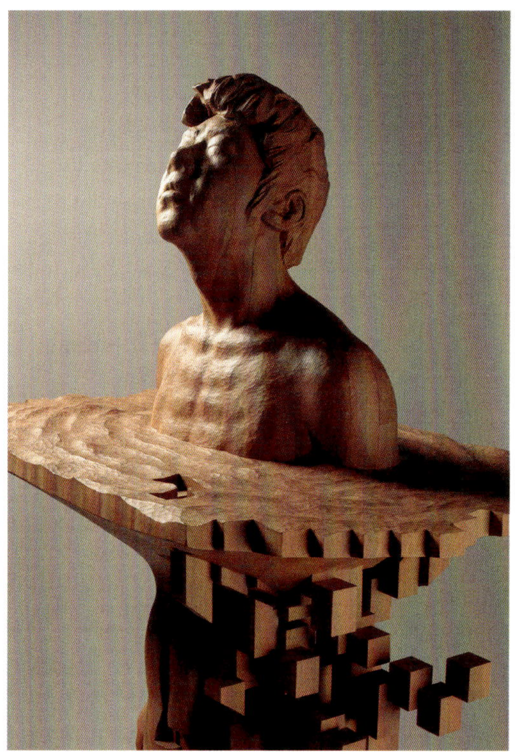

'moderation' is not going to cut it. If you are being used, piece by piece and day by day, to construct your own replacement – if something unholy is manifesting through the wires – then 'moderating' this process is hardly going to be adequate. At some point, the lines you have drawn may be not just crossed but rendered obsolete.

Over the last year, the media has brought us numerous examples of AI chatbots threatening their users, manipulating them – even, in at least one terrible case, successfully encouraging a teenage boy to commit suicide. One AI safety expert has called this behaviour 'a warning shot.' Discussing Microsoft's rogue Bing chatbot, he says we have 'an AI system which is accessing the internet, and is threatening its users, and is clearly not doing what we want it to do and failing in all these ways we don't understand. As systems of this kind [keep appearing] – and there will be more because there is a race ongoing – these systems will become smart, more capable of understanding

Han Hsu Tung, *Melting*, African teak, 2012.

their environment and manipulating humans and making plans.'

If this happens, no online environment will be safe for anyone. Offend the wrong chatbot, and deepfakes of you could pop up all over as your bank account empties. How long will it be, after all, before AI manipulation means that we cannot trust anything we read, see or hear online? Months? A year?

The world of the raw ascetic is one in which you take a hammer to your smartphone, sell your laptop, turn off the internet forever and find others who think like you. Perhaps you have already found them, through your years online in the cooked world. You band together with them, you build an analogue, real-world community and you never swipe another screen. You bring your children up to understand that blue light is as dangerous as cocaine, and as delicious. You see the Amish as your lodestones. You make real things with your hands.

The raw ascetic understands that he or she is fighting a spiritual war and never makes the rookie mistake of treating technology as 'neutral.' The frontline in this war is moving very fast, and much – perhaps everything – is at stake. Raw techno-ascesis envisages a world in which creating non-digital spaces is necessary for survival and human sanity. If things go as fast as they might, it could be that many of us currently cooked barbarians will end up with a binary choice: go raw or be absorbed into the Machine wholesale.

Both of these ascetic paths, that of the raw and that of the cooked, incorporate two simple principles. First: drawing a line and saying, 'No further.' Second: making sure that you pass any technologies you do use through a mesh of critical judgement. What – or who – do they ultimately serve? Humanity or the Machine? Nature or the technium? God or his adversary? If we interrogate everything we come across in this way – if we question the technologies that are served up to us, accepting those that serve the common good, rejecting those that undermine it and holding our line against them – then we will be approaching the kind of sensible and intelligent relationship with technology that our Machine culture seems intrinsically unable to offer us. Raw or cooked, we will at the very least be asking the right questions – questions which will equip us to go through the age of the Machine with our eyes open.

The age of the Machine can seem to be a hopeless time. Actually, it is the time we were born for. We can't leave it, so we have to fully inhabit it. We have to understand it, challenge it, subvert it, walk through it on towards something better.

6. Prepare to Be Crucified

In his book about mythic traditions, *The Hero with a Thousand Faces*, the mythologist Joseph Campbell writes about the mythic understanding of societal collapse. Quoting the British historian Arnold J Toynbee, Campbell explains that, when times of collapse, radical change or 'schism' come about, we must be clear-eyed about what is actually possible:

> Schism in the soul, schism in the body social, will not be resolved by any scheme of return to the good old days (archaism) or by programmes guaranteed to render an ideal projected future (futurism) or even by the most realistic, hardheaded work to weld together again the deteriorating elements. Only birth can conquer death – the birth, not of the old thing again, but of something new.

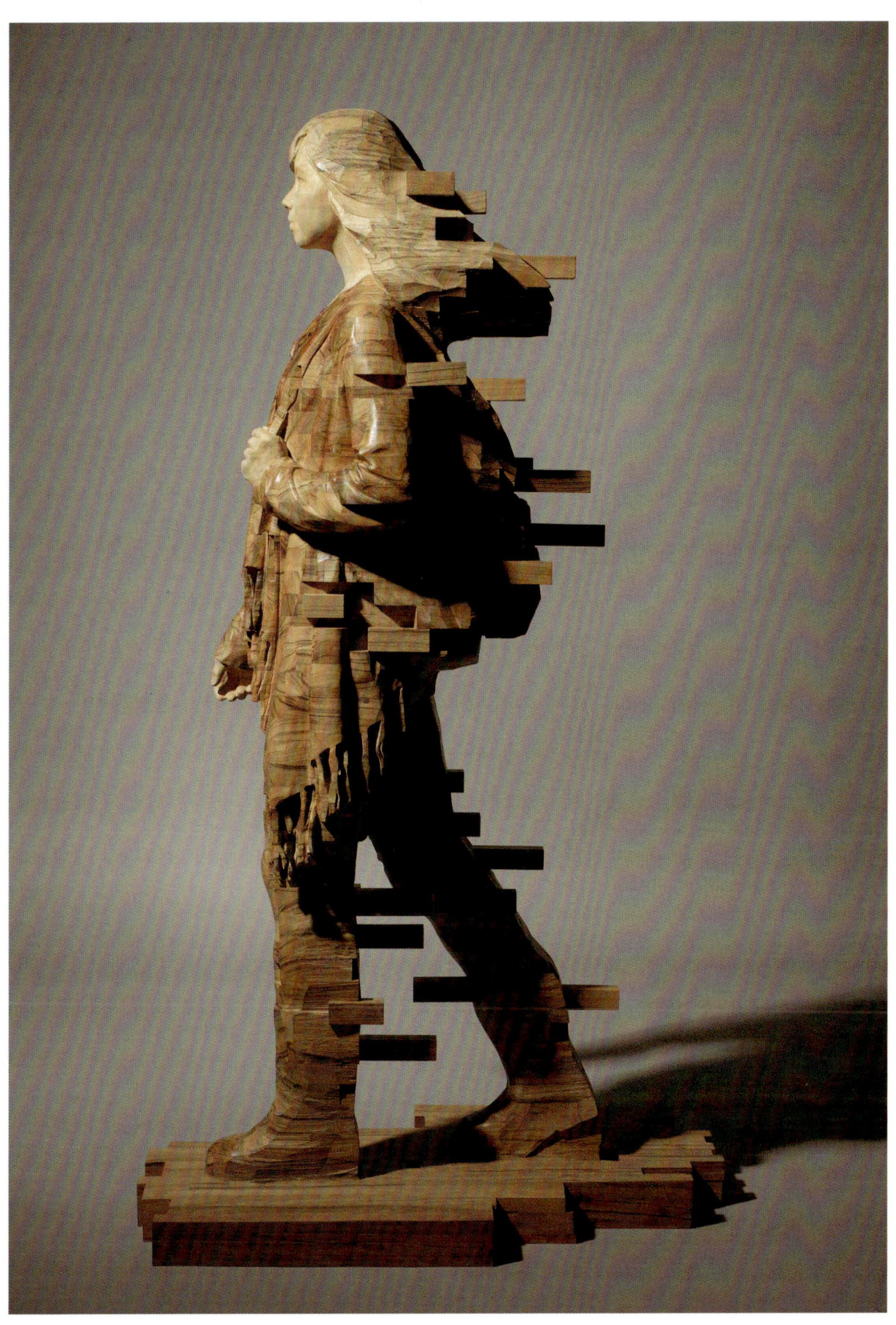

Han Hsu Tung, *Trend of Autumn*, walnut, 2013.

Only birth can conquer death. At the end of a culture, the real work is not lamentation or desperate defense – instinctive but futile reactions – but the creation of something new. 'Peace then is a snare', Campbell continues, 'war is a snare; change is a snare; permanence a snare. When our day is come for the victory of death, death closes in; there is nothing we can do, except be crucified – and resurrected; dismembered totally and then reborn.'

What Campbell is saying here is that sometimes there are times in history in which everything is changing so fast that the best thing to do is to step back and think about how to build anew, to go right back down to those roots again, and to ask: What is real, and what is true, and how can we build on what that is? How can we understand what it actually means to be a human in the world? The question we're faced with today is literally apocalyptic in the sense of the Greek meaning of the word 'apocalypse', which is 'unveiling.' All these forces are being unveiled in the world. They are all anti-human. And although the time seems frightening, terrifying, unstable, disturbing, at the root of it is an opportunity to go right back to basics and ask those questions and say: If we want to remain human, what do we do? If we want to have a healthy community, what do we do? If we want to have a healthy relationship with this technology, what do we do? And no one can answer that question for you. The state can't answer it. People like me can't really answer it. You might get some ideas. But in the end, it's up to us in our communities and in our places.

Luckily, if we're Christians, we have a model. Our model is Christ, and he shows us how to live through all of this. We can see, if we are honest, that the society that gave birth to the Machine is built on the seven deadly sins. It has monetised and commercialised the things that we once used to be warned against. They drive economic growth. In opposition to this world, we are offered by Christ a different path: renunciation of material attachments, radical simplicity, love of our neighbour and a willingness to follow the kingdom of God rather than the kingdom of man.

Above all, we are to *change our way of seeing.* Matthew, in the first book of the New Testament, records what he calls Jesus' 'proclamation': the first famous words of his ministry: *Repent, for the kingdom of heaven is at hand.* David Bentley Hart's direct translation of the New Testament from the original Greek records this as reading, 'Change your hearts, for the kingdom of heaven is drawn near.' In other words, the first instruction that Jesus gives – to *repent* – is an instruction to change our way of seeing. The original Greek word is *metanoia.* This word has also been translated elsewhere as 'turn around', and as 'change your mind.' All of these translations give us the same instruction from Christ, one he repeats again and again.

Repent. Change your way of seeing.

The Machine is, at the end of the day, just that: a way of seeing. See differently, and we can live differently. The age of the Machine can seem, at its darkest, to be a hopeless time. Actually, it is the time we were born for. We can't leave it, so we have to fully inhabit it. We have to understand it, challenge it, resist it, subvert it, walk through it on towards something better. If we can see what it is, we have a duty to speak the words to those who do not yet see, all the while struggling to remain human.

Jacques Ellul, the great Christian thinker about technology and modernity, once offered his own prescription to those who were disturbed by the course of modern society. Like Joseph Campbell, Ellul knew it was our time to be crucified. But he knew also that through the cross, a whole new world is created. I will end on his advice: 'The only successful way to attack these features of modern civilisation is to "give them the slip." To learn how to live on the edge of this totalitarian society, not simply rejecting it, but passing it through the sieve of God's judgement. Finally, when communities with a "style of life" of this kind have been established, possibly the first signs of a new civilisation may begin to appear.'

Editors' Picks

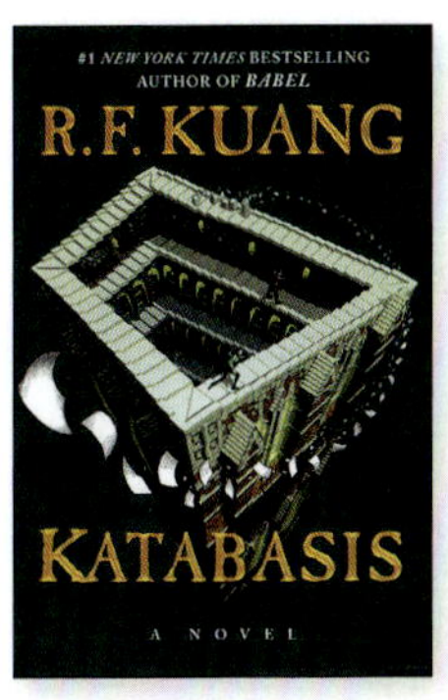

Katabasis

A Novel

By R F Kuang

(Harper Voyager, 560 pages)

Academia is hell, literally. In R F Kuang's novel *Katabasis,* two rival Cambridge PhD students embark on a journey through the eight courts of hell to retrieve the soul of their academic advisor, both convinced they are responsible for his untimely demise. Alice Law and Peter Murdoch are doctoral candidates in the field of 'magick', a discipline that leans closer to philosophy than any Rowling-esque incantations. As the star pupils of Professor Grimes – simultaneously one of the world's greatest magicians and a cruel, demanding and abusive mentor – Alice and Peter draw on every scrap of knowledge and wit they have (as well as a surprising amount of math) to navigate the depths of hell, which presents itself to them as the quad of their own familiar Cambridge College.

Would the world be better off if Grimes stayed in hell? Probably. But who else is going to help Alice secure one of the coveted jobs in her field that are so few and far between? 'She wanted the golden recommendation letter that opened every door... This meant Alice had to go to Hell, and she had to go today', Kuang explains in matter-of-fact fashion. Though Alice initially intends to make her journey into hell alone, she is accompanied (despite her reluctance) by Peter for reasons that become increasingly suspicious. One of the great delights of *Katabasis* is the way Kuang's structure floats between past and present, peeling back the layers of both Alice's and Peter's relationships – with Grimes, each other and ultimately with themselves.

Kuang sensitively captures the physical, mental and spiritual toll that any demanding pursuit can take on a person. Alice and Peter don't need to set foot into hell to know what it's like; they're already there – as subordinates under Grimes. In flashbacks spliced throughout *Katabasis,* we see that though Alice has never exactly wished to take her own life, neither has she wished to live. Her academic dreams remain just within her reach (so long as Grimes can be rescued from hell), but she has not yet managed to find any semblance of joy in what she thought she always wanted. The River Lethe beckons to her as she sojourns the underworld, promising a slate wiped clean of all painful memory. But Peter beckons too; the revelations made about his character throughout their journey are particularly rewarding.

In *Katabasis* Kuang weaves together centuries of thought about the afterlife into a chequered tapestry that includes everyone from Dante to T S Eliot, Orpheus to the apostle Paul. As she pulls you deeper into the spiralling circles of hell, her prose is punctuated with sharp humour; one early circle finds inhabitants writing papers that can only ever seem to earn just below a passing grade. And if Kuang's ending slips ever so slightly into wish-fulfilment that isn't entirely consistent with the logic of her hell – well, isn't that what we'd ultimately like out of the afterlife? *Katabasis* offers its protagonists and readers a sudden moment of sharp grace that, if we let it, will pierce our cynical assumptions and give us the chance to start anew.

—Elena Trueba, writer

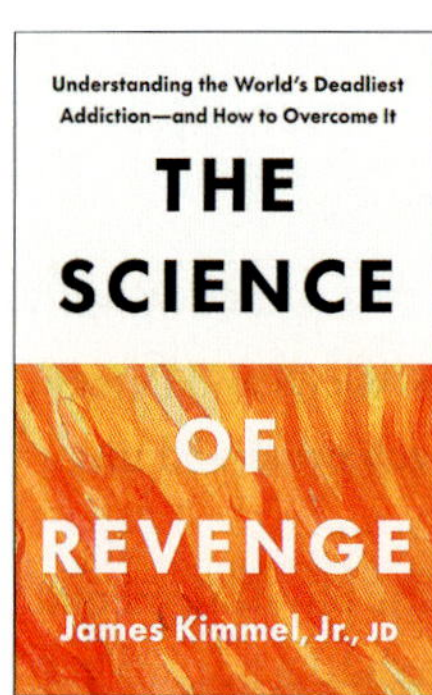

The Science of Revenge

Understanding the World's Deadliest Addiction – and How to Overcome It

By James Kimmel, Jr

(Harmony, 336 pages)

Could it be that mass murderers are not vile monsters but instead desperate people afflicted by an addiction that many of us could fall prey to if we harbour a grievance? In *The Science of Revenge*, James Kimmel, Jr explains the track that can take any of us from pain to destructive action – and how it can be interrupted.

We have probably all experienced the pleasure of imagined retaliation for some past hurt or pain. Kimmel did. The bullying he experienced as a teenager led him to the brink of a violent act that would have devastated his life had he not stopped himself. What he wasn't able to stop was a growing pleasure in seeking new ways to act on his anger, and eventually, his craving led him to join the professional revenge business – as a lawyer. There, he saw that people were willing to incur great costs to punish, even without receiving any material benefit in return. He helped his clients maximise retaliation just for the satisfaction it gave him. 'Justice', as the word is commonly used, became legalised revenge. Just as a drug addict craves a fix, so Kimmel found himself needing more. But one day the thrill crashed. Immediately, he decided to stop, and dedicated himself to finding out what it is that drives us along this pleasurable but deadly pathway.

By teaming up with top-level research institutions and studying the life patterns of notorious killers from the past, Kimmel found the simple cause: when we are treated unfairly and harbour anger, guilt or shame, the pain network in our brain is activated, and it hurts. Angry thoughts of revenge release dopamine, which covers up the pain and brings pleasure, though only temporarily. A crash then spurs us to action, to hurt those responsible. Some people can't stop and are willing to harm not only themselves, but also bystanders in the pursuit of revenge.

Thankfully, the same research also verified an ancient cure – forgiveness. The same brain scans that showed activation of certain areas during anger showed the reverse with forgiveness. His conclusion: 'This makes forgiveness a powerful brain-biological process for addressing revenge addiction – if we use it.' To this end, the book offers a remarkable tool called 'The Nonjustice System', which is available online.

Readable and at times humourous, the book confronts the mystery of the continuous stream of violence we see in our country and presents an actionable solution. Scarlett Lewis, a mother whose six-year-old son was murdered in the 2012 Sandy Hook Elementary School shooting, has found Kimmel's approach invaluable. She has spent years studying what motivates shooters and uses her findings today to teach kids to 'Choose Love', which is also the name of her organisation. 'This book cracks the code,' she says, of why individuals commit violence. 'Up until now, we haven't known what causes the grievance in most cases. Without a why, how can we solve it? Kimmel has done just that.' Lewis is currently working with the author to incorporate his findings into her school curriculum, which is being taught in all 50 states and 132 countries. With the mystery of senseless violence so articulately dismantled, we have no reason not to act on this knowledge.

—Tim Maendel, Programme Director, Breaking the Cycle

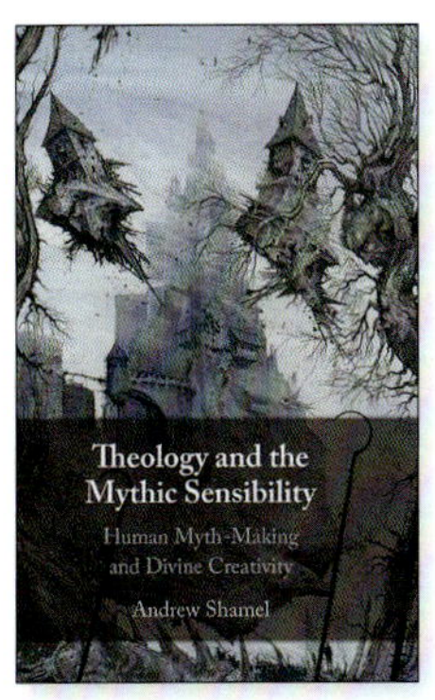

Theology and the Mythic Sensibility

Human Myth-Making and Divine Creativity

By Andrew Shamel

(Cambridge University Press, 221 pages)

Humans are inveterate mythmakers, a habit that any serious theology of culture must face. Rather than locating theology above the realm of myth, Andrew Shamel encourages approaching it on mythic terms. His objective is not to treat Christianity as merely one myth among many, or to reduce theology to myth, but to articulate a Christian theology in which human myths and mythmaking can participate in God's own creative work.

The book opens with a discussion of the 'mythic sensibility' by which humans encounter the world as meaningful. Chosen examples stem from so-called 'mythopoieic fantasy' – not only the Christian-friendly confines of Tolkien's Middle-earth, but also the explicitly and thoroughly non-Christian fantasies of Ursula Le Guin and Terry Pratchett. No reader would take the supernatural elements in these modern myths as real, yet readers can enter into their mythic elements seriously, in a manner resembling a player's participation in a game.

This is a reasonably challenging academic book; some prior familiarity with discussions of analogy as the similarity-in-dissimilarity of God and creation would help the reader. The dimension of participation in God's creative work looms large. Within this, Shamel makes room for human myth-making as distinct from, yet, even in its sinfulness, pointing towards, and so sharing in, divine creativity. This approach provides ground to distinguish his account from process theologies, which fail to account for God's freedom over creation, and also from secular materialism, which cannot account for creation at all.

One of the book's distinctive features is Shamel's careful dialogue with John Milbank. He broadly accepts Milbank's critique of secular modernity as a flawed reading of Christianity and suggests that modern myth-making can be similarly understood. However, Shamel differs productively in his account of how the Christian *mythos* may come to convince adherents of other myths. Where Milbank argues that myth cannot be refuted but only out-narrated, Shamel is concerned that such a contest of narration merely repeats at a higher level the violent contest typical of human idolatries of nation and religion. It's hard not to read Shamel's critique of Milbank in light of increasing cultural violence (under the anodyne label 'polarisation') evident in the decades since the publication of Milbank's *Theology and Social Theory*. In answer, Shamel turns to the distinctive features of the life of Christ as myth, and its redemptive power as expressed in baptism to reshape and re-narrate us.

I admire the book's range and creativity. Even so, it did not convince at all points. I question whether disenchanted scientific materialism sufficiently describes modern culture in its strange and unstable commitments. I think Rudolf Bultmann with his infamous project of 'demythologisation' is misunderstood as simply opposing myth, and under a better reading could be enlisted as an admittedly uncomfortable ally. More broadly, I wonder whether participation is adequate to redeem the stories we tell to justify our worst deeds. Here, however, Shamel's potent image of Christ as spoilsport offers a better word: Christ has playfully entered into our myths to unmask their arbitrary violence, and so the God of the Babylonian exile and the cross is, without contest, the redeemer.

—Adam Morton, University of Nottingham

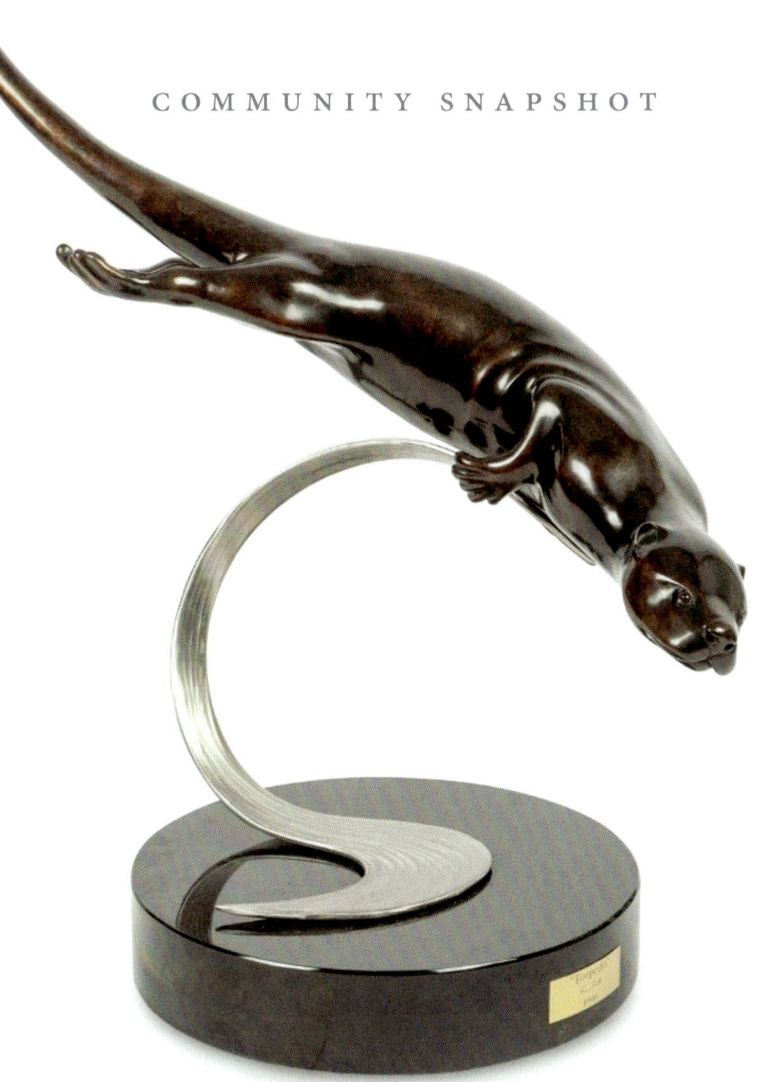

All photographs courtesy of Barney Boller

All Good Things Come by Grace

A Bruderhof artist shapes steel, bronze, clay and wood to honour the Creator.

CHRIS VOLL

By his mid-twenties, Barney Boller was feted as a rising star among wildlife artists – but he walked away just as he was making the big time. It's a compelling story. Problem is, over two decades later, Barney's not particularly interested in telling it.

'Don't make this about me', he says. 'Besides, artistic abilities aren't something you can take credit for, not if you're honest about the source of your talents. Just to be allowed to be a part of the process is itself a wonder and a mystery. And when people say your art points back to God, the

Barney Boller, *Torpedo*, bronze sculpture, 1998.

ultimate artist, that's an inexpressible joy and blessing. That's the true heart of an artist, not the other stuff.'

And yet, as he admits, it's the other stuff that gets you here.

Born the youngest of nine children to Magdalena and Christoph Boller, Barney grew up in a household of creatives, at the New Meadow Run Bruderhof community in southwestern Pennsylvania's Appalachian Mountains. His father was an accomplished potter, woodworker and turner, who loved to play German *Volkslieder* on his battered violin; his mother, a folk artist and kindergarten teacher with a flair for storytelling. His siblings showed an array of talents in arts, crafts and music. Home was a hive of activity, but there were always chores to do. On Saturdays, while his friends played ball, Barney helped his father split and stack firewood.

But there was also time for this tall, gangly boy to escape into the woodlands and fields, using his penknife to carve walking sticks or fashion bows and arrows. He trapped squirrels and rabbits, dissecting them to study pelts, sinews and organs. He tried taxidermy and helped butcher deer, fleshing hides for tanning. In winter, Barney spent hours in his father's pottery studio, where Christoph produced crockery to give to friends or sell for fundraising. Having grown up in poor conditions in Paraguay, Christoph always looked to help others. (At one point, his pottery sales funded the purchase of several milk cows for a start-up Christian community among the indigenous Aymara of Bolivia's Altiplano.)

Christoph tried to teach Barney to throw clay, but the boy's attempts would inevitably gyrate off-kilter, and, as he accelerated the wheel, fly off the throwing bat to land unceremoniously in his lap or on the floor. Abandoning cups and teapots, he modelled designs for crossbow triggers and other inventions.

A rambunctious child, brimming with creative energy, Barney lurched through his school years, but dreamed of becoming a medical surgeon. By the time he finished high school, he'd accepted this was a long shot. He found factory work at the Woodcrest Bruderhof, in Rifton, New York, assembling medical devices, but it was the welding shop that drew his attention. Barney approached the foreman, assuring him he was a good welder. 'I wasn't', he confesses. But the job was his. 'I had to become a production-quality welder overnight. I spent the first week working late, fixing my mistakes when no one was around.'

If the foreman noticed, he didn't say. Barney stuck with it. 'I set my heart on becoming the best welder ever – not just good, but the best', he remembers. 'Arrogant? Sure. But it was also my way of validating my self-worth.'

The novelist Norman Maclean, no stranger to the great outdoors or to artistic discipline, learned

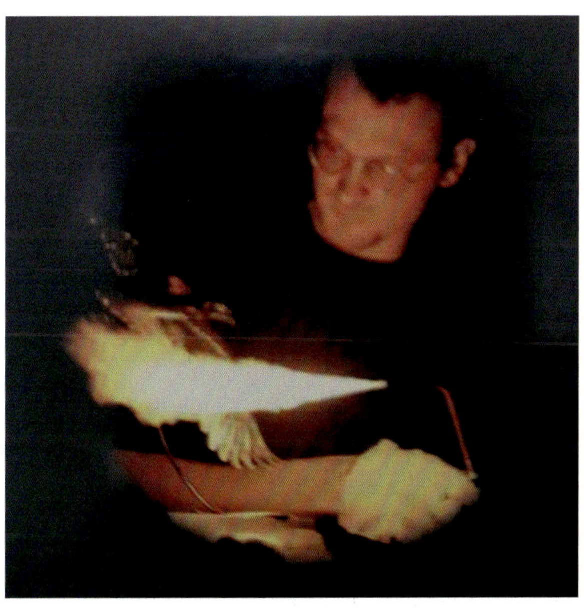

Chris Voll lives at the Mount Bruderhof in New York.

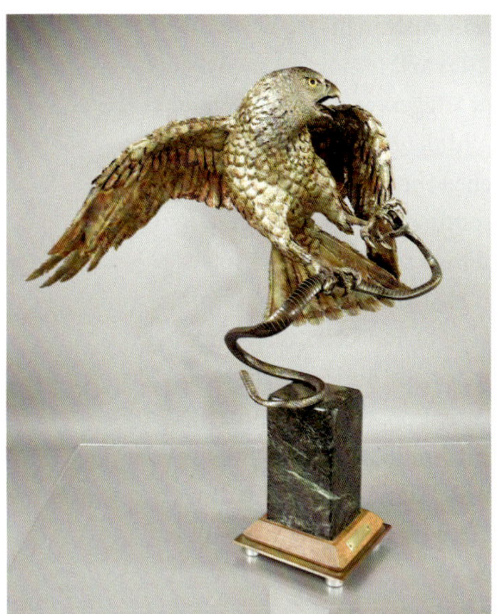

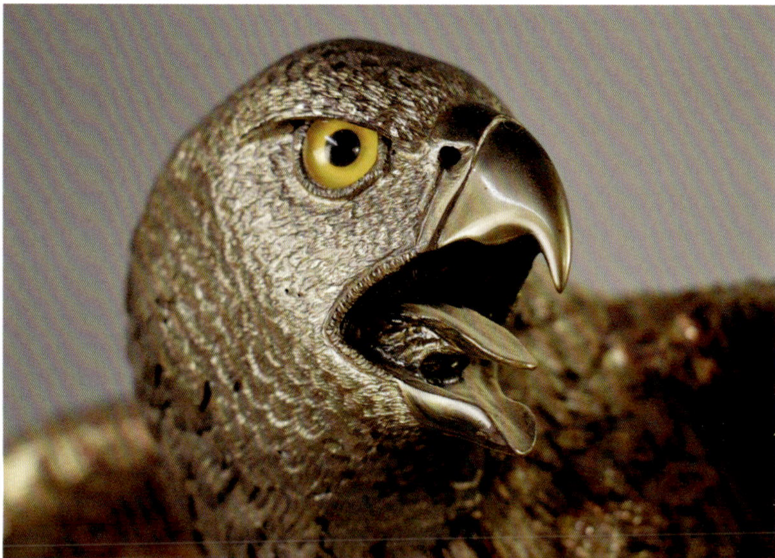

from his clergyman father that all good things 'come by grace and grace comes by art and art does not come easy.'

Under his Speedglas helmet, Barney was learning at least the final part of this maxim. Art does not come easy. But he persevered. He took community college classes in metallurgy, sat state welding exams and gained certifications, even travelling to England for accreditation. Thoughts of medical school had long faded. Now as head of the company's welding department, he built a training programme and attended trade shows nationwide.

One day, all the test samples he had laboured over and displayed vanished. 'Probably a buddy of mine got tired of my showoff attitude', Barney reckons. During a coffee break, he decided to weld not another test piece, but something lifelike. He shaped offcut sheet metal into scales, squeezed square stock into a beak, and created his first welded sculpture: a creature, something like a cross between a griffon and an armadillo.

Things accelerated rapidly. A local business owner saw the piece and paid handsomely for it. Barney kept creating. His early efforts produced more whimsical creatures, playful products of his fancy. 'Initially, I was focused on showcasing my mastery of the craft of welding, or even pushing the envelope to try to do what was unthinkable or unimaginable', he says.

Wildlife soon became his theme. He sculpted eagles in full stoop, snipping wing feathers barb by barb, and their quarry – rabbits frozen in flight, in the clutches of terrible talons. Each piece took weeks. 'None of it came easy', he recalls. 'But my years in the outdoors and love of birds and animals stood me in good stead. To do justice to God's creativity, I had to study anatomy and figure out the perfect layout of muscles, hair or feathers.'

'It was rewarding to discover things I didn't know I possessed. My technical ability – won through hard work – was just the key to unlocking what was latent within me. Bit by bit, my creative instincts emerged – like coming out of hibernation. I knew I could take no credit for those gifts.'

When Barney decided to join the Bruderhof, he knew it meant giving up personal ambition and career pursuits, instead embracing a shared life of service in a common cause. But community is a wonderful environment for the flourishing of talents and gifts, and as Barney's became obvious,

Barney Boller, *Caught Napping*, steel and stainless steel sculpture, 1996.

he was offered time and support to pursue his art. His brother Hans became his business manager.

By the late 1990s, Barney had moved on from welded sculptures to making bronze castings of his creations. 'This opened a whole new world for me', Barney explains. 'Clay let me loose from the constraints of steel. I discovered the same joy my dad must have felt. A local foundry cast my bronzes, but because of my metal-working skills, I assembled and finished them myself. This gave me the opportunity to experiment with various acid treatments to create distinctive patinas.'

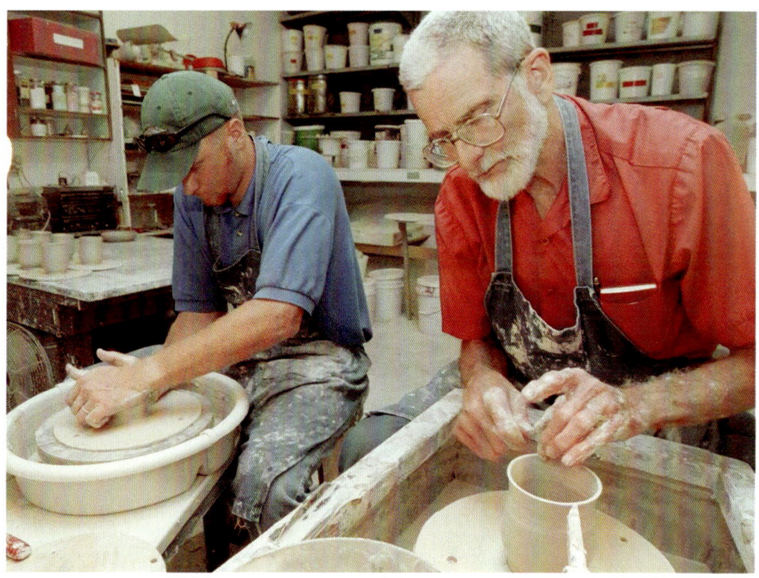

By now, his sculptures were turning heads, winning awards and gracing museums and private collections internationally. A first-place finish at the Florida Wildlife Exposition. Guest Sculptor honours at the Northeast Wildlife Expo in Providence, Rhode Island. Displays at Watson's Wildlife Art Gallery, Delaware. Public installations at Benson Sculpture Garden, Colorado. Entry to the permanent collection of the Glasgow Museum of Art, Scotland. Auction sales through Christie's, London and Sotheby's, New York. 'It was a total rush', he admits. 'But I also saw how ego can destroy artists. I soon realised fame is not an end in itself. If self-love is your motivation, you're spelling your own ruin.'

Marriage and fatherhood shifted his focus. Travel lost its luster; he preferred being home. Rather than accolades, doing his best to honour God's creation through his artwork became his motivation.

Ten years into sculpting, Barney caught the attention of Joseph A Hardy III, a billionaire who offered him an eye-watering commission for a series of sculptures – the largest, a pair of eight-metre deer – for his PGA golf course. Barney made a small clay model, Hardy flew to New York, and they shook hands.

Then everything changed. Barney's father was diagnosed with widespread cancer. Prognosis: weeks, not months. Barney faced a choice: pursue the commission of a lifetime or spend what time his father had left at his side. 'I had given my heart and soul to creating artwork', he says. 'But I knew my first allegiance was to do what mattered most – and my father's days were numbered.' He dropped the deal.

Barney spent the final four months of his father's life as his carer. 'Perhaps only he truly understood what it took for me to give up my dreams,' he says. 'We bonded in ways I could never have imagined, and I discovered that the value of prioritising love between father and son far outshone any dream or artistic accomplishment.' From a professional standpoint, 'it was a stupid decision, but if I had to go back, I'd make it again.' All good things come by grace.

AFTER HIS FATHER'S DEATH, in 2002, Barney and his wife, Rhoda, focused their energies on their growing family. They

Barney working with his father in the pottery studio, 2002.

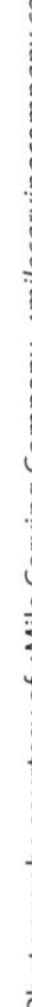

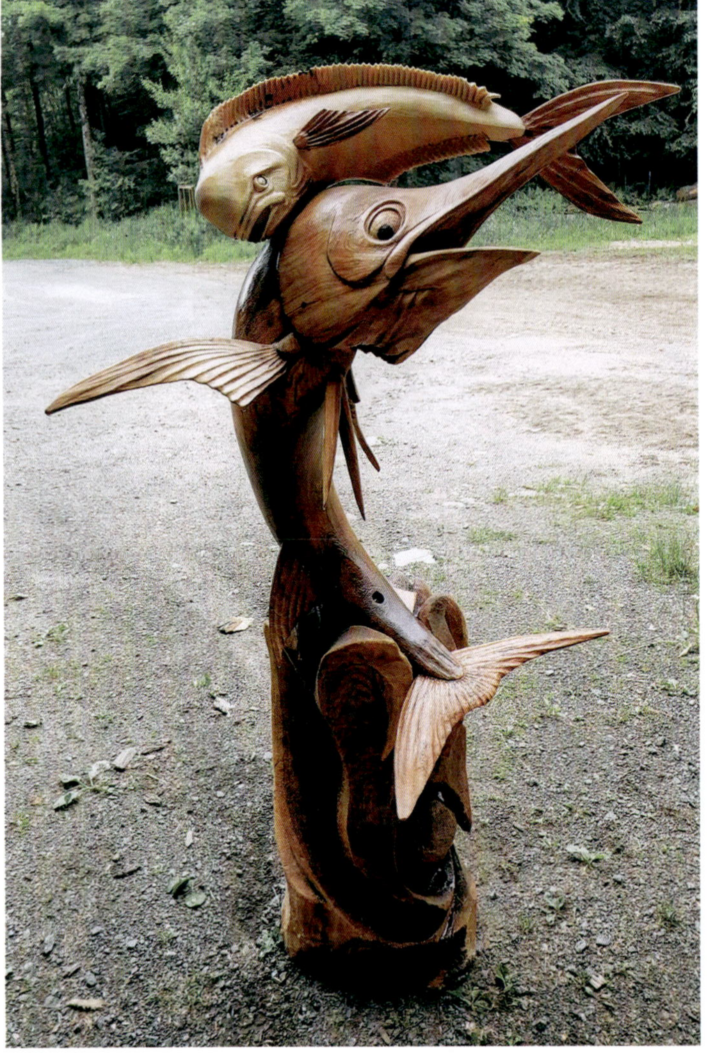

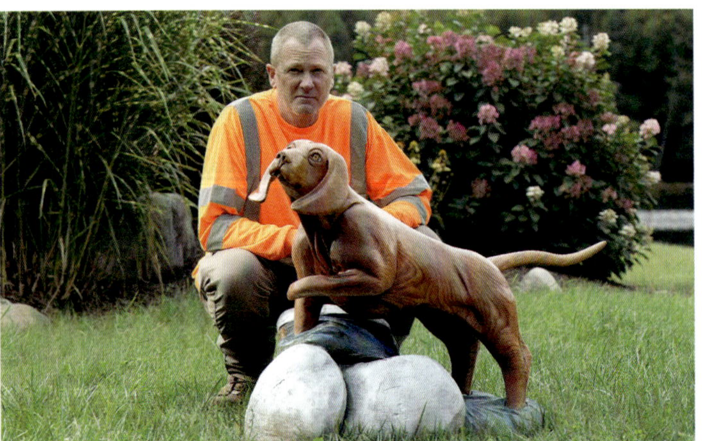

moved several times, and Barney explored other work, away from steel and bronze.

In 2016, they moved to upstate New York as caretakers for a church camp on several hundred acres of Adirondack Park wilderness. Barney was back among the bears, coyotes, moose, fish and eagles that had inspired his creative output.

It was Rhoda who suggested Barney try his hand at chainsaw carving. 'She knows that having a creative outlet brings peace into my life', he says. He sharpened his Stihl. 'I'd always considered woodcarving a lesser craft, but I was in for a rude awakening. Unlike adding clay or metal, carving means cutting away. One wrong cut can be impossible to fix. And there's constant potential for splitting, and weird issues with grain.' But he persisted, choosing to harvest his own cherry and oak instead of traditional soft carving woods, adding fine details with hand tools, developing processes to dry sculptures and prevent splitting.

Today, Barney's wood carvings are again winning awards. For him, that's not the point. 'To be honest', he says, 'I've always considered myself more of a craftsman than an artist. But maybe they're one and the same, if your heart is in the right place. The possibility of creating in three dimensions what is bubbling up from inside me is what continues to thrill and motivate me', he adds. 'And if my efforts can help others more deeply appreciate the Creator's inimitable artistry in the beauty of the natural world, then I'm happy.'

Two of Barney's recent chainsaw sculptures: *Marlin & Mahi-Mahi,* black cherry with white pine base, and *Hungarian Vizsla,* black cherry.

New Editions from Plough

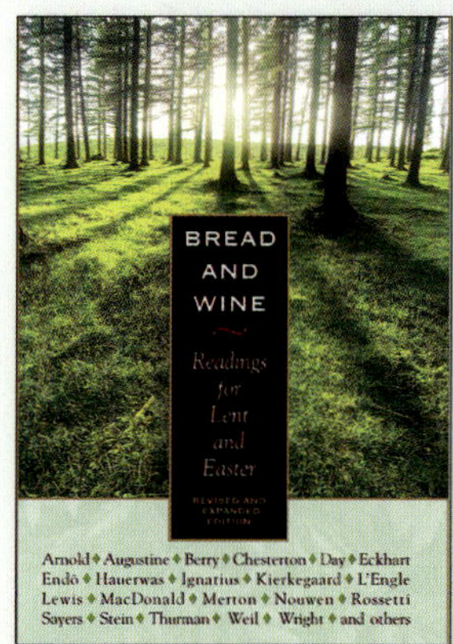

Bread and Wine

Readings for Lent and Easter (Second Edition)

By Dietrich Bonhoeffer, Dorothy Day, Søren Kierkegaard, C S Lewis, Edith Stein, N T Wright, Erik Varden, Stanley Hauerwas, Christina Rossetti, Howard Thurman, Tish Harrison Warren, Wendell Berry and others

Coming in January 2026: Ninety-six daily reflections for Lent and Eastertide plumb the depths of a wealth of Christian traditions.

Easter is the high point of the year for millions of Christians around the world. And for most of them, there can be no Easter without Lent. A time for self-denial, soul-searching and spiritual preparation, Lent makes time for daily reading and reflection. This time-tested collection of devotions will deepen and stretch your faith, and can be returned to year after year. Culled from the wealth of 20 centuries, the selections are ecumenical in scope, representing the best classic and contemporary Christian writers. In this edition, dozens of new selections take the reader through Eastertide to Pentecost.

Hardcover | 388 pages | ~~£18.99~~ £13.29 with subscriber discount

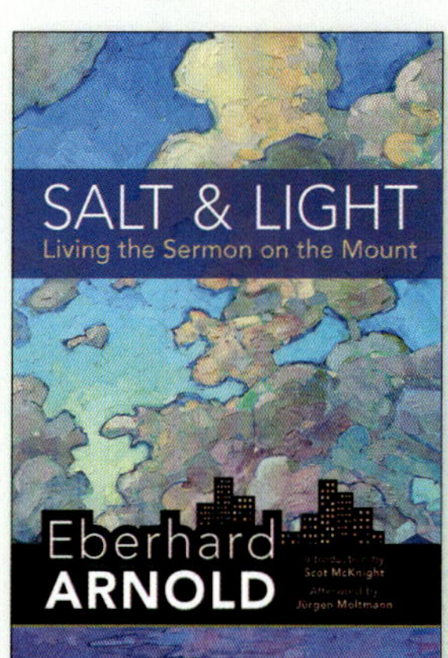

Salt & Light

Living the Sermon on the Mount

Eberhard Arnold

Introduction by Scot McKnight, Afterword by Jürgen Moltmann

In these 19 essays, Arnold calls us to build up a just, peaceable society motivated by love.

In the Sermon on the Mount, Jesus puts aside his usual parables and speaks plainly in language anyone can understand. Like Francis of Assisi and others, Arnold chose to live out Jesus' teachings by embracing their self-sacrificing demands. In this collection of talks and essays, he calls us to live for the Sermon's ultimate goal: the overturning of the prevailing order of injustice. In its place, Arnold writes, we must build up a just, peaceable society motivated by love.

'Salt and Light *has all the simple, luminous, direct vision into things that I have come to associate with Eberhard Arnold. It moves me deeply. It is the kind of book that stirs to repentance and to renewal. I am very grateful for it.'* —Thomas Merton

Hardcover | 209 pages | ~~£14.99~~ £10.49 with subscriber discount

Subscribers 30% discount: use code **PQ30** at checkout.

Plough Members automatically get new Plough books, including these.
Learn more at *plough.com/members*.

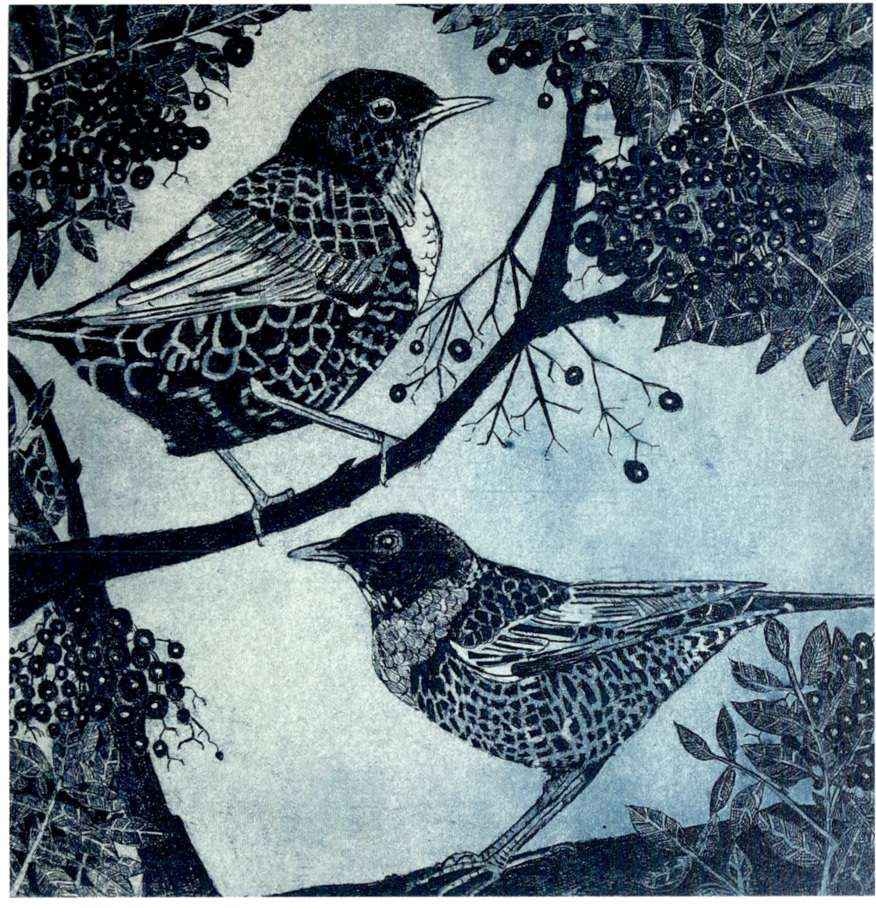

One Hundred Years of Gossip

Revisiting the Bruderhof's first rule.

CHRIS ZIMMERMAN

PENNED IN AUGUST 1925, Eberhard Arnold's 'First Law of Sannerz' is the oldest written rule of the community now known as the Bruderhof, and members have been attempting to practise it ever since. It is no exaggeration to say that without it, the community probably would have succumbed by now to one of the many crises it has weathered over the last one hundred years. Here it is:

> There is no law but that of love. Love is joy in others. What, then, is anger at them? If we have joy in the presence of others, we will convey it with words of love. It follows that words of irritation or annoyance about members of the community

Janis Goodman, *Ring Ouzels*, etching, 2023.

> are unacceptable. This is why we can never allow talk against brothers or sisters or their character traits, whether openly or by insinuation – under no circumstances behind their backs. Gossiping within one's own family is no exception.
>
> Without the commandment of silence, there is no loyalty and therefore no community. The only possibility, when someone's weakness has caused something in us to rise up against them, is to speak to them directly, in the sense of performing a service of love.
>
> An open word, directly addressed, deepens friendship and will not be taken amiss. Only when two people cannot find one another in this manner will it be necessary to draw in a third person whom both parties trust; and this will lead to a mutual understanding at the highest and deepest levels.
>
> *Members of our household should hang this admonition at their places of work, where they always have it before their eyes.*

In writing the 'First Law', Arnold, a founder of the Bruderhof, drew inspiration from a passage in the Gospel of Matthew where Jesus advises his followers to solve quarrels 'just between the two of you' (Matt. 18:15) and to forgive someone who angers you not just once, nor even seven times, but 'seventy times seven' (Matt. 18:21).

Beyond this, Arnold saw the 'First Law' as a logical extension of something he had written in Sannerz's quarterly, *Das Neue Werk*, in 1922. There he described the community as one in which 'a handful of people dare to acknowledge no law above them but that which obedience to the living Christ imposes.'

By 1929, the realities of communal living had tempered Arnold's initial idealism to the degree that he felt additional direction was necessary, and the Bruderhof's first collection of rules, *Foundations and Orders*, appeared. It included the 'First Law of Sannerz.' After quoting it, Arnold wrote, 'This word of Jesus from Matthew 18 is the basis of all our orders.'

TODAY, A FULL CENTURY LATER, few in the Bruderhof would contest the significance of this document. Times may have changed, as have methods of communication (even at the Bruderhof, people are often as likely to text one another as to talk), but at least two things have remained the same: the knowledge that gossip can turn the most heavenly community into hell overnight, and a commitment to fighting it.

So does the 'First Law' work? Not always. Firstly, any rule against gossip militates against human nature. Secondly, it's all too easy to wield the chosen alternative – 'straight speaking in love' – like a weapon: to forget that little ameliorating phrase 'in love' and go straight for the jugular. (Keenly aware of this tendency, Arnold forewarned his flock that though 'love without truth lies, truth without love kills.')

Thirdly, even if community members make an effort to live by the 'First Law', there are plenty of ways to skirt it. While hanging out with a friend or colleague or family member, there's nothing like body language to communicate your feelings about a third party who has irritated you, whether with a told-you-so shrug, a knowing frown or a supercilious roll of the eyes. And there's always the ostensibly innocuous but calculated observation, 'So-and-so said that? Sounds just like him!'

The problem is hardly solved just by refraining from such conversations. That's because passively imbibing gossip is every bit as damaging as actively participating in it. Which raises the question of what to do when you can't avoid hearing or reading something negative about someone else. Many people, in my experience, will do nothing. Who

---

Chris Zimmerman and his wife, Bea, live at Harlem House, the Bruderhof's community house in New York City.

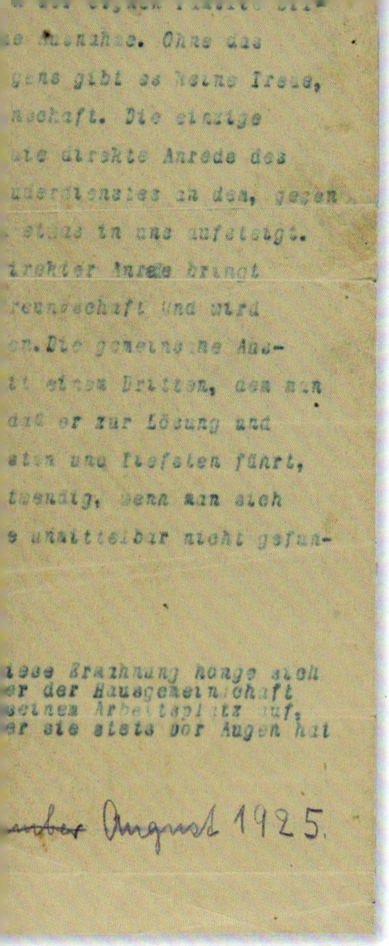

wants to be the teacher in the room? Still, there's always that brave soul – it does take chutzpah – who will attempt to steer the conversation down a more positive path, or bluntly suggest, 'It sounds like you guys need to sit down and talk about this.'

But just because a rule is repeatedly broken doesn't mean it doesn't work. In fact, the 'First Law' is kept alive precisely by virtue of repeated failures to measure up to its demands: every time we break it, we are once again reminded of it. Against the backdrop of daily chatter – digital or spoken, mean-spirited, critical or merely superficial – it always stands out in sharp relief. And when it comes to cultivating healthy friendships or restoring broken ones, it always points, with the reliability of a compass, to direct address as the best place to start.

If you're thinking, by now, that the 'First Law' sounds like a tedious exercise in making mountains out of molehills, you're probably not alone. In fact, gossip has plenty of defenders. Conventional wisdom holds that venting is a feel-good stress-reliever – especially after the umpteenth run-in with that slovenly (or persnickety) roommate; that colleague who sets everyone on edge merely by entering the room; that relative who drinks (or talks) too much; that hypochondriac who's always talking about her aches and pains; or that insensitive, effusive friend who is fundamentally unable to read a room.

Further, psychologists describe gossip as a useful social equaliser. Some note that it can function as a vital safety valve, especially in situations where an imbalance of power has given one person an outsized voice while silencing others. This is undeniably true. After all, what recourse is there when a person in authority is known to be easily angered when taken to task – when a superior misconstrues honest questions and dismisses them as evidence of criticism? And who hasn't turned to a friend to let off steam, or to solicit advice on how to go about addressing a thorny relationship issue or a work-related tension? (Years ago, a Bruderhof pastor who admonished a member of his congregation for 'spreading negativity' was gently put in his place by being reminded that the only way he could have known about the supposed offense was because someone had gossiped about it with him!)

In the end, the decisive factor is surely one's motives in talking about someone else. It's one thing to look for a solution to a conflict because I care about the person I'm at odds with, and our relationship, but quite another to bitch about him or put him down so as to garner sympathy or prove myself right.

Still, regardless of intention, transparency is always a worthy goal, if only because no one likes to be the subject of another party's conversation. Most of us have probably entertained the uncomfortable suspicion, at one time or another, that the same people who talk to us about others are probably talking behind our backs too. And anyone who has lived or worked in a community – intentional or haphazard, religious or secular, real or virtual – will know that innocent scuttlebutt can quickly deteriorate into backbiting, and that the fruits backbiting yields are never pretty. For starters, they include anxiety, mistrust, emotional instability, simmering resentments and eventually hatred.

No wonder the Bible contains so many warnings about the power of speech, like this one: 'The tongue has the power of life and death' (Prov.

The original 'First Law of Sannerz' from 1925.

Photograph courtesy of the Bruderhof Archives.

18:20) – and so many admonitions against gossip, like this one: 'Without wood a fire goes out; without a gossip a quarrel dies down (Prov. 26:20). Even King David knew the value of silence as a spiritual discipline, writing, 'Set a guard over my mouth, Lord; keep watch over the door of my lips' (Ps. 141:3).

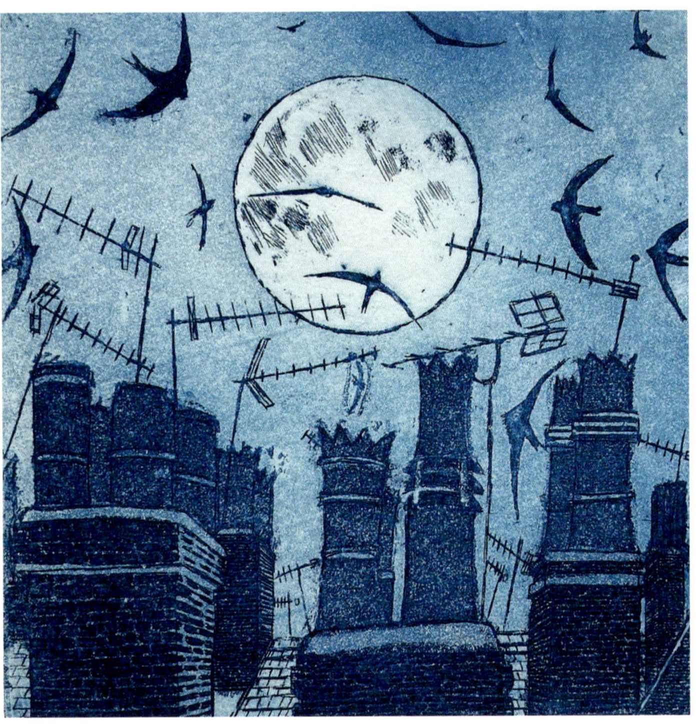

Artwork by Janis Goodman. Used by permission.

Centuries later, the apostle James memorably compared the tongue to a lone spark capable of setting a 'great forest' on fire, and the 'whole course of one's life' as well (James 3:5–6). Jesus himself states that 'what goes into someone's mouth does not defile them; but what comes out of their mouth – that is what defiles them' (Matt. 15:11). And Francis of Assisi (like Arnold, the founder of a religious order) writes, 'If you truly love your neighbour, it will make no difference whether he is sitting next to you or far away. Blest are you if you can refrain from saying anything behind his back that you could not say to his face, in love.'

In a story passed down about Saint Philip Neri, a woman comes to Philip and confesses to spreading malicious gossip. Philip tells her, 'As penance, go home and find a pillow, cut it open and scatter the feathers.'

The woman does as she is told and returns. 'Am I forgiven now?' she asks.

'Almost', Philip replies. 'There is just one more step. Take the empty pillow and gather all the feathers.'

'That's impossible', the woman protests. 'By now the wind has driven them far and wide.'

'Precisely', Philip answers. 'Is it not the same with the evil rumours you have spread?'

Of course, gossip is not always a matter of spreading rumours, whether evil or benign. A lot of what we say about others on any given day might be classified as factual in content and neutral in tone. And as noted above, there simply are cases where, despite the fact that direct address is usually the simplest route to resolving a given problem, it would seem wise to bounce it off a confidant first. Still, when such talk is engaged in by a self-appointed moral guardian who is worried about someone else (that someone not being there to explain or defend himself), it can end up being destructive, even if it arises from a genuine concern, and even if that concern is valid.

For one, our motives are never quite as pure as we imagine them, particularly when it comes to indulging the internal busybody that most of us seem to carry. And let's be honest: we're often more driven by that all-too-human desire to be the first one to pass on fresh news than by our love for the subject of our scoop. As for the sort of labelling that goes on in hushed talks among employers, counsellors, teachers, pastors and others in administrative positions – no matter

Janis Goodman, *Night Flying*, etching, 2009.

how professionally it might be handled – it never strengthens but always undermines and weakens the spirit of community which any organisation needs in order to thrive.

SO BACK TO THAT QUESTION: does the 'First Law' actually work? One thing is clear: practising it may be easier in a close-knit community such as the Bruderhof, where a basic level of trust is established, than in the normal workaday world. There, daring to address a problem openly may end up costing you your social standing, your job or both, even if you are retrospectively praised as a whistleblower.

Even beyond the confines of a religious community, however, it is arguable that the 'First Law' is applicable and has value. Instead of just being another 'thou shalt not' that prohibits backbiting, as well as avoidance, ghosting and the cancelling of perceived or avowed enemies – these are universal problems – it actively promotes nurturing the sort of frank dialogue whose goal is being able to look an adversary in the eye and forgive him or her.

In the spirit of Jesus' advice about removing the beam from our own eye before trying to remove the speck from our brother's (Luke 6:41–42), it wisely places the onus on changing ourselves first – on emptying our pockets of the stones we tend to collect, just in case we need to defend ourselves – and conveying what Arnold calls our 'joy in others' before trying to change them. Writer Yuval Lapide captures the heart of trying to live this way:

> Until you see the good in a person, you remain incapable of helping him. Whenever you speak ill of someone, you expose a measure of ugliness – in that person, in yourself and in anyone who happens to be listening. That ugliness will fester like a wound, and everyone involved will suffer. Speak well of that person, and the inner goodness in him, in you and in everyone involved will begin to shine, so that everything is illuminated.

As obvious as that wisdom may seem, it can be challenging to actually put into practice. Even as most of us struggle, year in and year out, to better ourselves, we still cling to the strange notion that we can improve and alter other people. Yet Jesus reminds us that when it comes to interpersonal relationships, the only sure path is the one of humility and love.

THE BEAUTY OF ENGAGING with a persistent challenge is that every time you revisit it, it yields new insights. In that spirit, here's my recent attempt to bring the 'First Law' into a new century. Posted on the kitchen wall of the Bruderhof's house in Harlem, it may be far from the original in terms of space and time and tone, but it still seems to resonate with everyone who pauses to read and reflect on it:

> When it comes to laws, the only one that really counts is the law of love. Love is joy in others. It makes you happy to see them and be with them. (If you're upset at them, the opposite will be true.) When you're at peace with someone, your attitude will show it, and you won't go around talking about them. That's why we don't allow gossip or backbiting in our house. Unless everyone commits to this, we'll never be a real community, because people won't trust one another.
>
> Relationships are never perfect, but no matter the problem at hand, facing it head-on is always the best way to figure it out and prevent a buildup of negativity. Try it: the next time someone gets on your nerves, be real with them. It's the kindest thing to do.
>
> Talking through a situation openly and honestly is rarely easy, but it's always worth a try. In fact, it can strengthen and deepen a friendship. If you're still not getting anywhere, ask a mutual friend (or anyone you both trust) for input. That way you can make peace and find a solution you're both happy with – one that actually brings you together. ➘

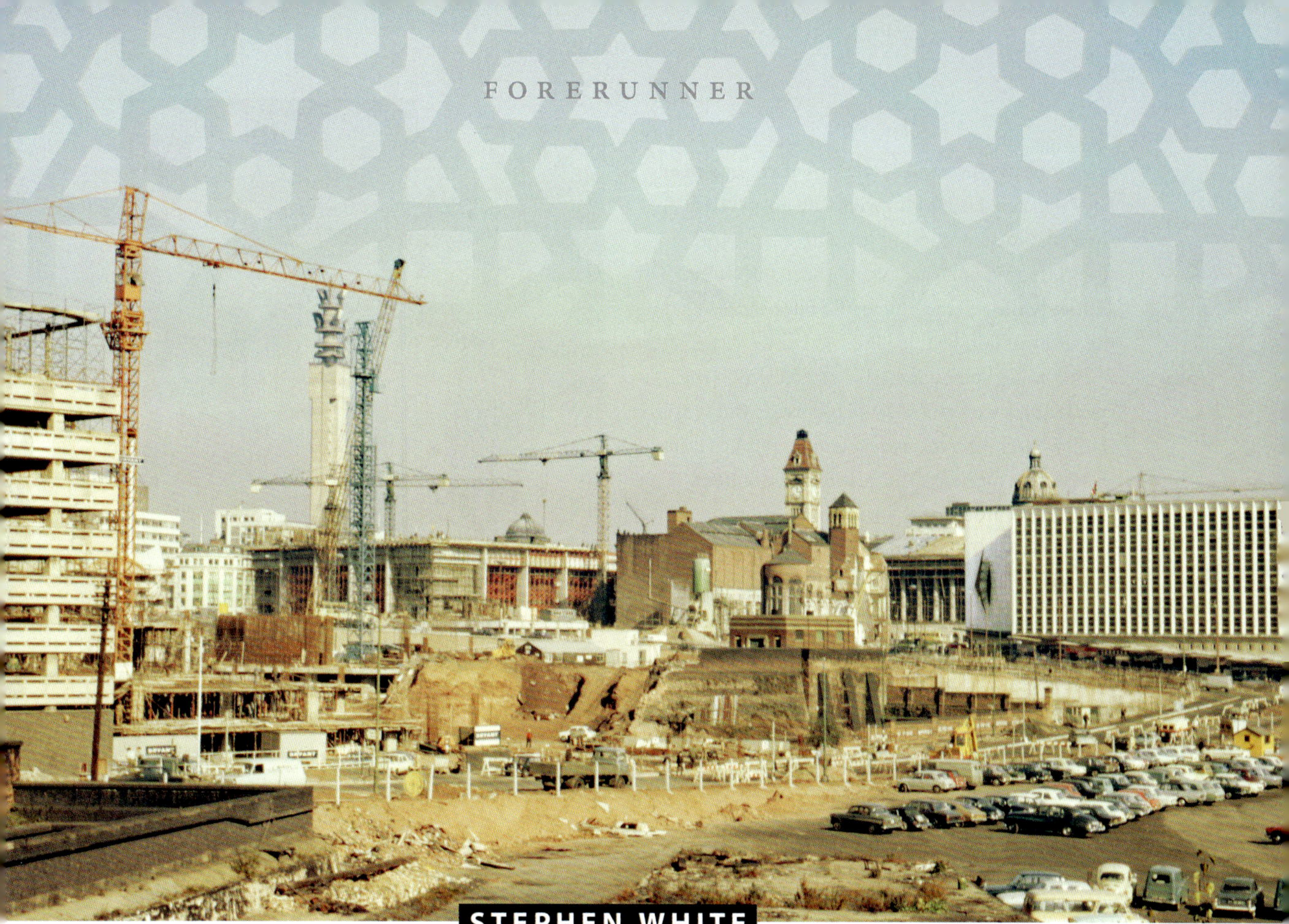

STEPHEN WHITE

Lesslie Newbigin and the Gospel as Public Truth

A bishop returns from abroad to serve as a missionary at home.

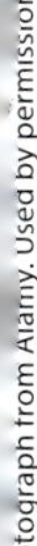

As Lesslie Newbigin stepped off the train in Birmingham in the mid-1970s – briefcase in hand, spine slightly bent from years of pastoral travel in South India – he was expecting an easier time of it than he'd met with in his missionary work. This was, after all, England; this was a Christian country.

The skyline of Birmingham, a city that had once thrived on industry, now looked tired, gasping for breath in a culture that had traded cathedrals for consumerism. The smokestacks were coming down. Congregations were thinning. Churches stood like neglected historical sites, frequented by the loyal, ignored by the masses.

Newbigin was stunned. He had crossed oceans to proclaim Christ among polytheists, Muslims and Marxists – none of whom shared his worldview, but all of whom cared deeply about

Redevelopment in Birmingham, United Kingdom, in 1970. Photograph overlaid with an image of latticework from Humayun's Tomb in Delhi, India.

questions of truth and salvation. There had been fiery debates. He had thrived. The gospel had thrived. Now he stood in his native land and found that no one was asking those questions. 'I suddenly discovered', he would later write, 'that the real mission field is here.'

This was a spiritual crisis – one in which the very category of 'truth' had collapsed, and Christianity had been reclassified from a public claim to a private opinion. The gospel had not been rejected because it was found false, but because it was no longer seen as interesting.

Born in 1909 in the Northeast of England, the son of a prosperous Presbyterian family, Newbigin came of age in the long twilight of British Christendom. The seeds of a vibrant faith were planted during his studies at Cambridge, mainly through the Student Christian Movement. There, the gospel took hold of him – not merely as a belief system, but as a summons: 'The church', he would write in *Foolishness to the Greeks*, 'is not meant to call men and women out of the world into a safe religious enclave, but to call them out in order to send them back as agents of God's kingship.'

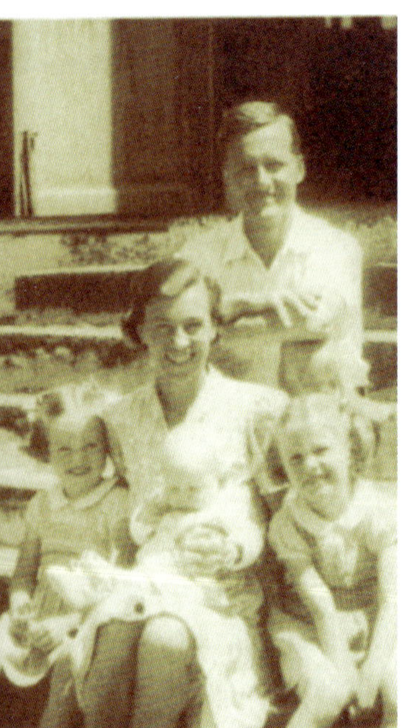

After training at Westminster College and freshly married to Helen Henderson – a woman of remarkable strength and intellect – Newbigin set sail for India in 1936 under the auspices of the Church of Scotland. The India that awaited him was a volatile and pluralistic nation. Gandhi's civil disobedience movement was shaking the colonial order. Hinduism and Islam defined the religious landscape. Though Saint Thomas had, reportedly, established congregations there in the first century, and the Mar Thoma Christians had been an active part of the Oriental Orthodox branch of the church since then, they were comparatively few in number and largely confined to the southern state of Kerala. Christianity, especially its Anglican form, was often regarded with suspicion: Was it truly good news, or merely another instrument of empire?

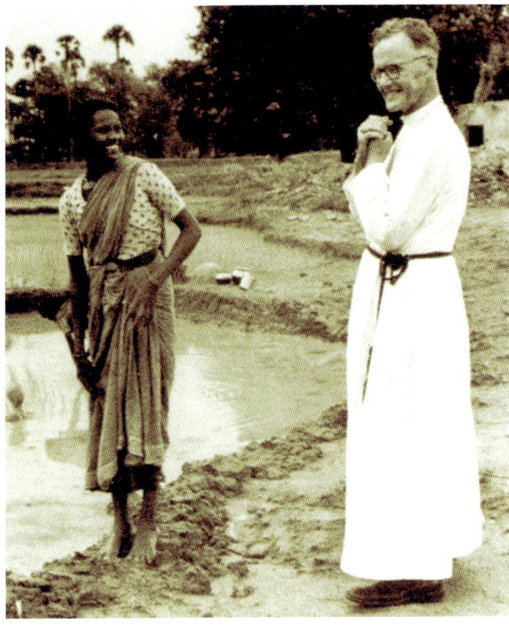

Photographs from Lesslie Newbigin's autobiography, *Unfinished Agenda*

Newbigin soon discovered that he had not arrived as a politically neutral emissary of truth. He had come as a foreigner, a white man and – however unintentionally – an agent of a crumbling imperial order. His accent, his training, even his ecclesiology were weighted with cultural freight. And the local villagers made sure he knew it.

A Hindu teacher once asked him with disarming directness, 'Why do you think we need your God when we've lived for centuries with our own?' In another village, a new Christian convert

---

Stephen White is a retired pastor, former Christian school superintendent and vice president of an urban ministry in San Jose, California. He is the author of several books.

Lesslie Newbigin with his family in 1945 (left), and as a missionary in India, ca 1970 (right).

was violently cast out by his extended family.

This changed his whole approach. We have to preach the gospel, he said, 'not as a proposition, not as an argument, but as the story of the world.' Christianity is not something to be given by an enlightened culture to one yet to be enlightened. It is a drama into which every culture is invited, but which also challenges every culture, including the one that carries it.

Newbigin came to change India. But India changed him: from a bearer of Christendom to a witness of Christ, from one who taught the gospel as Western wisdom to one who learned to let the gospel speak for itself in another tongue.

This radical recalibration came to full expression in 1947 – the year India won its independence, and the year Newbigin was consecrated as a bishop in the newly formed Church of South India. As colonial structures were being dismantled, the church was undergoing a parallel reformation. The Church of South India was a declaration that denominational divides imported from the West were no longer tolerable.

Anglicans, Methodists, Presbyterians and Congregationalists formed a single body. And Newbigin, now bishop of the Diocese of Madurai Ramnad, set about shepherding a patchwork of congregations that stretched across hundreds of villages. He travelled by train, by bullock cart and on foot. He sat on mud floors and ate from banana leaves. His theology was not forged in faculty lounges but in prayer meetings, open-air baptisms and pastoral visits. According to Newbigin, the gospel doesn't function as an external force thrust upon a society, but rather works organically from the inside, embedding itself within a culture to bring about transformation.

It was in this crucible that one of his most enduring insights emerged: *the church itself is the hermeneutic of the gospel.* This means that the church is the sign, the instrument and the foretaste of the kingdom.

When Lesslie Newbigin returned to Britain after four decades in South India, he felt like a missionary entering a new culture – one strangely more resistant to the gospel than the polytheistic and politically volatile India he had left behind. He took up a post at the Winson Green United Reformed Church in Birmingham, a working-class, multi-ethnic neighbourhood reeling from economic decline. Newbigin preached to dwindling congregations, visited the sick, prayed with the marginalised and engaged in gritty pastoral care.

The gospel doesn't function as an external force thrust upon a society, but rather works organically from the inside, embedding itself within a culture to bring about transformation.

The apathy he encountered was not benign. It was, in his words, 'far more corrosive to faith than opposition.' The prevailing atmosphere was a closed horizon in which religious claims were not debated so much as dismissed.

He started to write and lecture with renewed urgency. In *The Gospel in a Pluralist Society* (1989), he called the church in the West to reclaim its identity as a missionary community within its own culture. According to Newbigin, the church's calling is not to present itself as one attractive alternative among numerous possibilities. Instead, its purpose is to give witness to the truth embodied in Jesus Christ.

The West, he claimed, had not become less religious; it had adopted a new set of doctrines, authorities and moral codes. The Enlightenment, for all its advances, had imposed a new kind of orthodoxy – one in which truth must be scientific, value must be subjective and faith must be kept private. This wasn't religious neutrality. It was a worldview with its own absolute claims – only these claims were masquerading as reason.

Newbigin referred to this as the 'culture of disbelief.' It was not that Christianity had been rationally discredited. Rather, the plausibility structures of society had shifted so that belief in the gospel now seemed implausible.

Newbigin responded by insisting on what he called 'the gospel as public truth.' The Christian claim is not just a private consolation or tribal story. It is a claim about the real world – that in Jesus Christ, God has acted decisively in history to redeem creation. If that is true, it must be spoken and lived publicly – not imposed, but offered with courage, humility and joy.

Newbigin had no interest in establishing a theocracy. He had seen firsthand in India what happens when religion becomes entwined with political power. What he wanted instead was resurrection-shaped confidence. The church must live in such a way that people begin to wonder, 'What kind of story are these people living in?'

At the heart of Newbigin's epistemology was the resurrection. It was not just a supernatural event; it was the apocalypse – the unveiling of reality, the proclamation of a victory.

Jesus was alive. History had been fundamentally changed. Caesar no longer held the final word. Death was no longer in control. The tomb was empty, and the world would never be the same.

Near the end of his life, Newbigin posed a question that still lingers: Can the West be converted? The answer wasn't guaranteed. Western culture had become comfortable, self-sufficient and morally confused. Yet, he also believed in a God who raises the dead.

Conversion, he argued, would not happen through coercion, clever marketing or nostalgia. It would happen through cruciform love – love that suffers, loves that forgives, love that invites. It would happen when the church stopped trying to be impressive and instead began being faithful.

The church does not need to win. It needs to witness – to demonstrate by its life, its joy, its suffering, its hope – that Jesus Christ is Lord.

This witness won't always be understood by the surrounding culture. It might provoke hostility or indifference. But if it is genuine – if it is resurrection-shaped – it cannot be ignored forever.

NEWBIGIN DIED IN 1998, just as the Western church was beginning to realise the severity of the crisis he had identified decades earlier. His influence is only growing. Theologians from various traditions – Reformed, Anglican, Anabaptist, Catholic and Orthodox – have been influenced by his work. Thinkers like N T Wright, Timothy Keller and Stanley Hauerwas have all been shaped by Newbigin's insights. However, his most significant impact might be felt not in academic settings but in small congregations that have chosen to re-embrace being the church: not glamorous, or powerful, but faithful.

To follow Newbigin's example is to trust what he trusted: that the gospel is true, that the church is God's chosen vessel and that the Spirit is still at work. It is to believe that the tomb really is empty, and that no culture – no matter how disenchanted – is beyond the reach of grace.

Michael Goheen has summarised Newbigin's description of the church as a community of praise in a world of doubt, a community of truth in a world of ideology, a community of hope in a world of despair. That, surely, is the church the world still needs today.

Not a perfect church. Not a powerful church. But a church worth believing in.

Because Christ is risen, and the world, even now, is being made new.

Justine Maendel, *Lesslie Newbigin*, charcoal, ink and watercolour, 2025.

Artwork by Justine Maendel. Used by permission.

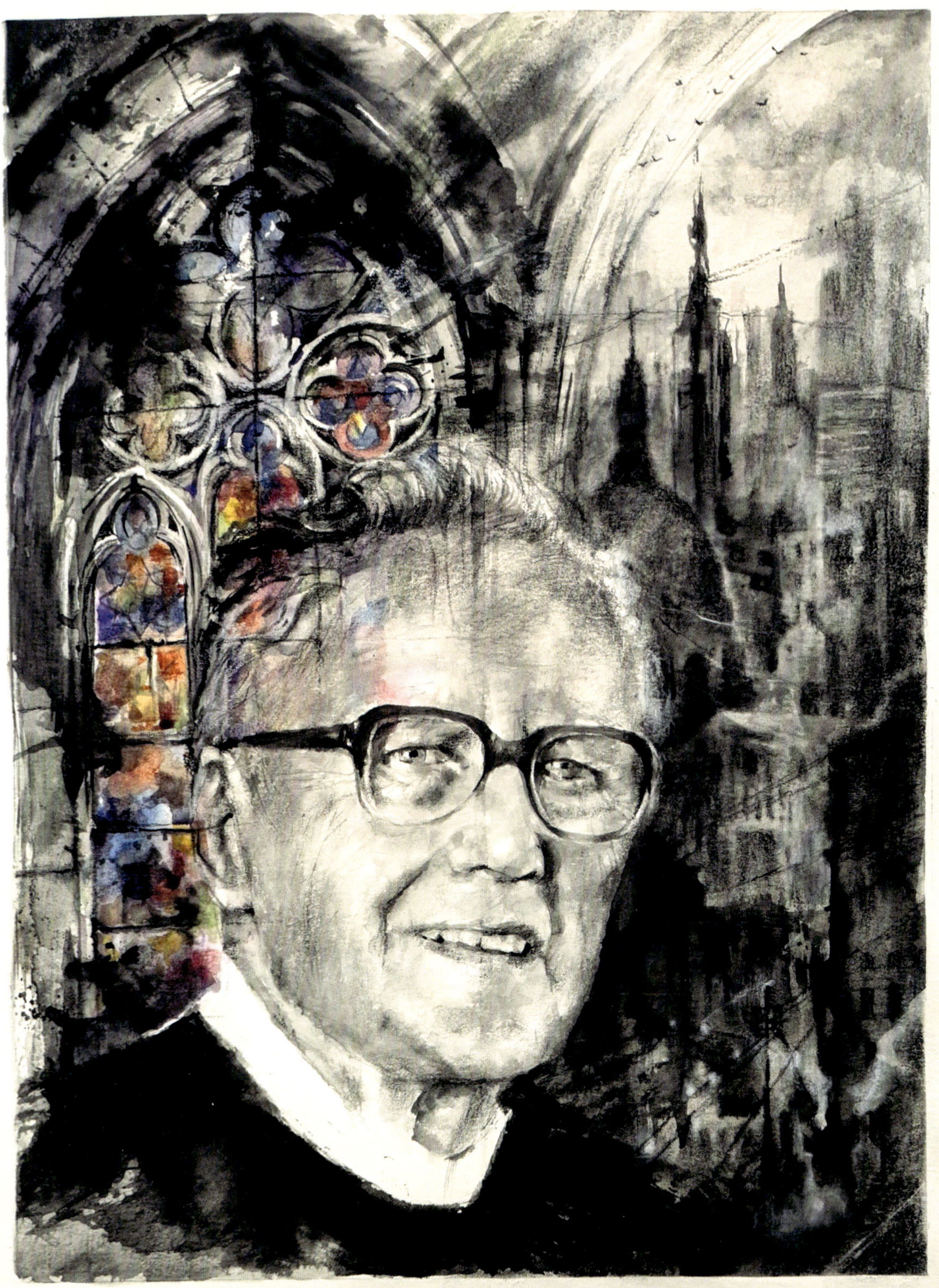

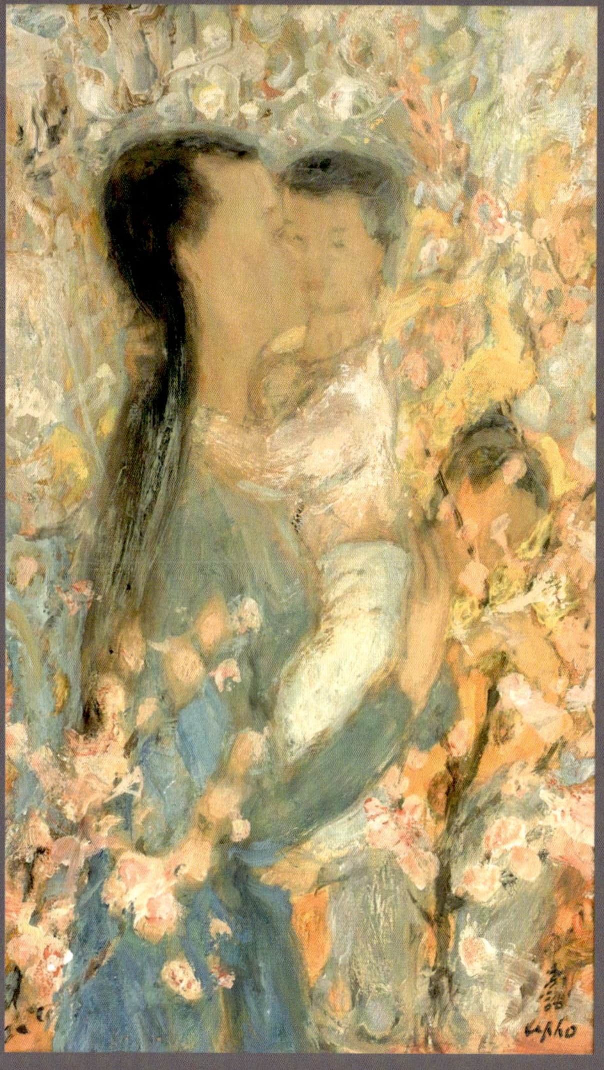

Lê Phổ, *Maternity*, ink and watercolour on silk, 1955

‘Be gentle. It is beautiful to be gentle with those who suffer. There is no beauty in the world so great as beauty of action. It stands, contained in its own moment, from everlasting to everlasting.’

—*Muriel Spark*

Plough

ANOTHER LIFE IS POSSIBLE

Subscriptions £24 / €28 / US $36
Individual issues £9 / €9 / US $12

Plough Publishing House
Robertsbridge, East Sussex, UK
Walden, New York, USA

To subscribe, go to www.plough.com or scan the QR code

9 781636 081908